DISSENT, INJUSTICE, AND
THE MEANINGS OF AMERICA

DISSENT, INJUSTICE, AND
THE MEANINGS OF AMERICA

Steven H. Shiffrin

PRINCETON UNIVERSITY PRESS   PRINCETON, NEW JERSEY

Second printing, and first paperback printing, 2000

Paperback ISBN 0-691-07023-7

The Library of Congress has cataloged the cloth edition of
this book as follows

Shiffrin, Steven H., 1941–
Dissent, injustice, and the meanings of America / Steven H. Shiffrin
p.   cm.
Includes bibliographical references and index.
ISBN 0-691-00142-1 (hardcover : alk. paper)
1. Freedom of speech—United States. 2. Hate speech—United
States. 3. Racism in language. I. Title.
KF4772.S448 1999
342.73'0853—dc21 98-23200

This book has been composed in Sabon

The paper used in this publication meets the minimum
requirements of ANSI/NISO Z39.48-1992 (R1997)
(*Permanence of Paper*)

www.pup.princeton.edu

Printed in the United States of America

10   9   8   7   6   5   4   3   2

For Neesa, Ben, Jacob, and Seana

Contents

Acknowledgments

ALTHOUGH writing a book is often a lonely enterprise, academic books are also a collegial effort. I have received helpful comments on various portions of this book from many people, including Bruce Ackerman, Kathy Abrams, Greg Alexander, Ed Baker, Cynthia Farina, Dick Fallon, Barbara Holden-Smith, Gerald Lopez, Sheri Lynn Johnson, Malcolm Litchfield, David Lyons, Tracey Maclin, Seana Shiffrin, Gary Simson, Winnie Taylor, Steve Thel, and David Williams. I also owe thanks to participants in workshops or conferences at Amherst College, Boston University Law School, Chicago-Kent Law School, Cornell University Law School, the Cornell Ethics and Public Life program, the University of Iowa Law School, and the University of Washington Law School, and to students in my seminars on constitutional law and political theory. In addition, I have been blessed with terrific research assistants: Neil Eggeson, Emmy Hackett, Julie Hilden, and Penny Zagalis. So, too, Jennifer Smith is the secretary to die for.

A somewhat different version of chapter one appeared as "The First Amendment and the Meaning of America," in *Politics, Identities, Rights*, ed. Austin Sarat and Thomas Kearnes (Ann Arbor: University of Michigan Press, 1995). I thank the University of Michigan Press for granting copyright permission. Chapter three appeared in the *Cornell Law Review*, and chapter five, together with the media section of chapter four, appeared in the *Indiana Law Journal*. I thank the editors for their assistance in the earlier incarnations of that work.

In particular, I would like to thank Malcolm Litchfield, acquisitions editor at Princeton University Press, for his support, his diligence, and his straight talk about all aspects of the project from start to finish; Karen Verde, for her smooth and hospitable coordination of the production process; Susan Ecklund, for her sharp copyediting; Shirley Kessel, for her intelligent work on the index; Sandy Levinson and Fred Schauer, who offered important suggestions while reviewing the manuscript for Princeton; Bruce Ackerman, whom I barely know, for attacking the end of what became chapter 1, thus inspiring me to write what has become chapter 3; Justices Stevens and Souter for infuriating me in the *Landmark* case, provoking me to write chapter 2; Cynthia Farina, who fights a brilliant battle to wring imprecision and exaggerations out of my writing; Julie Hilden, a remarkable editor, who did an awful lot to improve the style and the analysis in chapter 3; Barbara Holden-Smith, who kept my feet to the fire in chapter 3; Jerry Lopez, a wonderful friend and critic, who made a major mark on chapter 4; Sheri Johnson, not only for excellent criticism but also for her many suggestions for putting the book together (a few books were lost on the cutting room floor); and, of course, to my daughter, Seana Shiffrin, whose penetrating analysis has improved the manuscript in countless ways.

Some authors thank their spouses for their understanding in letting them pile up impossible hours to do their "important" work. You will not find that here. Thanks to Neesa Levine for resisting all such pressures.

Introduction

FREE SPEECH controversies involve debates about social power and cultural struggles about the meaning of *America*.[1] Should government be able to punish flag burners? Prevent tobacco companies from advertising products that kill more people every year than homicides, suicides, alcohol, illegal drugs, AIDS, and car accidents put together?[2] Prevent the Ku Klux Klan from making vicious racist attacks on groups that are guaranteed equal protection under our Constitution?

America means many things to many people. For most citizens, it is a cultural symbol that stands for the ideals of the nation. The flag represents *America*. To burn the flag is blasphemy that need not be tolerated. "It's a free country." To censor tobacco companies or the Ku Klux Klan is un-American. America stands for free speech. It is as simple as that.

Or is it? Freedom of speech clashes with so many other values in so many complicated contexts that it seems dogmatic to suppose a privileged position for free speech in all situations. Is free speech always more valuable than reputation, privacy, intellectual property, justice, consumer protection, morality, or public order? Free speech doctrine routinely denies any such privileged position.

Without suggesting that all free speech doctrine is appropriate, I will assume that its general approach is correct. Free speech protection should depend on a balancing of its values and harms in particular contexts. Because those contexts are so numerous and differentiated, I believe that a general theory of the First Amendment is impossible. Nonetheless, free speech rightly plays an important part in our culture, and the balancing of free speech values requires a sense of what is particularly important and what is not.

In *The First Amendment, Democracy, and Romance*,[3] I argued that dissent should be at the center of an appropriate theory of free speech. In this book I return to that perspective, but I emphasize two of the social functions of dissent: its place in cultural struggles about the meanings of America and its role in combating injustice. With this emphasis, I hope to make the case for dissent's special role more attractive in terms of both constitutional law and political theory. By dissent, I mean speech that criticizes existing customs, habits, traditions, institutions, or authorities. I do not suggest that dissent should always be protected. Knowing defamatory falsehoods about public figures, for example, are instances of dissent, but the case for protecting harmful lies is thin. Nor do I suggest that dissent is a necessary condition for free speech protection. Most religious and political speech should be protected whether or not it is dissenting. Even commercial speech should be protected. For example, bar associations should not be able to prevent attorneys from advertising their services in a nonmisleading way.

Dissent, however, is a practice of vital importance to the self-realization of many individuals, and even more important, a crucial institution for challenging unjust hierarchies and for promoting progressive change. It is also an important part of our national identity that we protect dissent. If a central insight of First Amendment theory is that dissent deserves special protection, it follows that the state should not be able to punish flag burners. If America stands for free speech and free speech stands for dissent, the flag stands for dissent. To punish flag burners, from this perspective, contradicts the meaning of America.

Commercial advertisers, however, are not dissenters. They deserve some free speech protection, but no special protection. Some might believe, however, that tobacco advertising must be dissenting because its product is socially stigmatized. In this respect, tobacco advertising has some elements of dissent, but it misses vital elements ordinarily associated with our valuing of dissent. Tobacco advertising is not an instance of the maverick, the rebel, or a social movement striking out against the current. It is an instance of the powerful influencing the market rather than one of dissent by the less powerful. Tobacco advertising is no part of a social practice that challenges unjust hierarchies with the prospect of promoting progressive change. Thus, it may have some First Amendment value in the dissent mold, but it does not deserve the full value that should be afforded to more classic instances of dissent.

The Ku Klux Klan would also claim to be dissenters, social outcasts who challenge the foundations of the system. Many who are attracted to a free speech theory accenting the protection of dissent might wish to stop right there. Arguably, however, the Klan says in public what many millions of white individuals think or come close to thinking in private. It may reflect the racist character of the society. Moreover, the Klan arguably silences those who would otherwise be dissenters. So understood, a focus on dissent in this context would not offer clear-cut guidance—which perhaps helps to explain why many see the hate speech issue as a difficult problem.

I argue that the hate speech question does not present a conflict between freedom and equality. On the one hand, I argue that our country is necessarily committed to the proposition that each citizen is worthy of equal respect. From that premise I suggest that hate speech implicates far less of First Amendment value than is frequently claimed by free speech advocates. If a major purpose of protecting dissent is to promote equality and justice, then it might be thought that the protection of speech by the Klan unnecessarily risks promoting inequality and injustice. On the other hand, I also argue that our country is racist to the core, and from that premise I argue that prohibitions of hate speech would not advance the cause of equality but would perpetuate inequality. Tolerating hate speech on this analysis should be a pragmatic concession to the needs of equality. It should be not a case for celebrating our glory as a nation but an occasion for shame. By contrast, I will argue that the case for regulation of hate speech is quite strong when the speech targets specific individuals.

Part One of this book, "The Meanings of America," ties important free speech issues in their own right to cultural struggles about the meaning of America. Although the theme of political identity runs through the chapters in Part One, other large issues are confronted, as well. Whether one thinks about flag burning, commercial advertising, or hate speech, for example, any serious examination of such issues runs straight into political theory. In chapter one, "The First Amendment and the Meaning of America," I explore flag burning and subsidies of the arts. In pursuing that discussion, I claim comparative advantages for a dissent-based theory over communitarian approaches on the one hand and postmodern approaches on the other. In chapter two, "Cigarettes, Alcohol, and Advertising," I discuss commercial advertising, with special emphasis on tobacco and alcoholic beverage advertising. In the course of that discussion, I explore the merits of a dissent-based approach against a politically centered approach to free speech, in particular the one put forward by Cass Sunstein. In chapter three, "Racist Speech, Outsider Jurisprudence, and the Meaning of America," I discuss racist speech and compare a dissent-based approach with outsider jurisprudence.

Part Two, "Combating Injustice," focuses on the relationship between dissent, the First Amendment, and combating injustice. To be sure, the chapters in Part One can all be characterized as dealing with injustice. For example, proponents of free speech argue that it is unjust to censor speech. Similarly, veterans would argue that it is unjust for government to call them to battle and then to permit individuals to blaspheme the flag that stands for their sacrifices. Public health proponents would argue that it is unjust for merchants of products creating severe health risks to market their products in ways that exploit children and adults alike. And some people of color would argue that a land permitting hate speech is not a land of justice. Nonetheless, Part One emphasizes cultural struggle. Part Two is concerned primarily with dissent's role in the theory and practice of combating injustice. Chapter four, "Dissent and Injustice," argues that the liberty of dissent combats injustice, and this aspect of dissent is a strong part of the case for its special protection. Indeed, I maintain that it is not enough to tolerate dissent; dissent needs to be institutionally encouraged. I explore the place of this contention in liberal theory. In terms of practice, I accuse the mass media in its daily operations and the Supreme Court in its jurisprudence of failing to live up to the goal of encouraging dissent. I also ruminate about the changes we might make in our institutions if we were to encourage dissent.

In chapter five, "The Politics of Free Speech," I confront those critics who recognize that the First Amendment has not been interpreted in ways that are sympathetic to the disadvantaged. These scholars argue that the First Amendment has been interpreted so often to help the wealthy and so rarely to help those who are subordinated that it should be regarded as a burden to justice and not a benefit. I have some sympathy with this view. I once considered writing an article entitled "What's Wrong with the First Amendment?" But I did not. There *is* a lot wrong with the First Amendment, but its benefits exceed its costs. Moreover, to say the very least, it is bad politics to oppose the First Amendment in a country whose national identity is linked so closely with free speech. In the end, we are better off contending that America aspires to be understood as committed to protecting and encouraging dissent, particularly the role of dissent in combating injustice. Better to struggle over the meaning of free speech and America. Better to hope to rescue progressive possibilities than to curse the darkness.

Part One

THE MEANINGS OF AMERICA

I

The First Amendment and the Meaning of America

POLITICAL pundits often proclaim the view that conservatives know how to tap into American values in a way that progressives do not. Consider this tiny masterpiece from Patrick Buchanan: "The arts crowd is after more than our money, more than an end to the congressional ban on funding obscene and blasphemous art. It is engaged in a cultural struggle to root out the old America of family, faith, and flag, and re-create society in a pagan image."[1]

Buchanan's value-packed epithets have much to teach American progressives, and the lessons are ultimately quite somber. But let us begin with the obvious, albeit the underappreciated obvious. Everyone understands that the "arts crowd" is engaged in a cultural struggle. From the perspective of the arts community, that struggle is ordinarily seen as one in which the country's cultural standards are improved or "elevated." Moreover, the arts community has a well-developed sense that the denial of funding to blasphemous art is contrary to the art community's understanding of the First Amendment. Indeed, the art community's sense of the First Amendment sometimes runs to the more demanding notion that it requires funding for the arts in general—although how much funding is not particularly clear.

What is less well appreciated is that the First Amendment itself is at the heart of America's cultural struggle, and that cases involving the arts are perhaps the easiest illustrations of a more general phenomenon. Although I will discuss the First Amendment ramifications of the selective denials of funding to controversial artists, I will focus on what may appear to be a digression from the arts, namely, the flag-burning cases.

But these cases are no digression. After all, the flag is a national art form designed to bring the nation together. Moreover, like those who sponsored the flag, those who fund the arts frequently seek to produce works that can induce a sense of national pride and accomplishment.

In a way, this makes sense of what otherwise might be inexplicable. The nation has spent considerable sums on art and on museums to house art. It invites citizens to come and appreciate that art. Yet, without sub-

stantial artistic education, education which the overwhelming majority of
citizens do not have, much of the art in museums cannot be appreciated
for its place in (or departure from) the tradition that precedes it. Museums, then, are designed in substantial part to show that the nation has a
great culture. Like the flag, they represent the *nation*.

In part because they are "our" museums, in even greater part because
"we" fund what goes into those museums, the public exhibits an interest,
even occasional outrage, when museums house materials that offend
deeply held values. Citizens ask why the public should have to pay for
materials they regard as offensive. But public displays of some art exhibits
would attract public outrage even in the absence of public funding. Take,
for example, the artistic representation of Christ—dipped in the artist's
urine. So, too, when someone burns a flag, the public response is outrage
whether or not public funds have been used to support the "performance." At such times, many members of the public (including Patrick
Buchanan) argue that such expressive actions so deeply offend cherished
traditions that they should not be tolerated.

But the law is not on Buchanan's side—at least, not yet. The public
must tolerate most offensive speech, including flag burning, and in some
circumstances is actually constitutionally required to pay for offensive art.
Of course, the latter conclusion is more controversial and more difficult to
reach than the first. Nonetheless, the path to the second conclusion follows from the first. In approaching the flag cases, therefore, we do not
digress. Indeed, we enter the forest from a spot where we can see it for
more than a collection of trees.

In approaching questions like flag burning and subsidies of the arts,
however, we have more to learn than lessons in First Amendment geography. These disputes give us more than basic insight about free speech
theory—important as that may be; in the end, they become an appropriate
vehicle for considering important aspects of the relationships among liberalism, radicalism, and national identity.

The First Amendment and the Flag

In 1988, during the Republican National Convention, Gregory Lee Johnson doused an American flag with kerosene and set it on fire. While the
flag burned, his fellow protestors shouted, "America the red, white, and
blue, we spit on you." Johnson was convicted for violating a Texas statute
that outlawed the knowing or intentional damaging of a state or national
flag in a way that the perpetrator "knows will seriously offend one or
more persons likely to observe or discover his action."[2] In *Texas v. John-*

son,[3] the U.S. Supreme Court held that Johnson's conviction violated his First Amendment rights.

On October 30, 1989, Gregory Lee Johnson appeared on the east steps of the U.S. Capitol in Washington, D.C. In protest against the Flag Protection Act of 1989 (which was passed to circumvent the *Johnson* decision), Mr. Johnson sought to burn another flag. As luck would have it, however, his flag failed to ignite. But several of his compatriots, including Shawn D. Eichman, succeeded in burning their flags, and the government proceeded to prosecute Eichman for violation of the very act he sought to protest. In *United States v. Eichman*,[4] the U.S. Supreme Court rebuffed the prosecutions and held once again that the First Amendment protects the right to burn a flag.

The Rehnquist Court has decided countless cases the wrong way, but this time the Court got it right. The flag-burning cases not only were rightly decided but also should stand as a fixed point in any reckoning of what the First Amendment is all about. Easy cases make good law. They can also open a window into the weaknesses of theory, and weakness of theory has pervaded the commentary surrounding the flag-burning dispute. Much of that theory is insufficiently rich. Its defense of free speech is excessively mechanical, and it possesses insufficient resources to explain why the flag-burning cases and the arts subsidy cases are as important as they are.

Proponents of flag desecration statutes argue that the expressive conduct associated with the burning of a flag should be recognized as an exception to the general principle that freedom of expression is ordinarily protected. In both *Texas v. Johnson* and *United States v. Eichman*, Justice Brennan invoked the "bedrock principle . . . that the Government may not prohibit the expression of an idea simply because society finds the idea offensive or disagreeable."[5] Moreover, he found "no indication—either in the text of the Constitution or in our cases interpreting it—that a separate juridical category exists for the flag alone. [The] First Amendment does not guarantee that other concepts virtually sacred to our Nation as a whole—such as the principle that discrimination on the basis of race is odious and destructive—will go unquestioned in the marketplace of ideas. . . . We decline, therefore, to create for the flag an exception to the joust of principles protected by the First Amendment."[6] Bye-bye to the proposed flag exception.

An air of inevitability punctuates Justice Brennan's line of reasoning: "We've never done it before; we would be inconsistent if we did; we won't do it." But the rush to judgment is a bit fast. Consider, first, the "bedrock principle." It is carefully phrased: "[T]he Government may not prohibit the expression of an idea simply because society finds the idea offensive or disagreeable." Only by resort to literalism does this principle pass First Amendment inspection. Candor dictates the recognition, for example, that obscenity is subject to restriction because people find it offensive. How does that recognition square with the bedrock principle? The conventional response is buried in Justice Brennan's formulation of the principle: "[T]he Government may not prohibit the expression of an *idea* simply because society finds the idea offensive or disagreeable." In other words, by prohibiting obscenity, the argument goes, no idea is suppressed. People are free to express whatever ideas they choose; they are simply barred from using obscenity as a method of expressing their ideas.

But now the hole is big enough for a truck, and Justice Stevens knows how to drive:[7] "The [flag-burning] prohibition does not entail any interference with the speaker's freedom to express his or her other ideas by other means. It may well be true that other means of expression may be less effective in drawing attention to those ideas, but that is not itself a sufficient reason for immunizing flagburning. Presumably a gigantic fireworks display or a parade of nude models in a public park might draw even more attention to a controversial message, but such methods of expression are nevertheless subject to regulation."[8]

This leads to an obvious question: Why would the protection of speech depend on judicial assessments of whether the speech contains an idea? My answer comes down to this: Justice Holmes was too eloquent for the First Amendment's long-term good.

In *Abrams v. United States*,[9] the Supreme Court upheld the conviction of Jacob Abrams for charges arising out of the printing of a leaflet that strongly opposed the "capitalist" invasion of Russia during World War I. In a ringing dissent, Justice Holmes stated: "[W]hen men have realized that time has upset many fighting faiths, they may come to believe even more than they believe the very foundations of their own conduct that the ultimate good desired is better reached by free trade in ideas—that the best test of truth is the power of the thought to get accepted in the competition of the market, and that truth is the only ground upon which their wishes safely can be carried out. That at any rate is the theory of our Constitution."[10]

The marketplace analogy was an elegant turn employed in a good cause, but there is no excuse for elevating it into a guiding framework. Free speech is an important principle, but there is no reason to assume that what emerges in the "market" is usually right or that the "market" is the best test of truth. Societal pressures to conform are strong, and incentives to keep quiet about the corruptions of power are often great. What emerges in the market might better be viewed as a testimonial to power than as a reflection of truth.

Nonetheless, owing primarily to the rhetorical power of a single paragraph, generations of students have been told that the primary purpose of the First Amendment has been to protect the now proverbial marketplace of ideas. Thus, when the Court sought to explain how the First Amendment and the prohibition of obscenity were compatible, it resorted to the suggestion that the prohibition did not exclude ideas from the marketplace. *Eo instanto*, we were supposed to imagine that Justice Holmes would have nodded in agreement.

Ironically, the same Justice Brennan who used marketplace theory to suppress speech in the obscenity context ultimately came to renounce his prior views.[11] But the technique lives on. It has been used to limit profane speech, and it rests at the heart of the dissents in the flag-burning cases.

Once the bedrock principle is shaken, it becomes less persuasive to insist that there is no possible room in the First Amendment for a flag exception. There is the stopping place problem ("if we create an exception today, the world will tumble tomorrow"), but exceptions to free speech protection are abundant (consider, e.g., libel, obscenity, perjury, and espionage). To be sure, as Justice Brennan suggests: "[The] First Amendment does not guarantee that other concepts virtually sacred to our Nation—as a whole—such as the principle that discrimination on the basis of race is odious and destructive—will go unquestioned in the marketplace of ideas."[12] But the creation of a flag-burning exception would not prevent any concept associated with the flag from being questioned "in the marketplace of ideas"; it would only prevent flags from being destroyed.

All this leads back to the bedrock principle. All is saved if it can be applied to the flag-burning dispute. Perhaps flag burning is like poetry in that the idea and the expression run together.[13]

But what an odd debate. Absent the power of Holmes's rhetoric and the perceived desire to justify the exclusion of particular categories of speech from First Amendment protection, who would have thought to suggest that the First Amendment was limited to ideas?[14] Imagine telling Walt Whitman: "If there are any ideas in *Leaves of Grass* go ahead and express them, but stop writing this offensive poetry." Of course, you may believe that expression and ideas run together in poetry, but how would you distinguish obscenity?

Perhaps your answer is that the obscenity exception should be overruled rather than distinguished. But if you are an advocate trying to persuade a majority of the Supreme Court, or a justice trying to put together a majority, you are trying to pers ᴅe people who are not about to dispense with the obscenity exception. Placed in that situation, of course, you could invoke the bedrock principle and proceed to duck. But the principle used in the flag-burning dispute does little to capture the free speech position. Who among us really thinks that protection for flag burning should depend on its relationship to poetry? Who among us believes that the heart of the issue can be reached by philosophical contemplation about what the word *idea* really means? Far from capturing the essence of the dispute, the marketplace of ideas metaphor defines the dispute in a way that puts free speech proponents on the defensive. If we need a metaphor, we could use a better one.

Content Neutrality and "Exacting Scrutiny"

The image of a content-neutral government has played an important role in First Amendment discussions in general and in the flag-burning dispute in particular. That image is related to the marketplace metaphor, but it is not the same. Consider, for example, the statute at issue in *Johnson*. The statute made it an offense to "deface, damage or otherwise physically mistreat [a flag] in a way that the actor knows will seriously offend one or more persons likely to observe or discover his action."[15] Respected commentators have suggested that the Texas statute "restricted the use of the flag as a means of expression *only* when it was used to convey *ideas* that are offensive to others."[16] But the dissenters in *Johnson* could give the statute quite a different gloss.

Johnson allegedly[17] burned the flag as part of a demonstration to protest the policies of the Reagan administration and of certain Dallas corporations. Certainly he knew that his actions would seriously offend one or more persons in the crowd witnessing the event. But nothing in the statute seems to require that his opinions be offensive. Many people might agree with Johnson's ideas about the Reagan administration and the Dallas corporations while still being offended by his method of communicating or drawing attention to those ideas.

On the other hand, it is hard to disagree with the Court when it says that violation of the Texas law "depended on the likely communicative impact of his expressive conduct."[18] Johnson can be taken to know that people would be offended by his flag burning precisely because it communicated an attitude of disrespect toward the flag. And, whether or not one calls the communication of that attitude the communication of an idea, it is the communication of a message[19] that offends most Americans, including Texans.

The stage was thus set in *Johnson* for the model of a content-neutral government. As Justice Brennan put it: "[Johnson's] political expression was restricted because of the content of the message he conveyed. We must therefore subject the State's asserted interest in preserving the special symbolic character of the flag to 'the most exacting scrutiny.' "[20]

But we must now confront the shell game of First Amendment doctrine. The rule in those cases where government restricts speech because of the content of the message is this: "Exacting scrutiny is called for—except when it's not."

Take the example of obscenity again. "Exacting scrutiny" was certainly *not* used in determining that obscenity was beneath First Amendment protection. In *Paris Adult Theatre I v. Slaton*,[21] the Court recognized that "although there was no conclusive proof of a connection between antisocial behavior and obscene material, the legislature of Georgia could quite reasonably determine that such a connection does or *might* exist."[22] This is the language of deference, not the language of exacting scrutiny. Even more telling, the Court explained that obscenity is beneath the protection of the First Amendment because it " 'intrudes upon us all.' "[23] It invades our privacy. But why doesn't the burning of a flag invade our privacy? Quite obviously, if there is a distinction to be made here, it cannot be derived from the model of a content-neutral government. Nothing in the idea of content neutrality can distinguish the flag example from the obscenity example. The interesting question is to determine that which accounts for the selective use of exacting scrutiny.

Geoffrey Stone has suggested that the Court employs exacting scrutiny for content-based restrictions except when low-value speech is at issue.[24] My own view is that Stone's account of the doctrine is brilliant and heroic, but seriously flawed.[25] Even if one accepted Stone's view of the doctrine, one would need an explanation of that which distinguishes low value from high value. Whatever the character of that explanation might be, except in rare cases,[26] it would not be a content-neutral explanation.

Finally, suppose that the First Amendment were said to bar any assessment of the value of speech and that First Amendment doctrine were revised accordingly. One might presume, for example, that obscenity doctrine and commercial speech doctrine would look quite different, since both areas have been influenced by judicial assessments of the value of the speech involved. But the leveling effect of content neutrality exposes its rhetorical poverty. Even if one wanted to protect commercial speech, the model of content neutrality would give us no explanation of why we might regard the flag-burning cases as somehow special. The books are filled with cases that violate the principle of content neutrality, and some of those cases have aroused more furor than others. If the Court had ruled that flag burning was not protected, I submit that First Amendment progressives would have been wounded by such a development far more than if a hawker of commercial goods or services were denied First Amendment protection. The question is: Why?

The First Amendment, Dissent, and Political Speech

Perhaps the flag-burning question touches a special chord within us because the government was attempting to suppress political speech. Undoubtedly, the suppression of political speech is revolting, but I do not think the concept of political speech gets at the heart of the matter. But we can appreciate that point only when we examine the alternative of dissent as a First Amendment value.

The flag-burning prohibition is uniquely troubling not because it interferes with the metaphoric marketplace of ideas, not because it topples our image of a content-neutral government (*that* has fallen many times), and not merely because it suppresses political speech. The flag-burning prohibition is a naked attempt to smother dissent. If we must have a "central meaning" of the First Amendment, we should recognize that the dissenters—those who attack existing customs, habits, traditions, and authorities—stand at the center of the First Amendment and not at its periphery. Gregory Johnson was attacking a symbol which the vast majority of Americans regard with reverence. But that is *exactly* why he deserved First Amendment protection. The First Amendment has a special regard for those who swim against the current, for those who would shake us to our foundations, for those who reject prevailing authority. In burning the flag, Johnson rejected, opposed, even blasphemed the nation's most important political, social, and cultural icon. Clearly, his alleged act of burning the flag was a quintessential act of dissent. A dissent-centered conception of the First Amendment would make it clear that *Johnson* was an easy case—rightly decided.

If dissent were thought to be at the heart of the First Amendment, there could be no evasion of the First Amendment issue. Any justice who looked at the case to find out whether Johnson had communicated an "idea" that might emerge in the metaphoric marketplace would clearly be in pursuit of the irrelevant. So, too, if dissent, as opposed to content neutrality, were thought to be at the heart of the First Amendment, our primary focus would be on dissent as a First Amendment value, not on the methodological niceties associated with the determination of whether the government's action was or was not content-neutral. To elevate content neutrality to a central place in First Amendment methodology—even as a guiding metaphor—would take too benign a view of content-neutral regulations.[27] The metaphor tempts us to forget that dissent smothered by government action is dissent smothered, even when the government's action is regarded as content-neutral.

A politically centered conception of the First Amendment—one that relies on the metaphor of the citizen-critic in an American democracy—might seem a more promising base from which to confront flag-burning statutes. And in many ways it is. After all, the flag-burning prohibition comes uncomfortably close to a seditious libel law,[28] and in the eyes of many the notion of seditious libel "has become a symbol—a symbol of the first amendment's ultimate opposite, what the amendment is today above all understood to have banished from the land."[29]

Perhaps one reason that flag-burning statutes arouse such strong feelings in American progressives is that they grievously affront *both* the dissent model and the political speech model.[30] The two models come together in finding the concept of seditious libel repulsive. From the political speech perspective, flag burning is protected political—dare I use the word—*dissent*. It is an attack on the political establishment, and if the political speech model protects anything, it is attacks on the political establishment. From the dissent perspective, flag-burning statutes are a particularly naked display of the conviction that government can suppress those who attack societal customs and traditions *just because* society holds its beliefs and symbols dear.

The political focus has its weaknesses, however. The flag is not just a symbol of government. Those who see a flag burned often feel that they have been personally assaulted. The action is perceived by them as an attack not merely on the existing government but on the society and the country of which they feel themselves a part. In short, flag burning has social and cultural dimensions that range beyond the political. Thus, the dissent focus is superior to the political focus because it encourages the view that people should be free to attack not merely politicians and government but deeply held customs, attitudes, and traditions that range beyond the political.[31]

Dissent and Communitarians

A significant advantage of a focus on dissent is that it serves to consolidate the values ordinarily associated with the First Amendment. Such focus does not liquidate liberty, freedom, equality, justice, tolerance, respect, dignity, self-government, truth, marketplace values, the checking value, associational values, cathartic values, or any other value that has been tied to freedom of speech or press. But the advantage of the dissent perspective runs even deeper: it implicates important cultural and communitarian values.

The aftermath of the *Johnson* decision and the debate surrounding it sheds substantial light on this important point. In response to *Johnson*, Congress passed the Flag Protection Act of 1989, which attached criminal penalties to knowingly mutilating, defacing, burning, maintaining on the floor or ground, or trampling upon any flag of the United States. Prior to adopting the Flag Protection Act, the Senate by a vote of 97 to 3 had passed a resolution registering disapproval of the *Johnson* opinion. The House had approved a similar resolution by a vote of 411 to 5, and President Bush had proposed a constitutional amendment to overrule *Johnson*. Opponents of the amendment argued that a carefully drawn statute might (or would) be upheld by the Court. Most liberal legislators supported such legislation. Although some feigned genuine appreciation for the action, the liberal's motivation is best captured in the following exchange from hearings of the House Subcommittee on Civil and Constitutional Rights on *Statutory and Constitutional Responses to the Supreme Court Decision in Texas v. Johnson* (1989):

> *Former Solicitor General Charles Fried:* "My good friends and colleagues, Rex Lee and Laurence Tribe, have testified that a statute might be drawn that would pass constitutional muster. [I] hope and urge and pray that we will not act—that no statute be passed and of course that the Constitution not be amended. In short, I believe the *Johnson* is right [in] principle." . . .
>
> *Representative Schroeder:* "I thought your testimony was eloquent. I think in a purist world, that is where we should go. But [we] are not talking about a purist world. We are talking about a very political world." . . .
>
> *Mr. Fried:* "There are times when you earn your rather inadequate salary by just doing the right thing, and where you seem to agree with me is that the right thing to do is to do neither one of these. . . . It is called leadership."
>
> *Representative Schroeder:* "It is called leadership. . . . But I guess what I am saying is if we can't stop a stampede on an amendment without something, isn't it better to try to save the Bill of Rights and the Constitution?"[32]

I suppose that progressives would be divided on this exchange. Many would side with Fried.[33] Many would support Schroeder. But few progressives were suggesting that a congressional statute (upheld by the Supreme Court) might be *worse* for the progressive cause than an amendment of the First Amendment.

Frank Michelman is one such progressive, and his argument is well worth considering. First, for many years Michelman has been attracted to and influenced by a communitarian perspective. For conservative communitarians, the flag-burning issue is easy. A minimum conservative communitarian requirement might be that Americans not physically degrade the one symbol that stands for the country.[34] Michelman, however, is not a conservative, and no progressive, whatever his or her communitarian leanings might be, is likely to uphold a flag-burning statute. Michelman's communitarian inclinations show up both in his discussion of the flag-burning issue per se and in his arguments for the proposition that a congressional statute (upheld by the Supreme Court) might be worse for the progressive cause than an amendment of the First Amendment. As I shall explain, these arguments will lead us to an appreciation of some of the differences between a communitarian approach and a dissent perspective—at the same time it reveals the communitarian dimensions of the dissent model.

In exploring Michelman's position, I should hasten to observe that he does not claim that a statute upheld by the Supreme Court *is* a worse alternative than an amendment. He suggests only that it *might* be worse and, in the end, concludes that both alternatives are equally bad: "[I]n the respects that ought finally to dominate our judgment the two come very much to the same thing."[35]

In support of the view that a statute upheld by the Supreme Court is just as bad as a constitutional amendment, Michelman first asks us to consider the situation from the perspective of "constitutional law" rather than that of the "scriptural Constitution." Constitutional law is the "body of normative material that the Supreme Court both creates and consults when it resolves questions about the legal validity of governmental actions challenged as unconstitutional."[36] This body of law includes principles, precedents, and doctrines, and is thus different from the "scriptural text we know as the Constitution."[37] As between the scriptural text and constitutional law, Michelman argues: "[I]t must be *constitutional law* that is the immediate concern of the practical-minded. . . . One could even ask why anyone ever cares at all what the scriptural Constitution says. Why is the prospect of constitutional amendment *ever* an occasion for practical concern? One answer, again obvious, is that while constitutional law is not identical with the scriptural constitution, neither is it independent of it. To the practical-minded, constitutional amendments matter—perhaps among other reasons—because of their anticipated effects on constitutional law."[38]

From the perspective of "constitutional law" as he has set it out, Michelman maintains that any opinion upholding a flag protection statute in the wake of *Johnson* would create dangerous doctrine. Even if the Court were to uphold the statute as a "flag exception" to ordinary First Amendment principles, Michelman argues that there could be no assurance that the opinion would stay confined. By contrast, an amendment could be carefully drafted to prevent a radiating effect. Indeed, the amendment could state explicitly that it "shall not be in any way relied upon in any case to which its terms are not directly applicable."[39]

As Michelman recognizes, there are other practical effects of amending the Bill of Rights that might concern progressives. It might legitimately be feared that " 'the appetites of many for quick ways to leap over constitutional barriers will be whetted. . . . With each amendment [curtailing the rights of dissidents], resistance would be lessened for the next amendment affecting an unpopular group.' "[40]

Nonetheless, Michelman has little patience for this line of argument: "This all seems dangerously close to declaring that the People cannot be trusted with self-government under this Constitution, at least not if the ring of fire around the Bill of Rights should ever be broken. . . . To speak as sharply as I can, I don't see how to distinguish our own resort to sacralization of the Bill of Rights from the kind of aversion and squeamishness towards open political conflict displayed by our adversaries who want to cast a special pall of sanctity over the stars-and-stripes. It seems to me that idolatry is idolatry, sacrosanction is sacrosanction, whether poured over the flag or over the Bill of Rights."[41]

In short, we should place more trust in democracy and be prepared to compete by argument "on the merits ungirded by mystique."[42] This does not mean we must shun "any nonmystical arguments we have that there ought to be a strong presumption against messing with the Bill of Rights."[43] It does seem to foreclose resort to an argument that would invoke those "mystic chords of memory that have kept the Bill of Rights, to date, an object of civil awe that mustn't be disturbed, upon pain of tempting a great Wrath."[44]

Finally, Michelman states that the best reason for preferring an amendment over a statute may "lie beyond a concern about constitutional *law*, in some other kind of care, some other sort of regard, that people feel for *the Constitution*."[45] I can only puzzle why this argument does not get more weight. One possibility is that Michelman ultimately finds the argument too mystical or insufficiently practical-minded, but, judging from his other writings, I doubt it. Michelman understands that symbols matter. Another stronger possibility is that it reaches beyond one of Michelman's principal purposes in the article, namely, to use the flag-burning controversy to explore the conventional wisdom that judicial interpretation is principled and guided by an external source and that amendments to the Constitution need not be principled.

What he says in connection with *"the Constitution"* is that a constitutional flag amendment would graft " 'a permanent blemish onto our most fundamental constitutional principle,' and would '[make] us a little silly, and a little less free, and a little less brave.' "[46] Michelman regards this "aesthetic and psychological" argument as particularly attractive because of its recognition that the Constitution assumes and pictures an "us," a political and moral community, a community that includes the majority, its opposition, and its dissenters.[47] Of course, our community falls short of what it ought to be, and he suggests that if our conceptions of community govern our "aesthetic"[48] response to proposed alterations of the Constitution "then one would have to consider, on behalf of a flag amendment, this argument: that some speech acts are so antithetical to any serious profession of aspiration toward political community, and so destructive of movement toward it, that a Constitution depicting that aspiration cannot shelter such acts against the community's prohibition, and at the same time retain the force of apparent moral seriousness."[49]

But flag burning, Michelman argues, is not paradigmatically at odds with political community: "Rather the flag burner charges the nation with betraying its ideals as the flag burner understands them and would have them (and herself) understood.[50] . . . Among modes of political expression, flag burning is not paradigmatically antithetical to American communitarian aspiration."[51]

In response to Michelman, I want to suggest first that his own premises lead, albeit not inexorably, to the conclusion that a flag-burning constitutional amendment would be a more serious loss for progressives[52] than a flag-burning statute upheld by the Supreme Court. As Michelman recognizes, a citizen's relationship to the Constitution is an important psychological connection. Indeed, the Constitution plays a special role in *constituting* who we are and who we aspire to be.[53] The flag amendment was uniquely threatening to progressives because it struck a *symbolic* dagger at the notion that the First Amendment is an important reflection of our "profound national commitment" to protect dissent. No doubt, the symbolic effect of a flag-burning statute upheld by the Supreme Court would be disheartening, but the relative rhetorical and constituting power of statutes, decisions, and the Constitution are not the same. The scriptural Constitution is a more important cultural symbol, and it constitutes us in ways that statutes upheld by the Supreme Court do not.

Moreover, from the perspective of encouraging a sense of belonging to a moral and political community (however aspirational), we should applaud the divide between constitutional law and the scriptural Constitution. If the Court had upheld the Flag Protection Act, liberals could say that what the Court says is not what *the Constitution* says. But if the Constitution were amended, it would be hard for them to avoid profound alienation. To experience the Supreme Court as a morally bankrupt institution can be an important psychological event in a person's political development; to experience the Constitution itself as embodying repugnant principles is a much more profound psychological moment. It encourages estrangement from a sense of moral and political community.

That estrangement might be somewhat less if one is a Michelman-type progressive (a "Democratic progressive"). If I read him correctly, Michelman would prefer to risk the Bill of Rights rather than settle for distrust of the People over democracy.[54] For some Democratic progressives—I do not claim that Michelman is one of them—a flag-burning amendment, albeit "ugly and dispiriting," is still a part of a Constitution in which the People rule, and if the People get it wrong in one amendment, they may well be persuaded to change. A flag-burning amendment would be no occasion for "dancing in the streets," but it would not necessarily be an occasion for feeling estranged from the moral and political community. Those Democratic progressives could believe that a flag-burning statute upheld by the Supreme Court and a constitutional amendment "come very much to the same thing."[55] In either case, the dominant feature of the Constitution—rule of the People—would be undisturbed.

I doubt Michelman himself would go so far. In his other writings Michelman exhibits no tendency to equate the people with the People. In *Law's Republic*, for example, the People is an aspirational concept and the constitutional community is an aspirational community.[56] Michelman is obviously offended by a political community that is not inclusive or is not open to dialogic questioning of its traditions and ideals. Nonetheless, the value he places on being a part of a political community makes him a more likely candidate to stay the course than some other progressives (the "Bill of Rights progressives").

The Bill of Rights progressives emphasize that some rights are sacrosanct, and the majority—even a supermajority—has no right to interfere. Of course, Article 5 of the Constitution gives the People the *power* to outlaw seditious libel, for example, criticism of the government in wartime, but more than a few progressives believe that the People have no *right* to do any such thing. Moreover, *if* the People enshrine their violation of rights in the Constitution, the Bill of Rights progressives are more likely than the Democratic progressives to be estranged. For them, the "mystic chords of memory that have kept the Bill of Rights, to date, an object of civil awe that mustn't be disturbed" have been an important psychological and aesthetic component of what the Constitution means and what the country means.

Moreover, the Bill of Rights progressives are at ease in distinguishing between their "own resort to sacralization of the Bill of Rights from the kind of aversion and squeamishness towards open political conflict displayed by our adversaries who want to cast a special pall of sanctity over the stars-and-stripes."[57] First, the Bill of Rights progressives themselves are unabashedly squeamish about certain forms of political conflict. For example, they do not want the polity to debate which church should be established as the national church; they do not want the polity to debate

whether the slave trade should be reinstituted; they do not want the polity
to debate whether the institutional press should be abolished, or whether
citizens should be prohibited from criticizing existing habits, traditions,
institutions, and authorities. By placing prohibitions on action in areas
such as these, the Constitution, with the full support of these progressives,
discourages political conflict over these issues. Whether or not it is fair to
say that the Bill of Rights progressives engage in "idolatry" or "sacrosanction" when they invoke the Bill of Rights as the centerpiece of the
Constitution and the country, their "mystical" appeals can easily be distinguished from those who would "sacralize" the flag. As Michelman recognizes throughout his article, the attempt to use legal penalties against
flag burners is a pure exercise of repression. But Michelman's objection
focuses more on the use of emotional appeals than on the object of those
appeals. What is missing from that argument (other than its privileging
of the People over the Bill of Rights) is an explanation of how the invocation of the People is any less a piece of mysticism than the symbolic use
of the Bill of Rights. Further missing is a delineation between building
an attractive psychological picture of the Constitution and engaging in
unacceptable mysticism. Without additional explanation, it seems that
one person's unacceptable mysticism is another person's attractive psychological and aesthetic ground.

In fact, the Democratic progressives and the Bill of Rights progressives
share mystical ideals that are not far apart. The Democratic progressives
long for informed democratic dialogue. Flag burning is seen as an important component of democratic dialogue because it, and other acts of
dissent like it, call attention to the failure of the country to live up to its
ideals. The Bill of Rights progressives seek to encourage and protect the
Emersonian dissenter,[58] and flag burners squarely fit that model. But the
dissent model is not premised exclusively on notions that individuals
thrive when they feel free to speak out. *It is not just a self-expression
model.*

The dissent model assumes that in large-scale societies powerful interest
groups and self-seeking politicians and bureaucrats are unavoidable. Injustice will always be present (although its severity can vary). Dissenters
and the dialogue that follows will always be necessary. On this premise,
dissent has important instrumental value. So, of course, does democratic
dialogue. Indeed, the dissent model would hope that dialogue would ultimately be spurred by the presence of dissent. In this respect the dialogue
model and the dissent model run together.

But instrumental value is also *not* the point of the flag-burning dispute.
From an instrumental perspective one might wonder why anyone should
care if people are free to burn flags. After a flag-burning amendment,
dissenters would still be free to burn copies of the Constitution or to melt

down images of the Washington Memorial, the Lincoln Memorial, or the Statue of Liberty.[59] Dissent would not be smothered by a flag-burning amendment.

No, the contest is about ideals. For the majority of Americans, flag burners were contemptuous of the community, and a congressional response was necessary to affirm the community's values. For these Americans, the flag stands for the country; for them, free speech is one thing; disrespect for the symbol that binds the nation together is quite another.

Opponents of flag-burning prohibitions also sought to affirm the community's values. But the values were different. For the opponents, particularly the Bill of Rights progressives, the American community is committed to the notion that dissent should be protected, and the First Amendment is the legal manifestation of that cultural commitment. For such progressives, the point of the flag-burning dispute was not the self-realization of the Johnsons of the world. Nor did such progressives lose sleep fearing that Johnson's truth would not emerge in the marketplace of ideas. (Few people had even the slightest idea of what he was trying to say.) Rather, such progressives forge their identity in a country that, in their mind, is (or ought to be) committed to protecting dissenters. To prevent people from burning the flag is to violate the First Amendment principles for which the flag ought to stand. It is to transform the very meaning of the country and thus to threaten the political identity of American liberals. The value of dissent, then, in this context is not that it fosters individual development or self-realization, or even that it exposes injustice and brings about change. The commitment to dissent and the First Amendment is of national symbolic value: it is a form of cultural glue that binds citizens to the political community.

The First Amendment and the Arts

It should now be clear that the cases involving the refusal to subsidize controversial artists are flag-burning cases with a doctrinal twist. Once again, the conservatives believe that the First Amendment is one thing but that our "public morality" is quite another. Again, whatever the progressives say, I do not believe that the issue involved concern over whether the photographer Robert Mapplethorpe's truth would or would not emerge in the marketplace of ideas, nor was this a contest about Mapplethorpe's self-expression. Again, this struggle was all about cultural ideals. For the conservative, the point is that our Constitution does not and should not provide protection for those who flout our customs and our morality. To the contrary, for the progressive, the point is that our Constitution has a special place for those who reject or leap beyond our prior understandings of tradition, order, and morality.

So understood, the doctrinal twist is of no constitutional moment. Money simply has no pride of place in this constitutional battlefield. To be sure, the conservative claim is readily understood. The Mapplethorpes of the world may have a constitutional right to produce and display their work, but surely taxpayers incur no constitutional obligation to subsidize that work. The failure to fund art is not its prohibition. Nor can it plausibly be argued that artists have a First Amendment right to government funds.

These observations, however, are quite beside the constitutional point and skirt the cultural heart of the dispute. The failure to fund art may well not involve its prohibition.[60] Nor is there any general right of artists to government funds. The progressives make neither of these claims. What the progressives do claim is that an artist cannot be denied funds for unconstitutional reasons.

Let us sneak up on the First Amendment point. Suppose a government funding agency as a matter of policy denies artistic subsidies to all black applicants. No doubt, everyone agrees that policy is unconstitutional, and no one would think it important to observe in that context that the failure to fund art does not involve its prohibition or that there is no general right of artists to government funds. Similarly, suppose a government funding agency as a matter of policy denies artistic subsidies to all Republicans. Here, there is no constitutional distinction between racial and political discrimination: both policies are unconstitutional.

Now suppose the government denies an artistic subsidy to a piece of blasphemous art or to a person who has produced blasphemous art. On the argument we have been following, that denial may or may not be unconstitutional. If the denial is based on the belief that the work in question or the work to be produced is unlikely to meet artistic standards, it is not open to constitutional question. On the other hand, if the work or the probable work is deemed to be *otherwise deserving* of artistic support, a subsidy cannot constitutionally be denied on the ground that the work is offensive. Under the First Amendment, dissenters have no right to be subsidized, but dissenters cannot be denied subsidies just because they are dissenters.

Owen Fiss partially denies this conclusion, and Robert Post denies it altogether. Fiss maintains that in a constitutional democracy the First Amendment is designed to protect "collective self-determination: to insure the fullness and richness of public debate."[61] From this perspective, he argues that the criterion of artistic excellence be supplemented by con-

cerns about the impact of fund allocations on public debate.[62] He suggests
that National Endowment for the Arts (NEA) administrators should give
consideration to the relative degree of exclusion of particular unorthodox
perspectives in the public square,[63] the degree of financial need of the
applicant,[64] and the extent to which the project illuminates issues of immediate national concern.[65] Fiss's desire to assure that unorthodox views
are subsidized, however, does not include the indecent. In his view, it is
permissible to choose decency as a criterion so long as the criterion is not
being used to disfavor the unorthodox.[66] Thus, from Fiss's perspective, a
project challenging orthodox views about sexuality or the distribution of
wealth could be selected over projects with the same views if the former
were more decent than the latter.

In my view, Fiss gives the NEA too little discretion, on the one hand,
and too much, on the other. I am sympathetic to the view that government
has a constitutional obligation to assure that the conditions for a robust
public debate are in place. I especially believe that government has an
affirmative obligation to assure that the society encourages dissent against
injustice whether in public or private hierarchies.[67] The role that the judiciary ought to play with respect to encouraging robust public debate or
dissent is more complicated, however. Even if the discretionary actions of
NEA officials or congressional directives to NEA officials were subject to
the Fiss regime, Fiss's easy assumption that the judiciary would enforce
the regime is hard to credit. If the judiciary were to enforce the Fiss regime,
all NEA grants would be open to immediate legal challenge. Judges would
be deciding on an ad hoc basis which issues need to be discussed on the
national agenda and which have been comparatively marginalized. Even
those who favor an "activist" judiciary may worry about the capacity
of judges to make those decisions, about the institutional costs to the
judiciary in doing so, and about the damage to the process of subsidizing
the arts that would be implicated by the costs and delays of litigation.
Apart from judicial roles, from the premise that government should support a robust debate, it does not follow that government should support
robust debate in all its programs. The government might support art on
the basis of artistic merit through the NEA and support unorthodox robust debate (including artistic and Philistine forms of expression) through
other programs.

Most surprising of all is Fiss's acceptance of an NEA restriction on
indecent speech. To his credit, what he says is at least guarded. In cases
where two projects support an unorthodox view, "a proper concern for
First Amendment values would not necessarily preclude the NEA chair-
person from taking decency into account. One must make certain that the
decency criterion is not being used to disfavor the orthodox, and one
should acknowledge that it might have a tendency in that direction, but

it is hard to rule out the criterion altogether. [C]ase-by-case judgements would be needed . . . to see whether the decency criterion is being applied in such a way as to systematically disadvantage certain perspectives and thus to impoverish public debate."[68]

What Fiss would permit is the failure to subsidize art that has already been deemed excellent on the ground that it is indecent. But art that is deemed indecent or offensive or potentially offensive is so regarded precisely because it challenges existing social customs, habits, and traditions. The constitutional wrong is achieved by using indecency in addition to artistic excellence, whether or not the wrong is compounded by "systematically disadvantaging certain perspectives" in a way that impoverishes "public debate."

If Owen Fiss is cautious about the use of the indecency criterion, Robert Post is more confident about its propriety. He argues, first, that free speech within bureaucracies is rightly limited. If an administrator tells a bureaucrat to give a speech supporting the policies of the administration, the bureaucrat has no free speech right to refuse.[69] The same principles apply to commands within the military,[70] and Post argues that they apply as well to directives within the NEA.[71] Although Post has made significant contributions to the literature in his discussion of the relationships between government as manager and as regulator of public discourse, to some extent I write on the opposite side of the fence. Post is undoubtedly correct in arguing that directives within bureaucracies ordinarily do not present serious free speech concerns.[72] Even from a dissent-centered perspective, government has a strong interest in running its programs, many of which involve speech. If every government employee could refuse to carry out orders to speak to the recipients of government programs in the name of dissent, substantial government interests would be unreasonably impaired. As I noted in the introduction, dissent is neither a necessary nor a sufficient factor for free speech protection. Whether speech should be protected invariably depends on the social context. There is a wide difference between employees dissenting within the workplace (which they generally should have the right to do) and refusing to carry out the orders of the organization (which they generally should not have the right to do).

Nonetheless, there are clear cases where employees have rights not to carry out orders and to say what they want to say. Within educational bureaucracies, for example, although public university professors can be directed to stick to the subjects they teach, the First Amendment would not permit university administrators to direct that professors adhere to a particular point of view in the classroom. Post, of course, recognizes that the managerial character of government action does not inevitably rule out First Amendment problems. He suggests that First Amendment issues are created when the speech of professionals is limited within bureaucracies in ways that do not permit them to exercise judgment according to their professional standards. He maintains, for example, that doctors in federal programs dedicated to preconceptional services should have been afforded a First Amendment right to counsel patients regarding abortion despite specific governmental directives to the contrary[73] and despite a Supreme Court decision to the contrary in *Rust v. Sullivan*.[74] This analysis could also be applied to university professors.[75]

I am not convinced, however, that the professional/bureaucrat line can do all the work that Post seems to suppose it can. I think it takes more argument to demonstrate that government directives limiting the professional judgment of employees or independent contractors in what they say is unconstitutional. I doubt it would be unconstitutional for the Justice Department to impose an official interpretation concerning case law that would limit prosecutors in what they tell police or what can be said in training prosecutors. Similarly, I do not think it should be generally unconstitutional for a government-run health maintenance organization to limit the kinds of advice that will be given to patients. On the other hand, if government in a managerial mode required doctors to violate their professional standards, I would recommend heightened judicial scrutiny, whether or not the requirement involved speech.[76] To my mind, *Rust v. Sullivan* was wrongly decided not because doctors are professionals but because poor women should be afforded rights to abortions, including the right to receive information about them, and because patients have a right to expect that government doctors will give them information about their legitimate medical options.[77]

Post's emphasis on the professional/bureaucrat distinction could itself invalidate an indecency requirement if an artistic subsidy program were not structured to get around it. Panels that recommend the approval of applications for artistic subsidies are composed of professionals, not bureaucrats. To impose an indecency requirement upon them would ask them to compromise their professional judgments. But the NEA could be structured so that artistic panels made judgments on the basis of artistic excellence, while an administrator excluded "indecent" proposals. Then Post could neither profit nor lose from the fact that government was directing employees in a managerial mode.

Post makes another argument that is importantly different. Rather than arguing for the marginality of free speech concerns within bureaucracies, he argues that government has a right to participate in culture building. In so doing, it necessarily discriminates on the basis of point of view. So far so good. It is not unconstitutional for government to create a flag or patriotic monuments or to sponsor antismoking campaigns. The government printing office produces many documents that present a specific point of view, and government support of such publications is not unconstitutional. Government has an interest in supporting its programs and in protecting the public interest. The Constitution does not prevent its entry into the marketplace of ideas. Nonetheless, the government's role as speaker and as subsidizer of speech is not uncabined. We have already mentioned that government should not constitutionally be permitted to discriminate on a racial or partisan political basis. In addition, if government enters the intellectual market, there should be First Amendment concerns about government domination. Post, of course, would not deny this, but he apparently would have judges make ad hoc decisions whether general subsidy programs did that. To my mind, these concerns are better addressed by doctrines that function to promote diversity and protect dissent when government embarks on a general program of subsidies without ad hoc determinations of government domination. Thus, broadcast licensees have First Amendment rights to make independent judgments about their programming,[78] and professors have First Amendment rights to make independent judgments about the content of their courses (within the prescribed curriculum). So, too, in the interests of diversity and dissent, I would argue that vetos on indecency grounds are unconstitutional. Those who serve on NEA panels should be able to make judgments of artistic merit, and those judgments should be respected independent of governmental assessments of orthodoxy and decency. A government administrator should not be able to censor such proposals in the interests of building the culture. Of course, if government could order broadcast licensees, professors, and NEA panels around, it would have an easier time in "building the culture," but the First Amendment is best interpreted to provide structural assurances that general subsidies be free from monolithic decision making or politicization whether in broadcasting, education, or art.[79]

Putting decision making concerning general artistic subsidies in the hands of artistic professionals, however, is not a perfect solution. Some dissent will still be muffled, albeit more subtly. Built into the conception of what counts as artistically valuable are a set of conventions and expectations. Those who break with these conventions may meet a chilly reception precisely because they broke with the conventions. In other words, artistic professionals (or the arts community) police the boundaries between art and mass culture, and between good and bad art. They, like academics, are masters of channeling conceptions of merit in self-serving ways. Just as power participates in the construction of knowledge, so it participates in the construction of beauty, the sublime, and the artistic. In the politics of aesthetics, dissent is frequently praised in the abstract and besmirched in the concrete.[80]

Nonetheless, the reliance on artists to make decisions about artists has countervailing advantages from a dissent perspective. Artists as a subgroup of the population are particularly likely to run against the current; they are more likely than others to appreciate the avant-garde.[81] Thus, the crisis over subsidies to controversial artists would never have arisen if artists had not first declared the works in question to be of substantial artistic value.

The First Amendment, Cultural Struggle, and National Identity

All of which returns us to Patrick Buchanan: "The arts crowd is after more than our money, more than an end to the congressional ban on funding obscene and blasphemous art. It is engaged in a cultural struggle to root out the old America of family, faith, and flag, and re-create society in a pagan image." From a legal perspective, part of this statement is pure gobbledygook. If work has serious artistic value, it is not obscene by definition. From a conservative perspective, the notion of obscene art is oxymoronic. From that perspective, work that is blasphemous or obscene cannot be sublime and *therefore* cannot be art.[82] But this is nitpicking. Buchanan is on to something, even if his statement reeks of overwrought conspiratorial designs. The artistic community is more likely to question the conventions Americans hold dear. And despite America's professed commitment to the First Amendment, few Americans want their values mocked in public.

The failure of liberals to command a majority of the American public, then, should not be surprising. The best liberal theory almost guarantees that liberals will occupy a minority. One need not read far in John Stuart Mill's *On Liberty* to find him writing "against the tyranny of the prevailing opinion and feeling; against the tendency of the society to impose, by other means than civil penalties, its own ideas and practices as rules of conduct on those who dissent from them."[83] That tyranny is with us now, and it always will be. If liberals seek to protect and promote dissent,[84] they will ride against the current. The only way for liberals to become a part of the majority on this kind of issue is to stop being liberals.

Nonetheless, it would be simplistic to regard liberals as carriers of the torch of dissent in American society, and not just because dissent is a multifaceted aspect of daily power relationships at every level of human existence. Liberals are often said to value freedom and dissent over community, but I think this characterization ignores political psychology and the liberals' characteristic attitudes toward change.

Consider another characterization of liberals that is just as frequently heard. Liberals are pragmatic realists who are prepared to compromise with the system in order to get something accomplished. Radicals believe that liberals "sell out" for prices that are far too low.

Why would liberals sell at too low a price (assuming they do, and surely they sometimes do)? First, there is the possibility that they miscalculate the possibilities for change. Second, and more interesting from the perspective of political psychology, liberals may want personal influence. Less frequently observed, however, and most interesting of all is the possibility that liberals crave community. It is one thing not to be a member of the majority; it is quite another to be a psychological outcast from the political community. By moving too far from the center, liberals risk marginalization and alienation. This is the posture of the true dissenter, and it involves difficult psychological burdens. My claim is that most liberals are loathe to accept these burdens.[85] Indeed, I suggest that in this sense, despite the common stereotypes, American liberals typically value community over freedom and dissent.[86]

From the same perspective, radicals defy the conventional stereotypes. They are often believed to value community over freedom, but this too ignores political psychology. Radicals are the political individualists of American society. They have the integrity to speak out against the dominant structure of the society even though most Americans have been socialized to deplore their views. They dissent more thoroughly than the liberals. This is not to say that radicals do not value community. Indeed, they may be more self-conscious about the need for community and their own personal needs than liberals. Instead of embracing a form of national identity, many radicals forge an identity with the workers of the world, the oppressed of the world, or the "arts crowd." But they also work hard at building a local community of like-minded individuals. Of course, this community building fits with the radicals' political perspective, but it also fits important psychological needs. To be at the political margin almost necessitates the building of networks that nurture the continuing capacity to dissent. Even these radicals forge a national identity of a sort. They criticize America more frequently than other countries and perhaps more bitterly because they feel attached[87] and responsible. As Henry Louis Gates, Jr., puts it, "[C]ritique can also be a form of commitment, a means of laying a claim. It's the ultimate gesture of citizenship. A way of saying: I'm not just passing through, I *live* here."[88]

Nonetheless, the liberals ordinarily forge a stronger connection to the community than the radicals in that liberals are more uncomfortable with and more resistant to feelings of alienation. Moreover, if I am right that liberals were more concerned about the cultural meaning of the First Amendment than about the self-expression of Gregory Johnson, the notion of liberal individualism needs substantial revision. The connection of liberals (and many radicals) to the country is not just a Hobbesian bargain; it is a form of nationalism,[89] a matter of cultural and political identity. It may be thought that this is a benign form of nationalism, and to a large extent it is. If political identity is bound up with the protection of dissent, nationalism would seem to strengthen, not to threaten, free speech.[90] Nonetheless, the liberal position on free speech rights has political costs. Some of the subtle political costs are intrinsically bound up with the flag-burning controversy or the controversy over funding of the arts. In order to uphold their position, liberals[91] have championed the view that this country values and prizes dissent, freedom, liberty, the marketplace of ideas, democratic dialogue, and/or controversy. This is what the country *stands* for, or so goes the argument.

This line of argument is part of the standard stock of the practicing liberal. The ideals of the country are X, but we've fallen short; therefore, we must do Y. In so doing, we will reconcile our theory with our practice. This stock argument has the force of exposing contradiction. Moreover, it takes a moral and political high ground, and it has a communitarian appeal urging its auditors to reaffirm their commitment to the ideals of the polity.

But the argument is mined with conservative aspects. "Ideals" are easily manufactured from pious statements by political, including judicial, leaders. To take those stated ideals seriously as a statement of what the country *in fact* stands for is to lose critical edge.[92] It is an argumentative strategy that functions to make the country look better than it is—even as it is used to condemn a particular practice.[93] Moreover, the style of argument promotes self-deception. To habitually use such arguments is to risk seeing the country through a distorted lens.

Nonetheless, in the legal world of constitutional interpretation, it would be a nonstarter to say that this country does not now and never has valued dissent *even if it were true*. To defend flag burning or blasphemous art as protected speech under the First Amendment, it is crucial to paint an argumentative picture that frames some value like dissent or its toleration as a vital ideal in the American culture.[94]

Necessary as the stock argument may be, the existence of the First Amendment as a cultural symbol masks the extent to which dissent is discouraged and subordinated.[95] Therein lies the paradox: the First Amendment serves to undermine dissent even as it protects it. Of course, the First Amendment protects dissent. It offers a legal claim for dissenters, and it functions as a cultural symbol encouraging dissenters to speak out. Nonetheless, the symbolism of the First Amendment perpetuates a cultural myth. It functions as a form of cultural ideology through which the society secures allegiance. It leads us to believe that America is the land of free speech, but it blinks at the "tyranny of the prevailing opinion and feeling," and it masks the extent to which free speech is marginalized, discouraged, and repressed. Even as it promotes dissent, it falsifies the willingness of the society to receive it, and it tolerates rules of place and property that make it difficult for people of modest means to address a mass audience.[96]

To get beyond the First Amendment paradox, one needs to take a broader look at the conditions of cultural struggle in America. One needs to ask how the political consciousness of the American majority is developed and why it is different in the United States than in other developed countries. To what extent does commercial art (i.e., advertising) play a role in molding the values of this culture? Does an advertiser-dominated medium adversely stack the deck against progressive politics? To what extent does the role of corporate money undermine the possibility of even incremental liberal reform? To what extent would mass media access by powerless groups affect the terms of cultural struggle? Is more thorough restructuring necessary? Desirable? Possible?

Issues like flag burning and subsidies for the arts raise important questions about the character of our culture. To fight about these questions is to reinforce the legitimizing myths of the society. Not to fight about them is a formula for political suicide. They are battles that need to be fought, but they should be placed in perspective: they are warm-ups for a larger war.

The First Amendment and Postmodernism

If the First Amendment paradox poses a challenge, some postmodernists pose a related but somewhat different First Amendment challenge. Their argument is not that First Amendment practice is a better description of the First Amendment values of the culture than its ideals. The argument is that the purportedly timeless ideals of the culture are utterly constructed, that they bear no relationship to any prepolitical reality, that the very idea of rights is suspect. Of course, the argument often goes deeper— to an interrogation of truth and of the very possibility of human subjectivity.[97] Postmodernists see themselves as well situated to question the foundations of scientific, moral, and political discourse, and they regard that undertaking as a politically powerful means of attacking hierarchy. Their perspective is valuable in showing the many ways in which power has constructed knowledge to the disadvantage of oppressed people.

Although I delight in the energy and ferocity of postmodernism, and believe that much work produced by postmodernists has contributed to our understanding of power and its abuse, I do not endorse postmodernism in any of its usual versions. I do not think it is necessary to be a postmodernist in order to attack and expose unjust concentrations of power, unjust hierarchy, the failures of grand theory or grand narratives, the pretensions of neutrality, or any of the authoritarian ways in which power constructs knowledge.[98] Indeed a non-postmodernist can launch such attacks without having to fend off conversations about relativism, skepticism, or nihilism. I do not see an attack[99] on truth or morals to be an important part of a fruitful political strategy,[100] particularly not one that has democratic aspirations and hopes to involve any large sector of the public.[101] More important, although postmodernism tends to focus our attention on some important issues, it distracts us from others. Among other things, postmodernism is a reaction to the failure of Marxism to speak to issues of difference. As Linda J. Nicholson writes: "Twentieth-century Marxism has used the generalizing categories of production and class to delegitimize demands of women, black people, gays, lesbians, and others whose oppression cannot be reduced to economics. Thus, to raise questions now about the necessary liberatory consequences of universalizing categories is to open spaces for movements otherwise shut out by them."[102]

To be sure, this is important work, and postmodernists, among others, have done it well. But the focus of postmodernism on the local and the particular tilts against all grand narratives, including narratives about the destructive impact of uncontrolled capitalism with its international conglomerates, together with their flights to exploitable labor and their political influence in national governments. As David Harvey writes: "[Postmodernism denies] that kind of meta-theory which can grasp the political-economic processes (money flows, international divisions of labor, financial markets, and the like) that are becoming ever more universalizing in their depth, intensity, reach and power over daily life. . . . The rhetoric of postmodernism is dangerous for it avoids confronting the realities of political economy and the circumstances of global power."[103]

Beyond truth, morals, and political economy, I believe in some prepolitical rights.[104] For example, I believe people have rights not to be gratuitously tortured[105] or held in slavery, and I believe that some free speech rights are prepolitical. I do not claim that I can *prove* there is a right not to be gratuitously tortured or that there is a right of free speech, but I am prepared to trust my reflective intuitions, even recognizing that such intuitions are socially constructed and even though they are often wrong. Socially constructed intuitions need not be wrong. Moreover, our inability to *prove* we are right does not mean we are wrong, nor does it mean we are disabled from believing we are right.

Finally, it is not clear that the stance taken by many postmodernists[106] toward rights is politically progressive. Critical race theorists,[107] among others,[108] have argued that reliance on the rhetoric of rights has been historically valuable. Perhaps they are wrong, but I do not think so. Few could deny that the rhetoric of rights has been a valuable tool in organizing grassroots emancipatory movements. Thus, James MacGregor Burns and Stewart Burns have chronicled the populist and broad-based character of "historic rights movements in which all participants are engaged in forging a dynamic, evolving people's charter of rights."[109] As the Burnses well understand and as some in critical legal studies[110] and critical race theory[111] have argued (influencing the Burnses as well as others), rights rhetoric has its costs. But which political strategy has the best overall chances is a matter of context. To rule out rights rhetoric altogether sweeps too broadly and too fast.[112]

Nonetheless, the postmodernist claim about rights has substantial value in the First Amendment context. Many, if not most, First Amendment claims involve issues of balancing and social engineering. They often depend on complex empirical and policy judgments. To what extent would a particular state interest be advanced by the state regulation in question? To what extent would speech be chilled by the regulation? Is the particular state interest as weighty as the particular free speech values imperiled by the regulation? What would be the consequences associated with other regulations that might impact on free speech values less severely?

Conceding that a legal right may be at stake, is it not a bit much for a First Amendment proponent to claim that his or her "rights" in any stronger sense have been violated in such a complex context? At least much of the time, I would agree that the existence of any such strong prelegal right cannot plausibly be defended.

Too easily, the rhetoric of First Amendment discourse projects a halo around the claim of the First Amendment claimant. To argue that the First Amendment dictates an outcome is to insist not merely on a legal right but also on a constitutional right with a Bill of Rights pedigree. Indeed, the invocation of rights smells of RIGHTS. It suggests that the proponents have a natural law right, an absolute right to that which they claim.[113]

And that is where the point of postmodernism has much to recommend it in First Amendment discourse. As William Connolly puts it, "The point is to refuse to curtail thinking in the name of guarding the faith."[114] Yet invocations of faith abound in First Amendment discourse. Perhaps the First Amendment faith does little harm when it applies to flag burning and the arts. But it is out of place when it comes to issues like pornography and hate speech. What is needed to address these problems is not faith but analysis. Whatever the role of the First Amendment in these circumstances, it should not be dictated by the fiat of faith. If the First Amendment is to nurture dissent, it must be open to dissent about its own role as well.[115]

Nonetheless, a postmodernist trap lies down this trail as well. If the First Amendment is no longer an absolute faith, its capacity to ground a political identity seems concomitantly diminished. Thus, the resort to dismissive conclusory assertions by many liberals in First Amendment contexts is understandable. If the First Amendment is an important part of a liberal's political identity, new challenges to free speech are psychologically threatening. If the First Amendment FAITH is dead, can the First Amendment itself be far behind?

But progressives cannot cling to a world of innocence. The innocent believe it possible to discover "some sort of truth which can tell us how to act in the world in ways that benefit or are for the (at least ultimate) good of all."[116] But the world of innocence was always a dreamworld in First Amendment law. Too many values interact in too many complicated ways for anyone to be able to hope or expect that something important need not be sacrificed. Many have blinked at this reality before, but issues like pornography and racist speech have opened more eyes.

Prior to issues such as these, progressives could comfortably sponsor a nation that treasured free speech *and* equality. Proponents of hate speech regulation argue, however, that historically disadvantaged groups are "silenced" by hate speech. In a sense this is an imperfect formulation. To be sure, many members of disadvantaged groups are silenced by such speech in the straightforward sense that their speech is chilled in many different ways. But the disadvantaged class as a class is "silenced" in a different sense, in that its members are not *heard* except through the distorting lens of hate speech. If truth emerges in the marketplace on issues of racism and sexism, perhaps it should be observed that it's a long wait. Thus, Cornel West can still speak of the ways in which black intellectuals are plagued by a "very deep racist legacy in which [they] are guilty before being proven innocent, in terms of perceiving them capable of intellectual partnership, capable of being part of a serious conversation."[117] And women are frequently perceived as sex objects before they are recognized as citizens.[118] Proponents of hate speech regulation argue, therefore, that values of free speech and equality collide in the hate speech context, and that equality is more important.

Most progressives have come to understand that the equality claim deserves a fair hearing, and they have resolved the issues in different ways. Many other progressives, however, have given these claims short shrift. It is difficult not to notice that many who confront these issues shout past each other, clinging to the world they want to see. This should not be surprising. Issues of racial, sexual, and political identity are emotionally charged, and notoriously so. I would not claim that these are easy issues. In chapter three, I will suggest that the issue of racist speech is itself quite complicated. It is not even easy to determine whether hate speech regulation would help disadvantaged groups or harm them. My own view, as I will argue in chapter three, is that such regulations would do some of both, and that some hate speech regulations should be upheld. But to some extent this is beside the point. Much of this debate is about symbols, not about important threats to free speech or about effective attacks on racism. And that places the hate speech issue in the picture I have been trying to paint here: from the flag to the arts, from racist speech to pornography, we ought not to underestimate the extent to which First Amendment debates implicate cultural struggles over the meaning of America.

II

Cigarettes, Alcohol, and Advertising

JAMES FENIMORE COOPER's novel *The Pioneers* still raises issues of contemporary importance. Set in Cooperstown, New York, the settling of
which was dominated by the author's father, the novel addresses such
issues as the fragility of the environment, the costs of "progress," the
authority of leaders and law, the pressures to conform, and the heroic but
anarchic character of independence.[1] Although the novel contains many
themes relevant to free speech, one stands out. At one point Judge Templeton's daughter, Elizabeth (Templeton is the character modeled after
Cooper's father) returns to the Templeton mansion after an absence of
many years. In doing so she displaces the head longtime housekeeper,
Miss Pettibone, who is relegated to the position of her subordinate. In
an effort to assert her new authority, the daughter tells the former head
housekeeper to call her *Miss* Templeton, not Betsy or Elizabeth. Some
pages later comes the passage of interest. Pettibone exclaims to another
employee, "I *will* call her Betsy as much as I please; *it's a free country*,
and no one can stop me."[2]

The notion that it's a free country runs through American life and literature in both the nineteenth and the twentieth century. Citizens invoke this
conception of the nation in support of free speech rights, frequently in
circumstances where no such right exists. The concept of "free speech in
a 'free country' " is not without ambiguity, but it seems to rest on an
individualistic, liberty-based idea of free speech. Thus, the basic idea
seems to be that no one has a right to interfere with the free speech of the
pioneer.

So it was. The "free speech in a 'free country' " slogan now resonates
with free markets. In this age, business corporations don a First Amendment cloak with shameless pride. Witness, for example, Philip Morris
purchasing the exclusive right from the National Archives to be the official corporate sponsor of the bicentennial celebration of the Bill of Rights
and participating in an extensive advertising campaign associating its
name with constitutional freedom.[3] Was this campaign an exercise of constitutional chutzpah, or did it proceed from a solid constitutional foundation? If America is the land of freedom, what is the constitutional status
of the advertising of products like tobacco or alcoholic beverages? What
should it be?

From some sources the answer has long been clear: time and time again, advocates for the affected industries and the American Civil Liberties Union (ACLU), among others, have told congressional committees that the First Amendment protects tobacco and alcoholic beverage advertising from extensive regulation or prohibitions. For many years, there was little foundation for this claim.[4] But a recent case, *44 Liquormart, Inc. v. Rhode Island*,[5] has cast a shadow over the regulation of such advertising.[6] That case has been interpreted by many journalists and commentators,[7] to imperil renewed regulatory efforts.[8] *Liquormart* is thought to represent a bold new charter of corporate freedom. Perhaps it does, but, as is so often the case in law, it may not. The pretenders to the throne of tomorrow may have longer to wait than they have let on. And wait, they should.

Liquormart reaches the right result,[9] but some of the opinions exhibit an overly broad view of the First Amendment. Just how many justices adhere to such a view requires a somewhat closer reading of the opinions than commentators have previously provided. Exploring the constitutional issues raised by the regulation of tobacco and alcoholic beverage advertising will lead us into some of the deepest issues in free speech. If such advertising does not rank high in the hierarchy of free speech values, we will need to know why. My suggestion will be that a free speech theory accenting protection for dissent fares better than a theory based in the protection of political speech or liberty.

The Liquormart Case

At one level, *Liquormart* was an easy case. With minor exceptions, the Rhode Island legislature had prohibited advertising the price of alcoholic beverages. Twenty years before the decision in *Liquormart*, the Court ruled in a landmark case (*Virginia State Board of Pharmacy v. Virginia Citizens Council*)[10] that a prohibition on prescription drug price advertising was unconstitutional. If Virginia could not outlaw the advertising of prescription drugs, it is hard, but not impossible, to see why Rhode Island could outlaw the advertising of alcoholic beverages. If Virginia sought to discourage the use of prescription drugs by artificially elevating their prices, it would have been forced to parade some pretty interesting views about doctors and pharmacists. Why would it seek to discourage the consumption of drugs recommended by doctors with the assistance of pharmacists? On the other hand, Rhode Island could argue that it would like to discourage the use of alcoholic beverages by elevating prices, and it could make this argument without exhibiting wholesale cynicism about the medical profession.

In assessing the worth of such an argument, the test to be applied was first developed in *Central Hudson Gas & Electric Corporation v. Public Service Commission.*[11] As the Court put it: "At the outset, we must determine whether the expression is protected by the First Amendment. For commercial speech to come within that provision, it at least must concern lawful activity and not be misleading. Next, we ask whether the asserted government interest is substantial. If both inquiries yield positive answers, we must determine whether the regulation directly advances the governmental interest asserted, and whether it is not more extensive than is necessary to serve that interest."[12]

By the time of *Liquormart*, only two justices were prepared to challenge the applicability of *Central Hudson*. Justice Scalia suggested on the basis of historical intent[13] that the test might be too strong, that is, commercial speech deserved little or relatively little protection.[14] Justice Thomas argued, on the other hand, that the *Central Hudson* test was too weak. When government attempted to suppress information in order to "protect" people from the truth, it contravened the antipaternalistic premises of the First Amendment, and he thought no test should salvage such action. For the seven remaining justices, the fighting issue related to the *strength* of the *Central Hudson* test in circumstances where government bans the dissemination of truthful information without regard to the manner in which it is disseminated. Justice Stevens, joined by Justices Kennedy and Ginsburg, wrote an opinion that was similar in spirit to that of Justice Thomas. To be sure, Justice Stevens was prepared to apply the *Central Hudson* test and Justice Thomas was not, but the version of the *Central Hudson* test propounded by Stevens was so stringent that one could reasonably suspect it might never be met.[15] Indeed, Stevens observed that his version of the test never had been met.[16] So understood, Justices Stevens and Justice Thomas wrestled over a distinction that might make no difference.[17]

Justice O'Connor, joined by Chief Justice Rehnquist and Justices Breyer and Souter, argued that the rush to transform *Central Hudson* into a stricter test was premature. The issue did not need to be reached, O'Connor maintained, because the statute at issue did not meet the relaxed version of the *Central Hudson* test.

Reading Supreme Court opinions requires one mathematical skill: an ability to count to five. As I have presented the case, five justices (Rehnquist, C.J., Breyer, O'Connor, Souter, and Scalia, JJ.) are unprepared to accept a stringent *Central Hudson* test at this point. Where, then, do commentators muster the confidence to assume that *Liquormart* opens a bold new era in commercial speech law? As I have presented the case, the status quo, imposing a moderate test, remains in place.[18]

Now for a confession: I have left something out. The same Justice Souter who signed Justice O'Connor's opinion (refusing to embrace a stringent test) also signed portions of Justice Stevens's opinion (embracing a stringent test).[19] Go figure. Perhaps Justice Souter found something to like in both opinions. Nonetheless, the commentators apparently count Souter as among the five who would offer commercial speech extraordinary protection in circumstances where government seeks to discourage consumption of tobacco or alcoholic beverages by regulating or prohibiting advertising, and they therefore conclude that *Liquormart* is a landmark.[20]

This widespread characterization of *Liquormart* is overblown. First, it begs the question of where Justice Souter really stands. Of course, it would have been nice, dare I say the judicial thing to do, for him to have written a concurring opinion in which he made his position clear. But he did not.[21] Second, the widespread forecast takes Supreme Court opinions more seriously than the justices do. District court judges have to take such opinions seriously, but the history of constitutional law and the history of the commercial speech doctrine provide a continuous record of cases in which justices twist the past to reach the conclusion they favor today. Thus, if Justice O'Connor writes an opinion, the commercial speech doctrine looks less protective than it does in the hand of Justice Stevens.[22] O'Connor is in the dissent one day and in the majority the next, and so it goes. Forecasting free speech law on the rhetoric of a single case is risky business. Perhaps Justice Souter was on to something after all. Why not sign two quite different opinions if the result is all that matters?

In this connection, it is important to observe that Justice Souter should not be regarded as the only culprit. Much of the analysis in *Liquormart* cannot be reconciled with the holding or the views expressed by many of the justices in *Edge Broadcasting Co. v. FCC*.[23] *Edge* rebuffed a challenge to a federal statute that prevented Edge Broadcasting, a North Carolina radio station located near the Virginia border, from broadcasting advertising messages for the Virginia lottery. The federal statute permitted lottery advertising in states, such as Virginia, where lotteries were legal and prohibited them in states, such as North Carolina, where lotteries were illegal. Edge Broadcasting wished to carry the Virginia advertisements because 92 percent of its listening audience resided in Virginia. The station seemed to be in a strong position. North Carolina outlawed lotteries and other forms of gambling, but it did not make it illegal for its residents to leave the state and gamble in Virginia. North Carolina's policy was to prevent its residents from being encouraged to gamble in state or out of state.[24] Of course, North Carolina could have no substantial interest in the gambling habits of Virginia residents. Given this background, Edge Broadcasting could argue that its message was unassailable for 92 percent of its audience. As to the North Carolina residents, the federal legislation was based on the kind of paternalistic premises that the First Amendment was purportedly designed to combat. Moreover, no showing had been made that the advertising successfully encouraged North Carolina residents to leave the state to participate in the Virginia lottery.

Justice White, joined by Chief Justice Rehnquist and Justices Kennedy, Souter, and Thomas, held that the statute directly advanced the governmental interest within the meaning of *Central Hudson* as applied to Edge Broadcasting despite the absence of evidence in the record showing that the advertising was effective. They also sidestepped the paternalism argument by stating: "Congress clearly was entitled to determine that broadcast of promotional advertising of lotteries undermines North Carolina's policy against gambling, even if the North Carolina audience is not wholly unaware of the lottery's existence. Congress has, for example, altogether banned the broadcast advertising of cigarettes, even though it could hardly have believed that this regulation would keep the public wholly ignorant of the availability of cigarettes."[25]

In a separate section of Justice White's opinion, joined by Chief Justice Rehnquist and Justices O'Connor, Scalia, and Thomas, the Court maintained that Congress could have outlawed lottery advertising altogether even in states where lotteries were legal, held that the regulation would directly advance the governmental interest even if there were no advancement as applied to Edge Broadcasting, reaffirmed that the *Central Hudson* standards required only a "reasonable" fit between the regulation and the interest sought to be served,[26] and concluded that this aspect of the test could be met whether or not the interest was served in the individual case.

Neither Justice White's opinion in *Edge*, an opinion joined by six justices on the current Court,[27] nor its holding can be reconciled with the broad rhetoric of Justice Stevens's opinion in *Liquormart*. *Edge* holds that legislation designed to prevent advertising of a legal service is to be scrutinized under standards that do not require evidence of the effectiveness of the advertising, that require only a "reasonable" fit between the regulation and the interest sought to be served, and that blink at the existence of paternalism.

In *Liquormart*, Justice Stevens, in a section of his opinion that attracted only three justices, tried to explain *Edge* by asserting that the advertising was for an illegal service.[28] But this is the same Justice Stevens who, dissenting in *Edge*, recognized the following: "Of course, North Carolina law does not, and, presumably, could not, bar its citizens from traveling across the state line and participating in the Virginia lottery. North Carolina does not make the Virginia lottery illegal. I take the Court to mean that North Carolina's decision not to institute a state-run lottery reflects its policy judgment that participation in such lotteries, even those conducted by another state, is detrimental to the public welfare."[29]

Despite Justice Stevens's claim in *Liquormart* that the advertising in *Edge* was for an illegal service, the facts are clearly to the contrary, as he himself recognized in his *Edge* opinion. Justice Stevens cannot avoid the fact that *Edge* upheld a paternalistic ban on gambling over his dissent. With six sitting justices on the Court who joined the *Edge* majority, it is hard to accept the glib proclamations that *Liquormart* is a landmark.[30]

Even if *Liquormart* were read for all it is worth, there would still be room for substantial regulation of tobacco and alcoholic beverage advertising. The *Liquormart* case dealt with commercial information; it did not deal with image advertising, Joe Camel, the Marlboro man, or the like.[31] Commercial information may receive more protection than musical jingles, rhetorical flourishes, and flashy images.[32] Moreover, the regulation in the *Liquormart* case was not specifically designed to protect children, and that distinction seems significant.[33]

Perhaps more interesting than the scope of *Liquormart* itself, however, is the challenge to free speech theory posed by cases like it. How broad should the free speech protection be, if any, and why?

The Fragile Case for Commercial Speech Protection

In arguing that commercial speech should enjoy constitutional protection, the Court has employed three main lines of argument. In a small class of cases, the Court has argued that the regulation of speech was paternalistic and that paternalism is foreign to the First Amendment. The Court has also argued that commercial information is vital to the consumer. Finally, the Court has suggested that commercial and noncommercial speech or political speech may be indistinguishable.

Paternalism

In *Virginia Pharmacy*, the Court considered the argument that prohibiting prescription drug price advertising helped preserve high-quality pharmacists by assuring that they would not be run out of business through discount advertising.[34] The pharmacy board purportedly feared that consumers would comparison shop and that the "professional" pharmacist could not survive. The Court objected to this "highly paternalistic"[35] approach and suggested an alternative, namely, that the high-quality pharmacist could advertise. Opening the channels of communication was considered better than closing them. The Court observed that the choice between the dangers of suppressing the information and the dangers of its misuse if freely available is one "that the First Amendment makes for us."[36]

Even ignoring the merits of the concerns about paternalism for the moment, it was a little odd to be told by the *Virginia Pharmacy* justices that the First Amendment had made the decision for them. After all, commercial speech had received no protection under the First Amendment in the history of the Republic until *Virginia Pharmacy*.[37] How thin the pretense that the justices were passive actors yielding to the clear mandates of a decision already made rather than active policy makers crafting new First Amendment law.

Turning to the merits, it is instructive to notice that the Court's hostility to paternalism is not unbridled. The Court is not so enamored with commercial speech, for example, that it is prepared to shut down the Federal Trade Commission (FTC). Yet the FTC engages in paternalism on a daily basis. It moves to prevent false and misleading advertising from being disseminated to the public.[38] A regime that was fully opposed to paternalism would close down the FTC on the ground that it is offensive for government to suppose that the public cannot separate the true from the false. I can see the opinion now: "The First Amendment has made the decision for us."

Of course, the public can be bilked, and government is permitted to regulate commercial speech in ways that would never be permitted with political speech. Imagine a Federal Political Commission with a roving license to censor false and misleading advertising in political campaigns. Here, at last, it might be appropriate to say that the First Amendment has made the decision for us.

Paternalism is permitted in the regulation of false and misleading advertising. It is also permitted in the regulation of economic activity.[39] Various opinions in *Liquormart* complained about the government's paternalism, but the objection lacked focus. Rhode Island sought to discourage consumption by making price competition difficult. Wherein lies the paternalism? Virginia may have supposed that consumers were making a mistake in shopping at discount pharmacies rather than frequenting "professional pharmacists," but Rhode Island was not supposing that consumers were making a *mistake* by purchasing alcoholic beverages at the lowest available price. Rhode Island was assuming that the collective decisions of consumers would lower prices and that their conduct would assist them in the *mistake* of consuming too much alcohol.[40] But the Court made it clear that combating that mistake was perfectly permissible provided it be done by other means. Thus, if Rhode Island had fixed prices for the paternalistic purpose of lowering consumption, its actions would have been entirely permissible under the Constitution.[41] It is the combination of paternalism and commercial speech that troubles the Court.[42] The paternalism argument thus rests on the assumption that commercial speech is particularly important. The argument does not stand by itself.

The Importance of Commercial Speech to the Consumer

Virginia Pharmacy asked whether commercial speech was "so removed from any 'exposition of ideas' . . . and from 'truth, science, morality, and arts in general, in its diffusion of liberal sentiments on the administration of government' . . . that it lacks all protection."[43] Notice that the question was not whether commercial speech was worthy of equal protection—only some. In support of this, the Court maintained that the "particular consumer's interest in the free flow of commercial information . . . may be as keen, if not keener by far, than his interest in the day's most urgent political debate."[44] Of course, the Court picked a convenient case to make the statement. One imagines an impoverished consumer struggling to survive on social security reading the paper to find the cheapest price for medically vital prescription drugs.

The statement would not resonate as well in *Liquormart*. An alcoholic's interest in liquor prices might be keener by far than the most urgent political debate, but I doubt we would call forth constitutional chamber music to celebrate the importance of an alcoholic's interest in liquor prices. Of course, I am making the argument too easy. Many consumers might be interested in liquor prices, not just alcoholics. And consumers are generally interested in information about products contained in commercial advertising. For some products, consumers' interest may be keener than the most urgent political debate; for some consumers, their interest in anything would be keener than the most urgent political debate. Would it not be elitist to suppose that literature and politics, for example, are more important than commercial advertising? If people want to consult advertising to make decisions about smoking or drinking, where does government get off interfering?

These questions simply reproduce the paternalism objection, and, to some extent, government already seeks to discourage smoking and the consumption of alcohol. Government's right to regulate in the economic sphere is settled. Thus, the Court has referred to the " 'common sense' distinction between speech proposing a commercial transaction, which occurs in an area traditionally subject to government regulation, and other varieties of speech."[45] Moreover, the Court has stated that commercial speech has been "afforded . . . a limited measure of protection, commensurate with its subordinate position in the scale of First Amendment values."[46]

The notion that commercial advertising enjoys a lower place in the scale of First Amendment values might stand up to a poll. Quick, send out Gallup to ask whether citizens value commercial advertising more than political speech, literature, and science. To recognize that commercials are influential and tolerated need not entail the conclusion that citizens enjoy the deluge of manipulation. Commercial advertising, however, might be lower in the scale of First Amendment values wholly apart from anything George might find. The First Amendment may have a social dimension that transcends the materialism of the culture. It may seek to preserve a certain kind of polity, and supporters of the First Amendment need not be at all embarrassed in suggesting that some speech, such as political speech, is more important than commercial speech.

The Relationship of Commercial Speech to Political Speech

Of course, the Court has suggested that political speech is centrally important to the First Amendment—many times.[47] In a breathtaking passage, *Virginia Pharmacy* suggested that commercial speech was a form of political speech:

> So long as we preserve a predominantly free enterprise economy, the allocation of our resources in large measure will be made through numerous private economic decisions. It is a matter of public interest that these decisions, in the aggregate, be intelligent and well informed. To this end, the free flow of commercial information is indispensable. And if it is indispensable to the proper allocation of resources in a free enterprise system, it is also indispensable to the formation of intelligent opinions as to how that system ought to be regulated or altered. Therefore, even if the First Amendment were thought to be primarily an instrument to enlighten public decisionmaking in a democracy, we could not say that the free flow of information does not serve that goal.[48]

For the moment, we can go along with the game and suppose that the private allocation of resources is part of public decision making in a democracy. We should further notice, however, that government allocation of resources is also part of public decision making in a democracy. That one predominates over the other (for many wealthy corporations, of course, free enterprise is the exception, not the rule) seems quite beside the point. Even if we suppose that commercial advertising is political, protection of "political speech" in this context seems dramatically less important than in others if all that is at stake is the efficient allocation of resources. Moreover, since government frequently departs from free enterprise with constitutional blessing, perhaps the proper allocation of resources as seen by the market should not be privileged after all.

If the government seeks to discourage the consumption of tobacco for public health reasons, why should we assume that it interferes with the proper allocation of resources? If it taxes to discourage consumption, no constitutional issue is even presented. Why should allocation of resources be a First Amendment worry?

In making its argument from democracy, the Court further observes that the free flow of commercial information is also crucial for the formation of opinions in a democracy.[49] This seems exactly right, but beside the point. Of course, the closing of the *Wall Street Journal* would be a blow to democracy.[50] The Court trades, however, on its failure to make a distinction between commercial *information* and commercial *advertising*. There may be some who believe that the free flow of commercial information in commercial advertising is crucial for the formation of opinions in a democracy, but I would guess that the majority of them work in the advertising industry.

This is not to deny that advertising as a whole lacks political impact. Advertising generally may contribute to a materialistic culture, to a belief that consumption and high living standards are all important (or crucially important), and that may affect elections. But that is a far cry from the assumption that citizens decide to vote for a presidential candidate on the basis of information contained in a magazine advertisement for any particular product (or set of products), let alone Camel cigarettes.

Even if it were possible to equate commercial advertising with political speech, however, I would argue that a politically centered approach to the First Amendment has serious deficiencies, particularly as compared with a dissent-based approach.

The Deficiencies of a Politically Centered Approach to Free Speech Theory

Both dissent-based and politically centered approaches to free speech would rightly put commercial speech at the margin. Commercial advertisers are not dissenters. As I mentioned in the introduction, however, some might believe that tobacco advertising must be dissenting because its product is socially stigmatized. In this respect, tobacco advertising has some elements of dissent. There is a serious question whether judges should be asked to make ad hoc decisions about whether particular advertisements are or are not dissenting. I think it better to make decisions about the general category without resort to ad hoc decisions within it. If ad hoc decision making were appropriate, however, it would be appropriate to concede that tobacco advertisers ask people to consume a controversial product and that this at least implicitly criticizes the conventional wisdom. Some might argue that implicit criticism is not enough, but, as I suggested earlier, there is a more important point. Tobacco advertising misses vital elements ordinarily associated with our valuing of dissent. Tobacco advertising is not an instance of the individual striking out against the current. Instead, it is an example of the powerful influencing the market rather than one of dissent by the less powerful. Tobacco advertising is no part of a social practice that challenges unjust hierarchies with the prospect of promoting progressive change. Thus, it may have some First Amendment value in the dissent mold, but it does not deserve the full value that should be afforded to more classic instances of dissent.

In some respects, a politically centered approach has an easier time in putting all commercial advertising at the margin. Commercial advertising, even tobacco advertising, is not political speech, despite the resource allocation theory put forth by the Supreme Court. Although a politically centered approach seems to work well in this case, it has some serious weaknesses.

The politically centered approach is most typically associated with the work of Alexander Meiklejohn, who argued that freedom of speech should be regarded as a deduction from our democratic commitment to self-government.[51] Citizens in a democracy are entitled to engage in discussion about public issues and are entitled to criticize political leaders in uninhibited, robust, and wide-open debate. Under Meiklejohn's approach, speech relevant to self-government is absolutely protected under the First Amendment; speech not relevant to self-government is beyond its scope and is said to be fair game for government regulation so long as due process requirements are respected.[52]

Nonetheless, Meiklejohn's theory of the First Amendment is seriously flawed. If it is construed to protect political speech in its garden-variety sense, then it removes philosophy, literature, and science from First Amendment protection. In an effort to blunt this criticism, Meiklejohn maintained that philosophy, literature, and science were areas from which the voter derived "knowledge, intelligence, sensitivity to human values: the capacity for sane and objective judgment which, so far as possible, a ballot should express."[53]

On this standard, however, virtually all speech is potentially political, including commercial advertising and gossip. Voters can derive their values from any speech, including their daily private speech interactions. On this account, Meiklejohn cannot sustain a well-founded distinction between the political and the nonpolitical.

Cass Sunstein, however, has developed a sophisticated theory of free speech, which he traces to James Madison, that is designed to rescue Meiklejohn's theory from its most serious flaws and to elaborate the implications of a politically centered theory across a broad range of important issues.[54] First, and most important, Sunstein does not relegate nonpolitical speech to the low level of protection that would have been afforded through the due process clause. Instead, he is at pains to stress that most nonpolitical speech (save for many of the usual exceptions, such as fraud, perjury, and the like) would be afforded a generous measure of protection, albeit not as much as most political speech.[55]

Regulations of political speech would be subject to the most exacting scrutiny unless the regulations promoted deliberative democracy by the citizens at large.[56] From Sunstein's perspective, the central purpose of the Madisonian First Amendment is to safeguard and promote a deliberative democracy, a government where there is broad discussion about matters of public concern among citizens, and between citizens and their representatives.[57] From this perspective, restrictions on seditious speech would be quite suspect. But regulations of broadcasting designed to foster discussion of public issues would be viewed with favor.[58]

Sunstein not only departs from Meiklejohn in the degree of protection he would afford to most nonpolitical speech but also characterizes *political speech* differently. He states that speech is political "when it is both intended and received as a contribution to public deliberation about some issue."[59] Thus, much literature would be political; much would not—depending on its intent and its reception.

This sketch of Sunstein's presentation will suffice to launch a discussion comparing a politically centered conception of the First Amendment with a dissent-centered conception. In my view, the focus on political deliberation is rooted in an unrealistic conception of democracy and leads to a misguided emphasis in free speech theory. According to Sunstein, free speech theory supposes a government by the people. He argues that if most citizens do not attend to public issues well or in depth, the Madisonian system cannot function.[60] He seems to concede that we do not have a Madisonian system now but argues that we could have one if we could structure a system with better education and public affairs programming.

Contrast Sunstein's conception of democracy with that of Joseph Schumpeter, who described American democracy as a system in which elites periodically sought the votes of the citizenry so that they could run the country until the next election.[61] From Schumpeter's perspective, elites with superior knowledge governed, not the people.[62] This perspective is clearly overdrawn. There are too many issues on which politicians turn to opinion polls in deciding how to vote to make the Schumpterian description credible. But Sunstein's world, which seems to imagine a nation of policy wonks, also seems overdrawn. To be sure, Sunstein does not expect citizens to spend all or most of their time studying issues of the day.[63] He does demand, however, a system that generates broad and deep attention to public issues,[64] an ambitious system involving widespread public deliberation.[65]

Sunstein's concern about the lack of public political participation and his call for public deliberation of political issues can be contrasted with the work of some scholars who believe the problem is best addressed in less political terms. For example, instead of calling for more political participation, Robert Putnam calls for more civic participation, without

regard to the political character of the associations involved. Putnam fa-
mously argues, for example, that more Americans are bowling, but they
are bowling alone. He contends that television and other contributing
factors have caused a serious decline in participation in a variety of associations, from PTAs to Rotaries. He suggests that people who do not associate with each other do not trust each other. Such lack of trust is infectious,
leading to less social motivation and less trust of governmental institutions.[66] Sunstein's scholarship precedes Putnam's most recent work, so it
is hard to know what Sunstein would say about it, but an explosion of
commentary already exists. If one reads the literature in its worst light,
one imagines a group of citizens in separate homes watching television
and cursing the darkness, emerging from their homes only to shoot fellow
citizens on the freeway as they travel for a brief sojourn at the local bowling alley. But many commentators question the Putnam thesis. Some
doubt that civic participation has in fact declined;[67] others observe that,
even if participation has declined, rates of participation in the United
States are higher than in any other country in the world.[68] On the other
hand, political participation rates on some measures are higher. Advocacy
groups, relying on the mail and checks from supporters, have grown enor-
mously in power and influence, contributing to political debate.[69] At the
same time, voting rates remain low,[70] and distrust of government and
other institutions is demonstrably high.[71]

My own inclination is to side with those who believe that participation
in associations can be a stabilizing or destabilizing force depending on
the responsiveness of government, and that mistrust of our major institutions may exist because they deserve to be mistrusted.[72] The role of money
in politics, the upward redistribution of wealth, continuing discrimination (despite promises of equality), continuing revelations of corruption,
and the fact that it takes two wage earners to purchase what one wage
earner could purchase not so many years ago—each contributes to an
abiding distrust in the major institutions of our society. Whatever one's
reaction to the Putnam debate, however, the production of a running national seminar on issues of the day involving most citizens seems to be a
herculean task.

Citizens who come home from hard days at work are unlikely to devote
deep attention to public issues, and we know they do not.[73] Nor should
we fault the viewers of *Seinfeld*, *Murphy Brown*, or *Frasier* for being entertained, although Sunstein seems to have little patience for those who
spend time on "silly" situation comedies instead of public affairs.[74]
Sunstein argues that people might be "educated" to turn toward the programming he recommends, and he claims that this is not unacceptably
elitist.[75] It is not if, but only if, the Madisonian view has been accepted.
Aside from the thinness of support for the view that the mass of the popu-

lation might be educated to change their viewing habits, the amount of time that would be required for truly deep attention to the public issues of the day is substantially more than most people have available.[76]

Would it be a good thing if we all knew more about public affairs than we do? I should think so. Would be a good thing for the mass of the population to transfer their time to a gigantic study hall on politics, away from the diverse ways in which they now spend their time? Not necessarily.[77] Will they do so? Not on your life.

Given the unrealistic posture of Sunstein's conception of democracy, it is hard to believe that it somehow reflects the central meaning of the Constitution. Moreover, if our country depends on the enactment of the Madisonian conception, we are doomed. At the same time, the Sunstein ideal seems vastly superior to the Schumpeterian ideal. Elites running the country without popular intervention for years at a time would be a prescription for corruption, injustice, and inequality.[78] The dissent perspective in part is a compromise between the Sunstein and Schumpeter perspectives.

The dissent perspective would argue that the policies, prescriptions, and privileges of the elite need to be challenged on a regular basis by enough people to make a difference. If the population is widely educated on public issues and involved to the extent Sunstein desires, so be it. But widespread and deep deliberation may not be necessary to combat injustice. If, however, elites rule without the challenge of diverse, lively, and powerful dissent, the country is in grave danger precisely because it is undemocratic. Protection for dissent is a necessary feature of any respectable democracy.[79]

To a large extent, Sunstein recognizes the latter point. The dissent and political deliberation conceptions overlap in important ways. The desire to promote political deliberation by the citizenry is substantially motivated by an appreciation for the value of dissent. Although Sunstein remarks that his approach does not "place special stress on the dissenter,"[80] he recognizes that his approach overlaps with a dissent-based approach in that both are "intended to promote diversity of view and to allow critical scrutiny of current conventions."[81] Nonetheless, the dissent approach is better suited to handle some of the areas Sunstein tries to treat from a political deliberation perspective. Consider Sunstein's treatment of literature. Literature that is intended to contribute to social deliberation and that is received as such falls within the political category and receives extraordinary protection.[82] What of nonpolitical literature (leaving aside questions about the quantity of political material that needs be present to qualify literature as political)? In my view, Sunstein rightly argues that such literature will receive generous protection under his scheme, among other things, because government should not be permitted to prohibit even nonpolitical materials merely because they are deemed to be offensive. To the extent he suggests that "offense" drives most literary censorship, he is surely right.[83]

To take it from a more general perspective, speech reinforcing the status quo will always be present, and it will flourish without legal reprisal, but authorities will always be tempted to criticize critical speech if they can get away with it. Nonetheless, it would be a mistake to suppose that the temptation in Western democracies is greatest with respect to political speech. The tradition of free speech is too well established to permit politicians to censor their opponents without the expectation of serious public reprisals. The temptation to censor arises when speech challenges existing conventions, habits, and traditions to the point that people are offended. Politicians are then tempted to cater to the censoring instincts of the masses. When Sunstein argues that speech may not be suppressed merely because people find it offensive, therefore, he rightly recognizes that the protection of dissent is fundamental to a free society.

This explanation seems more credible than one that relies on the political or nonpolitical character of literature in free speech theorizing. Let there be no confusion, however. I do not claim that literature is important only when it dissents or that dissenting literature is always important. Literature's insights into the human condition need not depend on their dissenting character. I do claim that literature needs constitutional protection especially when it attacks existing customs, habits, traditions, institutions, and authorities. The need for protection closely tracks the impulse to censor.

Sunstein's political emphasis is also unconvincing when he turns to the issue of privacy for the names of rape victims. Sunstein argues that a state may legitimately protect the privacy of such victims because the disclosure of their names is not political within his definition.[84] Suppose, however, that a reporter writes a story in which he maintains that we live in an excessively dangerous society, and includes the name of a rape victim in the course of the story. Surely such a story is intended (and would be received) as a contribution to public deliberation about the issue of crime. So understood, it would meet Sunstein's requirements for classification as political, and Sunstein nowhere states that he is prepared to determine which facts are important for political stories and which are not. If the goal is to protect privacy, the political/nonpolitical is not a reliable dividing line.

Laws intended to protect the privacy of rape victims, on the other hand, do not seek to suppress a category of speech that is dissenting in character. From a dissent perspective, such laws regulate speech at the margin. This does not mean that a case for speech protection in this context cannot be made (though I have not been persuaded by the attempts);[85] it does mean that the dissent perspective provides a clearer focus than the political perspective.

The political emphasis, however, is even more troubling when it is used to evaluate regulations of corporate speech. From the political perspective, when wealthy corporations speak about public issues, they contribute to political dialogue, and arguably deserve the highest degree of protection. Regrettably, this would seem to be true even if a corporate advertiser of products were to craft her advertisement to meet Sunstein's definition. On the other hand, the political perspective is based in a conception of democracy that prizes political equality. Corporate speech forces a choice between political equality and political deliberation, and Sunstein opts for the wrong choice. He argues that regulations of corporate political speech discriminate against corporations.[86] He suggests that regulations of the wealthy, including corporations, should probably survive constitutional scrutiny, but he regards the singling out of corporations for special treatment as objectionable.

There is a Catch-22 to Sunstein's discussion of this issue. In *Buckley v. Valeo*,[87] the Court declared it unconstitutional to restrict the political expenditures of the wealthy, thus privileging political deliberation over political equality. Subsequently, *Austin v. Michigan State Chamber of Commerce*[88] upheld a statute prohibiting corporations from making political expenditures, although they could use treasury funds to solicit voluntary contributions to an independent segregated fund administered and controlled by corporate officers. Sunstein objects to *Austin*.[89] But it seems quite odd for Sunstein to tell the state of Michigan that its action was unconstitutional on the ground that it should have prohibited expenditures by the wealthy when *Buckley* had already declared any such prohibition to be constitutional anathema.[90]

In fairness, Sunstein is unsure whether that conclusion of *Buckley* is correct.[91] He does believe some other reform proposals are available that might make it unnecessary to prohibit speech by corporations or speech of the wealthy, and he suggests that the availability of these proposals might be a sufficient basis to block speech-restrictive election reform.[92]

From a dissent perspective, Sunstein's analysis seems to blink too much at the realities of political power. When legislatures seek to regulate the speech of the powerful on grounds of political equality, a dissent perspective would not suggest that the courts should pull out a rubber stamp. On the other hand, courts should be generous in assessing such regulations because the legislature seeks to advance important constitutional goals. It should not be fatal if the legislation is overinclusive (some corporations are poor) or underinclusive (some persons are wealthy). Regulations designed to secure justice in the polity need not be perfect. Justice should not be delayed because nonviable alternatives are conceivable.

In the final analysis, the most serious problem with a politically centered conception is its restricted attention to the problem of injustice. A dissent-based approach proceeds from a moral condemnation of unjust hierarchies wherever they may be inside or outside of government—whether or not they relate to "public issues." A politically centered approach to free speech treats unjust hierarchies as of crucial importance only if public issues are involved. The many millions of people who are unjustly treated in the workplace, for example, deserve rights to dissent whether or not their concerns are of general interest. A dissent-based approach recognizes this, while a politically centered approach does not.

Conclusion

Tobacco and alcoholic beverage companies want to sell their products. Advocates of regulation want to protect the public health. If this were all that were at stake in this dispute, the advertisers would have little public support. But there is more. For many, this dispute has far-reaching implications for the meaning of America.

"It's a free country. I can say what I want," many Americans say, and they believe that slogan captures the essence of free speech. The notion of a free country, however, is itself too empty a bottle to satisfy the need for free speech theorizing. It is a bottle that is too easily filled in many different ways.[93] Nonetheless, my suggestion is that an important clue to free speech puzzles lurks in the text of Cooper's book *The Pioneers*. The person who speaks out on behalf of free speech in a free country is not a corporation hawking its wares or seeking to dominate the election process; nor is it a media conglomerate exploiting the privacy of an individual. If it were, the passage would be robbed of its rhetorical power. The person who speaks in *The Pioneers* is not even engaged in political speech. No, the speaker is challenging the insensitive exercise of power by a person she believes is carrying hierarchy to excess. In short, Miss Pettibone represents more than freedom; she represents those who speak out against authority and injustice. Miss Pettibone was a dissenter, and greater attention to that fact will help us to understand that a free country need not protect tobacco companies or alcoholic beverage companies when they encourage people to consume products that cause needless death and suffering.

III

Racist Speech, Outsider Jurisprudence, and the Meaning of America

MORE THAN thirty years ago, Harry Kalven, Jr., one of the leading legal scholars of the twentieth century, wrote a book in which he attempted to analyze the impact of changing race relations and the civil rights movement on First Amendment law.[1] Kalven, who observed that African Americans did not often resort to the courts to combat racist speech,[2] was "tempted to say that it will be a sign that the Negro problem has basically been solved when the Negro begins to worry about group-libel protection."[3]

Times have changed (although few would claim that the plight of African Americans has basically been solved).[4] African Americans are deeply concerned with the problem of racist speech in American society, and they are not alone. Many have urged that punitive sanctions be imposed against the perpetrators of such speech.[5] Perhaps the most persuasive writings have come from practitioners of outsider jurisprudence,[6] a thriving school of thought in American law schools.[7] In the area of race relations law,[8] outsider jurisprudence frequently builds from the lived experience of people of color.[9] It utilizes particularistic analysis and is hostile to false pretensions of universality and neutrality.[10] Its general orientation is pragmatic, and its mission is to combat racism and injustice. From this perspective, rules affecting race relations depend for their justification on the extent to which they combat the racism present in the existing set of power relations; certainly, if they entrench those power relations, the rules are not legitimate. In an effort to combat the power of racism, practitioners of outsider jurisprudence have for the most part argued for the imposition of sanctions against some forms of racist speech.[11]

Unfortunately, no practitioners of outsider jurisprudence sat on the Supreme Court when the famous cross-burning case, *R.A.V. v. City of St. Paul*,[12] arrived on its docket. Partly because of their absence, the Court simply bungled the First Amendment job in its most important encounter with racist speech in the last forty years.[13] The United States has two First Amendments. One is studied in law school, and consists of an extremely complex body of doctrine that few claim to understand. The other is, in some sense, understood by every citizen; it is an important part of the stories we tell ourselves about the meaning of America.

Both First Amendments were tarnished in *R.A.V.* In ways that have yet to be fully appreciated, the case restructured, transformed, complicated, and distorted doctrine. Because it restructured the First Amendment so dramatically, and because its doctrinal adventures are set against one of the most explosive of free speech topics—the relationship between speech and race—*R.A.V.* deserves sustained inquiry. Finally, *R.A.V.* tells a story about the First Amendment that affords a better window into the weaknesses of conservative thought on the subject than any recent case.[14] Those weaknesses are particularly important, for the stories we tell ourselves about the meaning of the First Amendment do more than influence the outcome of concrete cases; they also help construct the social and political identity of American citizens. Beyond tarnishing the First Amendment, *R.A.V.* missed opportunities to provide fresh thinking about racist speech and to provide direction for lower courts in how they should approach these questions.

In this chapter, I propose to discuss First Amendment doctrine and the larger symbolism of the First Amendment as they relate to racist speech. In my view, the argument that First Amendment values (such as truth, autonomy, self-expression, and liberty) dictate that racist speech cannot be regulated is ultimately indefensible. I develop that argument at some length, but the main purpose of this chapter concerning racist speech is to open discussion about an issue that has received little attention, perhaps because First Amendment arguments play so large a role in our political identity. My tentative conclusion is that the racist character of our society should be considered a barrier to much regulation of racist speech, not the values protected by the First Amendment. I argue that regulation of racist speech that is not targeted against any specific individual or small group of individuals will be counterproductive in a society as racist as this. On the other hand, I believe that individuals who are the victims of racist speech that is targeted against them should have a right of redress even if the affording of such redress is counterproductive to themselves or to a larger group. Moreover, because I believe First Amendment issues are (after all the arguments are aired) of minor importance in this area, I think that the victims of racist speech should have the primary voice in determining whether sanctions should be imposed in this area. If policy in the end should turn on judgments about whether people of color would be helped or hurt by the regulations, they should have the primary voice in determining what risks they wish to take. My argument, therefore, seeks to close a discussion about the First Amendment (of course, it will not) and open a discussion about the effectiveness of hate speech regulations in a racist society.

The first section of this chapter provides a brief description of the facts and holding of *R.A.V.* The second section provides a deeper description of the doctrinal architecture of Justice Scalia's majority opinion. In order to make the discussion more concrete, I compare that doctrinal structure with the approach taken in the commercial speech area and show that the two approaches are incompatible.

The third section shows a more general failure: Justice Scalia's framework provides neither a cogent explanation of the doctrinal framework of First Amendment law nor a sturdy basis for justifying *R.A.V.*'s result. Moreover, the Court's purported concern with content discrimination in First Amendment law is thoroughly compromised.

The fourth section shows what really drives the *R.A.V.* opinion: a particular, implicit conception of the meaning of America. Equally important, this section contrasts this understanding with other competing explications of the meaning of America and shows that the *R.A.V.* opinion is at a loss to deal with them. The fifth section examines Justice White's concurrence, demonstrating how the absence of an outsider jurisprudential perspective leads him into serious error in his assessment of the St. Paul ordinance. This section also takes issue with Justice White's apparent focus on injury, arguing that injury should be neither a necessary nor a sufficient condition for the imposition of sanctions. Finally, it explores Justice White's suggestion that the "fighting words" doctrine does not require the prospect of violence and argues that some personal insults should lose constitutional protection whether or not a breach of the peace is likely.

The sixth section discusses whether racist comments that are *not* targeted against particular individuals or a small group of individuals should receive constitutional protection. It argues that positive First Amendment values are not sufficiently breached by nontargeted racist speech to outweigh the harm caused by such speech. Nonetheless, this section concludes that the racist character of American society makes it unlikely that racist speech regulation could be effective.[15] In the process, it proposes a different conception of the meaning of America than those implicit or explicit in the opinions of Justice Scalia, Justice White, and in the St. Paul ordinance: one that overlaps with, but is somewhat different than, that of outsider jurisprudence. In conclusion, the final section retraces how these different understandings of the meaning of America might bear on resolving racist speech issues.

The *R.A.V.* Case

During the night of June 21, 1990, a group of teenagers burned a cross within the fenced portion of the yard of a Black family that lived in a predominantly white neighborhood in St. Paul, Minnesota.[16] One of the perpetrators, "R.A.V.," was prosecuted under a broadly worded hate speech ordinance,[17] which he challenged on First Amendment grounds. The Minnesota Supreme Court rejected the challenge,[18] and R.A.V. appealed.

Justice Scalia's opinion for the U.S. Supreme Court accepted the Minnesota court's construction of the ordinance, which limited its scope to "fighting words"[19] based on race, color, creed, religion, or gender. Moreover, Justice Scalia purported not to reach the question of whether the fighting words doctrine should be reconsidered or whether the ordinance could constitutionally reach all of the expression it sought to proscribe. Instead, the principal defect he spied in the ordinance was that it discriminated on the basis of subject matter: "[E]ven as narrowly construed by the Minnesota Supreme Court, the ordinance is facially unconstitutional. . . . Displays containing abusive invective, no matter how vicious or severe, are permissible unless they are addressed to one of the specified disfavored topics. Those who wish to use 'fighting words' in connection with other ideas—to express hostility, for example, on the basis of political affiliation, union membership, or homosexuality—are not covered. The First Amendment does not permit St. Paul to impose special prohibitions on those speakers who express views on disfavored subjects."[20]

No doubt, Justice Scalia was right: the ordinance exhibited both content and subject matter discrimination on its face.[21] Moreover, he determined that the St. Paul scheme embraced a form of point-of-view discrimination as well: "One could hold up a sign saying, for example, that all 'anti-Catholic bigots' are misbegotten; but not that all 'papists' are, for that would insult and provoke violence 'on the basis of religion.' St. Paul has no such authority to license one side of a debate to fight freestyle, while requiring the other to follow Marquis of Queensbury Rules."[22]

But that was not the end of the matter. Justice Scalia entertained the argument that point-of-view discrimination might be permissible if a sufficiently powerful justification were provided. St. Paul argued that the ordinance was justified despite any point-of-view discrimination "because it is narrowly tailored to serve compelling state interests."[23] Justice Scalia recognized that helping to safeguard the basic human rights of groups historically subject to discrimination was a compelling state interest.[24] He argued, however, that clearing the compelling state interest test did not take the ordinance the full distance. He maintained that the " 'danger of censorship' presented by a facially content-based statute"[25] required a showing that such a statute was necessary to serve a compelling state interest. The ordinance failed this test, he concluded, because of the "existence of adequate content-neutral alternatives. . . . An ordinance not limited to the favored topics, for example, would have precisely the same beneficial effect."[26] In other words, a pure fighting words statute would avoid the impermissible discrimination.

Commercial Speech and Racist Speech

Although I propose to show that Justice Scalia's opinion has many weaknesses, its basic premise is sound: although many categories of speech have been described as "unprotected" (such as obscenity and some forms of defamation), the purported status of a category of speech as "unprotected" does not necessarily justify discrimination within the category. It would, for example, be unconstitutional to tack on additional penalties just because the victim of an unprotected form of defamation or fighting words was a Republican.[27] More difficult to determine is the test to apply when content discrimination takes place within a category of unprotected speech. Justice Scalia maintains that the appropriate test to apply is a form of strict scrutiny, but some doctrinal savagery is required in order to make that conclusion presentable.

Despite significant questions about its current vitality, which I will discuss in due course, *Posadas de Puerto Rico Associates v. Tourism Company*[28] can help to fill out important details of Justice Scalia's analysis, as well as revealing some of the obstacles to its success. Puerto Rico there engaged in a blatant form of subject matter discrimination. It permitted commercial advertisements generally and advertisements for horse racing, the lottery, and cockfighting in particular. Nonetheless, it prohibited advertising of *casino* gambling aimed at Puerto Rican residents.[29] In testing the constitutionality of this discriminatory approach, the *Posadas* Court did not utilize any form of strict scrutiny; instead, it applied a relaxed version of the *Central Hudson* test.

A case like *Posadas* raises a difficult question for Justice Scalia's approach: if less than strict standards are employed to deal with subject matter discrimination within a category of *protected* speech (even recognizing that commercial speech receives less protection than other forms of protected speech),[30] how could one justify strict scrutiny to examine subject matter discrimination within a category of *unprotected* speech?

Justice Scalia does not directly respond to this question, but he does maintain that the "prohibition against content discrimination . . . applies differently in the context of proscribable speech than in the area of fully protected speech."[31] Specifically, he points to four circumstances in which content discrimination is permissible. None of those circumstances distinguish *Posadas*.

The Reason for the Lower Level of Protection

Justice Scalia first observes that "[w]hen the basis for content discrimination consists entirely of the very reason the entire class of speech at issue is proscribable, no significant danger of idea or viewpoint discrimination exists."[32] He provides an example from the commercial speech area. A state could "choose to regulate price advertising in one industry, but not in others because the risk of fraud (one of the characteristics of commercial speech that justifies depriving it of full First Amendment protection) . . . is in its view greater there."[33] On Scalia's view, such subject matter discrimination would be unproblematic because no idea or viewpoint discrimination is present. Instead, the justification for the regulation is the risk of fraud, and the risk of fraud is itself one of the reasons that commercial speech is proscribable.

How does *Posadas* fit into this analysis? Not very well. The advertising of casino gambling is not based on any of the reasons that justified the lower place commercial speech occupies in the First Amendment hierarchy. In developing the commercial speech exception, the Court first attempted to justify treating deceptive, misleading, or fraudulent speech differently from other forms of protected speech because of the durability or hardiness and the verifiability of commercial speech.[34] But these justifications do not justify a ban on the advertising of true commercial speech such as was present in *Posadas*. Indeed, apart from declaring that commercial speech traditionally gets less protection,[35] or invoking "common-sense,"[36] or worrying that the treatment of commercial speech on a par with noncommercial speech would "dilute" the speech that really counts,[37] the Court has not provided an explanation for the lesser protection of commercial speech. It has not justified the tradition, explained the common sense, or explored the reasons that dilution might come about.[38]

Consider now why Puerto Rico was said in *Posadas* to oppose the advertising of casino gambling. According to the Tourism Company's brief, it did so fearing not fraud but " 'the disruption of moral and cultural patterns, the increase in local crime, the fostering of prostitution, the development of corruption, and the infiltration of organized crime.' "[39] I daresay *none* of these were the kinds of reasons invoked to justify the commercial speech exception. Nonetheless, the Court applied a relaxed standard.

It was enough that the state advance directly a substantial governmental interest by means no more extensive than necessary to further that interest, and the application of that test in *Posadas* was even less strict than it sounded.[40] In any event, strict scrutiny it was not. If strict scrutiny was not appropriate in *Posadas*, we are owed an explanation regarding why it was appropriate in *R.A.V.*

Secondary Effects

Justice Scalia's second exception is the "secondary effects" doctrine: "Another valid basis for according differential treatment to even a content-defined subclass of proscribable speech is that the subclass happens to be associated with particular 'secondary effects' of the speech, so that the regulation is 'justified without reference to the content of the . . . speech.' "[41]

Renton v. Playtime Theatres, Inc.,[42] is an important example of the secondary effects principle. *Renton* upheld an ordinance that zoned adult bookstores and theaters differently from other bookstores and theaters. The City of Renton said it passed the ordinance not primarily out of concern for the content of the films or the direct response of audience to such films, but rather for secondary effects such as the deterioration of neighborhoods (crime, property values, the environment).[43] Because the city's alleged purposes were founded on secondary effects, the Court did not classify the ordinance as content-based.

Renton's failure to recognize the ordinance as content-based is quite remarkable. The result of the secondary effects doctrine, after all, is that some communities like Renton may let *Bambi* be shown in a local theater while excluding sexually explicit films. Moreover, a strong part of the reason for stringent scrutiny of regulations directed at content has been that hostility toward the speech may lie behind the recitation of other interests. Indeed, substantial grounds exist for believing that the Renton City Council in fact passed its ordinance out of hostility to sexually explicit films.[44]

A more generous reading of *Renton* (with some support in subsequent opinions) might focus on the interests put forth by the state (rather than its motivation) and ask whether those interests are jeopardized by the communicative impact of the activity the state seeks to regulate. Thus, one could argue that the prostitution associated with adult theaters—and the resulting decline in property values—is caused not by the communicative impact of the activity but by the physical concentration of potentially receptive clients. This reading has significant difficulties, however. First, it should not make a difference that the state regulates the content of a film because that content draws people to the theater, rather than because of the impact the film has on them once they get there. More important, the causal analysis of this argument is at least open to question. It is difficult to believe that the erotic arousal caused by the content of the films is unconnected with the sexual commerce that follows.

But let us assume that *Renton* and the secondary effects doctrine are models of constitutional analysis. Does *Renton*, so conceived, shed light on the relationship between *Posadas* and *R.A.V.*? Certainly, many of the

state concerns in *Posadas* are *Renton*-like. Nonetheless, the *Posadas* case
is not on a par with *Renton*. To make the cases more alike,[45] *Renton*
would have to have involved the *advertising* of adult theaters. But on that
understanding, it becomes more difficult to see *Posadas* as a secondary
effects case. For the *advertisements* to cause any of the harm of concern
to Puerto Rico, the audience for the message would have to be directly
persuaded by the message to gamble.[46] Moreover, one of the principal
interests argued by the Tourism Company, the disruption of moral and
cultural patterns,[47] would seem to follow directly from an audience response to the advertisements: Puerto Ricans are persuaded by advertisements to gamble in casinos, their morality will be undermined, and the
culture subsequently damaged. In other words, the state seems concerned
about the morality of casino gambling but not the morality of cockfighting, and it therefore outlaws the advertising of one but not the other.
Obviously, that is point-of-view discrimination.

Incidental Effects

Justice Scalia unhelpfully combines a third category of cases, the "incidental effect" cases, with the "secondary effects" line of cases.[48] Under the
incidental effect theory, if a statute is directed at conduct generally, and
hits speech incidentally as one form of the conduct, there is no content or
subject matter discrimination of First Amendment interest because the
statute is not directed at speech.[49] So, as Justice Scalia recognized, if a
legislature prohibits sexual harassment (whether by physical or symbolic
means), the imposition of penalties for sexually harassing speech would
not violate any First Amendment prohibition against content discrimination.[50] Similarly, it would seem to follow that if St. Paul were to prohibit
racial harassment (whether by physical or symbolic means), the imposition of penalties for racially harassing speech would not violate any First
Amendment prohibition against content discrimination. Although this
feature of the opinion is obviously significant, the incidental effect principle on which it relies does not distinguish *Posadas* because the Puerto
Rican statute in *Posadas* was directed exclusively at speech, that is, commercial advertising of a certain sort.

The Catchall Category

Finally, Justice Scalia suggests that there might be another exception for
cases where "[t]here is no realistic possibility that official suppression of
ideas is afoot."[51] *Posadas* hardly qualifies for this exception because the

hostility to the idea of participating in casino gambling screams out from the recitation of the legislature's interests in morality and the culture. In the end, it seems obvious that *Posadas* cannot be passed off under any of Justice Scalia's exceptions.

Content Discrimination and *R.A.V.*

Some might argue that the approach used in *Posadas* is the aberration, not *R.A.V.* Indeed, the method employed by *Posadas* was subsequently questioned by the Court in *Liquormart*. To be specific, with the single exception of Justice Scalia, eight justices thought the relaxed scrutiny employed in *Posadas* was insufficiently demanding.[52] As I explained in chapter two, however, the fighting issue in *Liquormart* was how strict the scrutiny should be, and that issue was not resolved. Moreover, as I also mentioned in chapter two, *Posadas* was not overruled, and Justice Stevens's attempt to distinguish *Edge Broadcasting*, a paternalistic anti–gambling advertising case, did not secure a Court majority. Perhaps even more important, whatever the strength of the commercial speech standard in a case like *Liquormart*, the commercial speech test set out in *Central Hudson* ordinarily calls for a less than strict standard even though content discrimination of otherwise protected speech is involved.[53] Yet *R.A.V.* applied strict scrutiny to content discrimination of otherwise unprotected speech.

The irreconcilability of *R.A.V.* with general commercial speech doctrine is part of a larger failure: Justice Scalia's framework provides neither a cogent explanation of First Amendment law nor a sturdy basis for justifying *R.A.V.*'s result. In attempting an overview of the exceptions he parades, Justice Scalia suggests that each provides a basis for concluding that the subject matter restrictions at issue are legitimate because they are not "even arguably 'conditioned upon the sovereign's agreement with what a speaker may intend to say.' "[54] Or, as he also puts it: "There is no realistic possibility that official suppression of ideas is afoot."[55] This description of the case law breathes new life into the expression about ostriches hiding their heads in the sand. When the government outlaws threats against the president,[56] casino gambling advertisements,[57] lottery advertisements,[58] or the burning of draft cards[59] or when it engages in a campaign of zoning adult theaters out of neighborhoods,[60] no one but a person wearing a black robe and possessing a strong will to believe or befuddle could possibly suppose that "[t]here is no realistic possibility that official suppression of ideas is afoot."[61] Point-of-view discrimination arguably permeates these categories. If point-of-view discrimination were as significant an evil as the Court often supposes, one would think that a demanding test would have been applied in some of these cases. But many of the justices presumably share the governmental view that advertisements for casino gambling, the burning of draft cards, and the kinds of films shown in adult theaters are not worth much. They either do not look for point-of-view discrimination or else devise tests that command them not to look. Perhaps they cannot see the ways in which they themselves discriminate.

But Justice Scalia was sharply on the lookout for such discrimination in *R.A.V.* Regrettably, he was more cavalier when it came to discussing the possibility that the St. Paul ordinance fit within one of his own exceptions. Recall that Justice Scalia had allowed subject matter discrimination "[w]hen the basis for content discrimination consists entirely of the very reason the entire class of speech at issue is proscribable."[62] It could well be argued, as Justice Scalia recognized in footnote seven, that "the ordinance merely regulates that subclass of fighting words which is most likely to provoke a violent response."[63] Justice Scalia first responded that St. Paul had not made the argument. But to make it clear that it would not have mattered if St. Paul had made the argument, he opined that it "appear[ed] unlikely" that the subclass covered by the ordinance could be so described.[64]

Is this description really unlikely, however? Consider Justice Frankfurter's related remarks about group racial or religious libel: "Illinois did not have to look beyond her own borders to await the tragic experience of the last three decades to conclude that wilful purveyors of falsehood concerning racial and religious groups promote strife and tend powerfully to obstruct the manifold adjustments required for free, ordered life in a metropolitan, polyglot community. From the murder of the abolitionist Lovejoy in 1837 to the Cicero riots of 1951, Illinois has been the scene of exacerbated tension between races, often flaring into violence and destruction. In many of these outbreaks, utterances of the character here in question, so the Illinois legislature could conclude, played a significant part."[65]

Even if racial and religious insults did not specially give rise to the possibility of violence, what of the related argument that racial, religious, and gender insults are especially serious instances of the kind of "words . . . which by their very utterance inflict injury"[66] in the fighting words context?

Here we approach the heart of the matter. Justice Scalia responds: "This is word-play. What makes the anger, fear, sense of dishonor, etc. produced by violation of this ordinance distinct from the anger, fear, sense of dishonor, etc. produced by other fighting words is nothing other than the fact that it is caused by a distinctive idea, conveyed by a distinctive message. The First Amendment cannot be evaded that easily."[67]

That the injury is caused by a distinctive message is obvious; that the First Amendment prevents protection against that injury by prohibiting the message, however, is the issue to be decided. Notice that if R.A.V. were prosecuted under a nondiscriminatory fighting words statute, the offense would normally be triggered by uttering a distinctive message. Absent unusual circumstances, if R.A.V. insulted a person's driving ability, a jury could reasonably find that no fighting words were present. If R.A.V. insulted a person's race, however, the distinctive character of the message would contribute to a jury determination of a fighting words violation. Thus, a jury could determine that racist speech was especially damaging. The puzzle is why the St. Paul City Council could not do the same. It is simply not the case that the First Amendment absolutely prohibits the regulation of injuries caused by messages. Indeed, Justice Scalia's suggestion that a fighting words statute is a content-neutral alternative to the St. Paul ordinance authorizes the ad hoc application of its terms to "distinctive messages."

Justice Scalia does not clearly deny that the injuries of concern in the ordinance are qualitatively different than the kinds of injuries triggered by fighting words as a class. He comes closest to discussing the point when he builds on an assertion that the fighting words category implicates an unacceptable "*mode* of expressing *whatever* idea the speaker wishes to convey."[68] He then says that "St. Paul has not singled out an especially offensive *mode* of expression—it has not, for example, selected for prohibition only those fighting words that communicate ideas in a threatening (as opposed to a merely obnoxious) manner. Rather, it has proscribed fighting words of whatever manner that communicate messages of racial, gender, or religious intolerance. Selectivity of this sort creates the *possibility* that the city is seeking to handicap the expression of particular ideas."[69]

Precisely. But quite beside the point. If the argument is that a particular subject matter implicates the very risks the category was designed to cover, but in a more severe way, what difference does it make that the category of speech involved is not the most offensive *mode* of speech? The question is whether the speech causes the most serious forms of injury. Since when has the mere possibility of idea discrimination in regulating less than fully protected speech become of such enormous constitutional import?

Obviously, it would have been easy enough to write an opinion in which the existence of the state's substantial interest in deterring racial, religious, and gender injuries was sufficient to justify the ordinance. Claims that the ordinance was motivated by hostility to the content could have been swept aside by reference to the kinds of devices used in cases involving commercial speech or adult theaters.

It would not have been an occasion for "dancing in the streets,"[70] however, had the Court resorted to any such device. Intellectual dishonesty is no virtue. There is no point in pretending that St. Paul lacked hostility to the underlying message. Of course, St. Paul was hostile to the messages it sought to criminalize—which is not to deny that the injuries were of concern to those who passed the ordinance.

The question is whether and when such hostility should be constitutionally fatal. Justice Scalia's apparent response to the question is that such hostility is constitutionally fatal if the Court is prepared to recognize its existence and if the legislation in question is unable to pass a test of strict scrutiny.[71] But this is unduly simplistic; we have already seen that the Court has not subjected subject matter discrimination within categories of speech receiving less than full protection to the kind of strict scrutiny that Justice Scalia supposes is the usual First Amendment standard. Even if Justice Scalia's recharacterization of the cases involving less than fully protected speech were on the mark, there would be no easy skip to the conclusion that strict scrutiny was appropriate.

Strict scrutiny is ordinarily employed when the state attempts to use content discrimination against otherwise protected speech, for example, to regulate the time or place in which such speech can be uttered. Thus, when Chicago prohibits speech near a school except speech pursuant to a labor dispute, the Court employs strict scrutiny to test the constitutionality of the content discrimination.[72]

But idea discrimination is not always a constitutional sin, and strict scrutiny is not a given. In determining that obscenity or some forms of defamation are unprotected, for example, the Court has forthrightly balanced or deferred to the interests proffered by the state. Why, then, is strict scrutiny appropriate for regulation of racist speech but not for defamation or obscenity?

Consider obscenity. The Court in *Paris Adult Theatre I v. Slaton*[73] asserted that the distribution of obscene material is not protected under the First Amendment because such material debases human personality, violates the social interest in morality, and interferes with the state's right to maintain a decent society. In short, it is not good speech. Whatever slight value it may have is said to be outweighed by "the social interest in order and morality."[74] Indeed, the very definition of obscenity is filled with decisions about value. To be obscene, material must first appeal to prurient interests; second, it must be a patently offensive depiction or description of sexual conduct; and third, it must *not* have serious literary, artistic, political, or scientific value.[75]

The third prong of the test is obviously phrased in terms of value. The prurient interest part of the test, however, is also an especially clear example of point-of-view discrimination. Appeals to prurient interest are defined as appeals to a "shameful or morbid interest in nudity, sex, or excretion"[76] and cannot be taken to include appeals to "normal" interests in sex.[77] That is, appeals to interest in "good, old fashioned, healthy"[78] sex are constitutionally protected even if they are patently offensive to contemporary standards and lack serious literary, artistic, political, or scientific value. Appeals to "abnormal" interests in sex are criminalized when the other requirements are satisfied.[79]

If it is fair to ask whether obscenity's contribution to truth is outweighed by the social interest in order and morality and to base an answer on what a legislature could quite reasonably determine (a far cry from strict scrutiny), then why are the same question and scrutiny inappropriate for racist speech? If obscenity can be judged by whether it jeopardizes the "right [to] maintain a decent society,"[80] why is racist speech not subjected to the same test?

Perhaps the answer is that the suppression of obscenity does not involve the suppression of "ideas."[81] But *this* is "word-play."[82] To distinguish between decent sex and morbid sex is obviously point-of-view discrimination. Moreover, opponents of obscenity object to a variety of themes: the notion that sex is a casual affair, the idea that sex is an "animal connection" rather than a human relationship,[83] and the implicit denial of the need for a public morality.[84]

Obscenity law, then, is an instance in which content discrimination, subject matter discrimination, and point-of-view discrimination coincide, yet strict scrutiny is not employed, and the legislation is not invalidated. This leaves two possible responses. One might be: "So much the worse for obscenity law. Let us get rid of it." No doubt many liberals would take this view, but the Court is not prepared to afford obscenity full constitutional protection—and Justice Scalia is adamant on the subject.[85] Justice Scalia needs to reconcile his approach to racist speech with his approach to obscenity.

Alternatively, one might might argue that, unlike racist speech, obscenity is not political (except for obscenity that has political value but *not* enough to deserve the label of "serious" political value) and that political speech is particularly privileged. Here much depends on the definition of "political." Assume for the moment that feminist conceptions of the political[86] are ignored (so that obscenity is nonpolitical). Is it clear that a racist insult implicates politics? We can assume that the perpetrator of a racist insult holds politically controversial views, but we can also assume that the disseminator of obscene materials holds politically controversial views about the themes contained in the materials. Does this make either of them political?

In a sense, the answer does not matter because the underlying assumption of the political argument (that strict scrutiny applies to political speech and that point-of-view discrimination is not permitted) is itself misplaced. The law of defamation, much of which involves political speech, makes this point clear. The rhetoric of strict scrutiny has not been employed in defamation cases. Rather, the Court has balanced the interest in reputation against the interests in freedom of expression,[87] and that balancing process has produced a complex set of rules.[88] Perhaps defamation can be distinguished from racist speech on the ground that the former does not involve idea discrimination. Notice, however, that the law of defamation involves a form of content discrimination that has predictable discriminatory impact. If you say nice things about powerful people, the defamation laws will not bite you; if you say critical things, you are at risk.[89] This is content-neutral in that any defamatory criticism is subject to these laws, but the general deterrence of criticism is arguably as serious a concern as the deterrence of a particular defamatory statement.

Perhaps more serious from a First Amendment perspective, defamation laws, like "pure" fighting words statutes, cannot be enforced without the authorization of ad hoc point-of-view discrimination by judges and juries. In many defamation trials, the state is forced to determine (often with the help of a jury) whether particular critical statements are true or false. These statements may involve public officials, public figures, or private persons. They may be of vital import in the marketplace of ideas. Nonetheless, the judicial branch of government makes an official determination of whether the point of view expressed by the defendant about the plaintiff is true or false and, if false, whether it is subject to monetary sanctions. This official governmental determination of truth and falsity is pure point-of-view discrimination. Moreover, the impact of this process is not confined to trials. Anyone publishing a critical statement about someone he or she believes might sue must take into account what a typical jury is likely to think about that statement. As a consequence, some critical statements are easier to make than others. Obviously this entire process deeply implicates First Amendment values.

It is, therefore, a nonstarter to suggest that under the defamation laws "ideas" are (or should be) protected and only statements of fact are subjected to scrutiny.[90] This just leads to the question of why ideas are more important than assertions of fact. Surely assertions of fact make important contributions to our understanding of society and its government. Assertions of fact are afforded a measure of protection under the First Amendment; no one has put forth a compelling argument that they are less important than ideas. Assuming we could define an "idea" in the first place, we would be at a loss to explain why facts or assertions thereof are less important. Indeed, a major part of the rationale for protecting opinions in defamation law has been that they say so *little* that a jury could not reliably determine their truth or falsity.[91] A marketplace of ideas with-

out facts would be bankrupt. The intrusion of defamation laws into the marketplace of ideas *and* facts discourages many true assertions of fact and entails a genuine First Amendment loss.

My point, however, is not that defamation laws should be regarded as unconstitutional. My point is that defamation laws permit point-of-view discrimination—without applying strict scrutiny—because the interest in reputation is thought to outweigh the interests in freedom of expression in particular contexts.

Does racist speech differ? Racist speech laws single out particular ideas for special regulation; defamation laws do not. This no doubt is a distinction. However, since (as I have argued) defamation laws license ad hoc point-of-view discrimination by juries and likely cause writers and publishers to take the potential unpopularity of their positions into account in deciding whether to publish critical statements, this distinction seems to make little difference. To discern whether it does, we need a firmer grip on what is wrong with idea discrimination or point-of-view discrimination in the first place.

Content Discrimination and the Meaning of America

Justice Scalia's opinion does not provide much assistance. He maintains that the rationale of the prohibition against content discrimination is the "specter that the Government may effectively drive certain ideas or viewpoints from the marketplace."[92] That concern, however, is difficult to take seriously in the context of *R.A.V.* St. Paul prohibited only a small class of "fighting words," words that make a slight contribution to truth[93]—just a particular socially unacceptable *mode* of presentation, in Justice Scalia's view. It is hard to see how that raises the "specter that the Government may effectively drive certain ideas or viewpoints from the marketplace."[94]

Even more telling is Justice Scalia's content-neutral alternative to the St. Paul ordinance: a "pure" fighting words statute, which, he maintains, could serve the valid governmental interest in basic human rights of members of groups historically subject to discrimination.[95] But this content-neutral alternative would drive the very same ideas and viewpoints (along with others) from the marketplace. Thus, Justice Scalia cannot plausibly claim to be concerned about this result.

However facially content-neutral a fighting words statute might appear to Justice Scalia, juries or judges would inevitably make content-based judgments in applying the statute. Justice Scalia, for example, complains that the St. Paul ordinance discriminates between statements based on race (which it reaches) and statements based on political affiliation, union membership, and sexual orientation (which it does not). Nonetheless, under Justice Scalia's content-"neutral" ordinance, a judge or jury could make on an ad hoc basis the same type of distinction the St. Paul City Council was not permitted to encode as a rule, deciding, for example, that comments about race are fighting words but that comments about union membership or politics are not.

Nonetheless, there is something about explicit content discrimination that has piqued Justice Scalia's concern.[96] The root of that concern (and that of other justices as well), I suspect, is at once symbolic and substantive. He is attracted to a particular vision of America—as a nation that spurns paternalism and tolerates different points of view, however hateful. It is a nation that is formally neutral in race relations (affirmative action programs, from his perspective, are undesirable),[97] ideally neutral in the economic market (although the Constitution does not guarantee this), and neutral in the "marketplace of ideas." Of course, government will engage in programs that have differential impact on groups and ideas, but substantive equality is not the goal of the Constitution.

From this perspective, there is little to be said for general racist speech statutes such as the St. Paul ordinance. If such statutes target group libel, they are paternalistic and intolerant. If they are applied against fighting words, and if one of the rationales is that victims tend to internalize hostile messages, they can be paternalistic. If the statutes are based on hostility to the message expressed, they can be intolerant. Moreover, as Justice Scalia specifically argues, content-neutral alternatives exist to guard against the harm.

Of course, Justice Scalia's perspective is not unqualified. Government can enter the intellectual marketplace (even if it skews it in important ways) to communicate its own messages.[98] Moreover, government can take the value of speech into account in determining its degree of constitutional protection. A model of antipaternalism, tolerance, and neutrality has difficulty explaining why, for example, commercial speech and obscenity get less than full protection. Moreover, as we have seen, substantial point-of-view discrimination is immanent in existing law, a body of law that Justice Scalia for the most part accepts.

Beyond the doctrinal tensions, however, we should question how attractive the picture of the nation implicit in Justice Scalia's First Amendment jurisprudence really is. Antipaternalism[99] and toleration[100] are strong American values, and there is much to be said for (and against) the idea of a neutral government, particularly one that plays no favorites in the intellectual market. Justice Scalia's national picture is certainly one with deep roots in American culture.

Nonetheless, there are other important stories to be told about the nation. For example, one could describe a country that has historically evolved from a nation of slavery into a nation with a profound constitutional commitment to racial equality and ultimately to gender equality. Similarly, the country has evolved from the existence of state-established churches to a nation where religious equality is a constitutional given in every state.

These stories may be exaggerated conceptions of the country, but they are important parts of the ways we explain and talk about our constitutional culture. Often these stories and ideals can innocently be held out as mutually consistent. In the racist speech context, however, they seem to compete, and innocence is no longer possible.

In choosing between these competing stories, outsider jurisprudence proposes an egalitarian solution: pick the story that benefits those who have been subordinated. I would note, however, that prominent practitioners of outsider jurisprudence balance competing stories about freedom and equality. Mari Matsuda does not advocate a ban on all racist speech;[101] even Catharine MacKinnon does not advocate the abolition of all sexist speech.[102] Perhaps these positions are purely strategic; for the moment, it does not matter. At a minimum, Matsuda, a strong proponent of outsider jurisprudence, is at pains to recognize the existence of competing stories.[103]

In contrast, Justice Scalia's approach to racist speech is relentlessly simplistic. He does not take the competing story seriously. That is why it is clear to him that a comprehensive fighting words statute is an obvious alternative to the St. Paul ordinance, despite the fact that it ignores the equality story and lacks the St. Paul ordinance's symbolic power. Justice Scalia has a response to this, but he does not have an argument: "[T]he only interest distinctively served by the content limitation is that of displaying the city council's special hostility toward the particular biases thus singled out. This is precisely what the First Amendment forbids."[104]

Justice Scalia's description of the government's interest dilutes it unfairly. St. Paul's interest, of course, is not in allowing its city council to have a special moment of pique. Rather, it is to establish not only that religious, racial, and gender epithets are particularly harmful but also that, as a matter of public morality, such epithets are a public disgrace.

Regarding to the latter point, Justice Scalia insists that this kind of proclamation of public morality is precisely what the First Amendment forbids. But this is naked assertion, a selection of one story over another. How is it that a state's attempt to establish public morality in outlawing obscenity is not also precisely what the First Amendment forbids? If interests can be balanced against each other, why can't constitutional stories be set beside each other and accommodated?

I do not mean to suggest that Justice Scalia's overall position is hopeless. We can only speculate, however, about how he reconciles his positions on racist speech, obscenity, and defamation. I suspect he thinks that obscenity is nonpolitical smut unworthy of protection; that defamation, although political, causes harm for which there has traditionally been a remedy (plus, he is no fan of the press); and that racist speech is political in character (although he would agree it can be regulated if the statute is not targeted by subject matter or if it is directed at conduct generally) but not ordinarily the source of traditionally recognized or serious harm. Those who object to racist speech, he may believe, are often too thin-skinned. Of course, it is one thing to assume that racist speech is political and quite another to suppose that racist speech in the form of fighting words is political—as if fighting words were a form of dialogue or debate in the public sphere.[105]

The authoritarian simplicity of remarks like "This is precisely what the First Amendment forbids"[106] does not sit easily with the deeply compromised vision Justice Scalia actually holds. I do not mean to say that complexity can be avoided. I do mean to suggest that if content neutrality is the First Amendment emperor, the emperor has no clothes.

Once it is recognized that a reference to content neutrality is not a conversation stopper, the City of St. Paul's story becomes difficult to dismiss abruptly. St. Paul, by passing its ordinance said in effect: We understand that idea discrimination is a deep intrusion into First Amendment values, but the toleration of racial, religious, and gender epithets has serious implications for equality and our public morality. Our concern about those issues is so great that a symbolic commitment to prohibiting those epithets is of more importance than the first amendment story. Indeed, the very existence of the first amendment story and our willingness to trump it shows how strongly our community values equality and public morality.

On this understanding, St. Paul cannot fairly be understood to have little appreciation for First Amendment values. Instead, it has adopted a First Amendment story very different from Justice Scalia's. Recall that its ordinance, as construed by the state supreme court, applies only to fighting words.[107] If someone gives a public speech involving racial superiority but no fighting words are addressed to any individual or small group, the ordinance does not apply. Perhaps St. Paul shares Justice Brennan's story about our "profound national commitment to the principle that debate on public issues should be uninhibited, robust and wide-open."[108] On this understanding, St. Paul's conviction is based on appreciation for life in an exciting and diverse country. It need not be committed to the view that racial inequality might be a fine idea and that the intellectual marketplace can decide. Opposition to racial inequality was, no doubt, an important part of the reason St. Paul outlawed racial epithets.

This is certainly a different First Amendment story than the one Justice Scalia implicitly tells, and yet all Justice Scalia can say on behalf of his own story is either irrelevant (since his own alternative would drive even more ideas from the marketplace than St. Paul's) or an exercise in pure fiat ("This is precisely what the First Amendment forbids"). Moreover, his opinion in *R.A.V.* provides little direction for legislatures and lower courts on a key issue: assuming that fighting word statutes are constitutional, what are fighting words?

"Fighting Words"

Justice White's opinion, joined by three other justices, speaks to the question of what fighting words are, but in terms that need elaboration and qualification. Justice White believes the St. Paul approach was flawed not because it reached too little speech (as Justice Scalia would have it) but because it reached too much; in other words, it was overbroad. There are two problems with this argument. First, it seems clear that Justice White misinterprets the ordinance. Second, he criticizes the ordinance for not being specific enough about the nature of the injuries that would suffice to trigger sanctions. As I will argue, this focus on injury is not helpful. Nonetheless, I will suggest (at some length) that there may be substantial merit in Justice White's further suggestion that direct personal insults (whether or not they are likely to trigger violence) are rightly distinguished from racial insults that are not targeted at particular individuals.

The Overbreadth Issue

In retrospect, it is more than a little odd that Justice White authored an opinion declaring the statute to be overbroad. For many years, Justice White led the Court in limiting that doctrine's reach,[109] successfully championing the view that those whose own conduct is unprotected should not prevail in challenging a speech statute without a showing that its overbreadth is "real and substantial."[110] As written, the St. Paul ordinance was surely a ripe candidate for a real and substantial overbreadth finding, but since the Minnesota Supreme Court constructed the statute narrowly, restricting it to fighting words, Justice White's enthusiasm for the overbreadth argument is somewhat difficult to understand.

As written, the St. Paul ordinance is sweeping: "Whoever places on public or private property a symbol, object, appellation, characterization or graffiti, including, but not limited to, a burning cross or Nazi swastika, which one knows or has reasonable grounds to know arouses anger, alarm, or resentment in others on the basis of race, color, creed, religion or gender commits disorderly conduct and shall be guilty of a misdemeanor."[111]

One doesn't need to get up early in the morning to appreciate that placing a symbol on public or private property (with consent), "which one knows or has reasonable grounds to know arouses alarm, anger, or resentment" on the grounds specified in the ordinance, might be protected in a wide variety of circumstances. Any controversial placard concerning race, gender, or religion is likely to provoke anger in others. If the St. Paul ordinance had been read for all it was worth, few would rush to defend it.[112]

Justice's White opinion did not deny the power of a state court to provide a narrowing construction,[113] nor did he argue that there was anything untoward about the particular narrowing construction in this case. He made no claim, for example, that the construction was so novel that the defendant could not have anticipated it.[114] In considering the overbreadth issue, then, the justices were required to take the statute " 'as though it read precisely as the highest court of the state has interpreted it,' "[115] and Justice White recognized this.[116]

Here, however, Justice White went astray. Although he properly examined the text of the Minnesota Supreme Court's opinion, not just that of the ordinance, his rendition of the opinion—joined by three of his fellow justices—is eccentric. According to Justice White, the Minnesota Supreme Court ruled that the ordinance prohibited fighting words but understood fighting words to include any expression that " 'by its very utterance' causes 'anger, alarm, or resentment.' "[117] From that premise it was an easy ride to the conclusion condemning the St. Paul ordinance: "The mere fact that expressive activity causes hurt feelings, offense, or resentment, wrote Justice White, does not render the expression unprotected."[118]

One might be initially suspicious of this interpretation, for it is difficult to understand how it could have been seen by Justice White or by the Minnesota Supreme Court as a *narrowing* construction. The ordinance, as construed by Justice White, seems to cover exactly the same speech covered by its literal terms, namely, speech reasonably likely to cause anger, alarm, or resentment on the grounds specified in the ordinance.

To be sure, the Minnesota Supreme Court did say something that *left alone* would have justified Justice White's reading: "Unlike the flag desecration statute at issue in *Texas v. Johnson,* the challenged St. Paul ordinance does not on its face assume that any cross burning, irrespective of the particular context in which it occurs, is subject to prosecution. Rather, *the ordinance censors only those displays that one knows or should know will create anger, alarm or resentment based on racial, ethnic, gender or religious bias.*"[119] If the Minnesota court had stopped there, no doubt Justice White would have been on the mark. But the court went on:

> *In re S.L.J.*, 263 N.W. 2d 412 (Minn. 1978), this court narrowly construed Minn. Stat. 609.72, subd. 1(3) (1990), which prohibits "offensive, obscene, or abusive language or . . . boisterous and noisy conduct *tending reasonably to arouse alarm, anger, or resentment in others*" (emphasis added) *to refer only to "fighting words," S.L.J.* 263 N.W. 2d at 419, *thereby preserving it in the face of an overbreadth attack. Similarly limited to expressive conduct that amounts to "fighting words"*—conduct that itself inflicts injury or tends to incite immediate violence, see *Chaplinsky v. New Hampshire*, 315 U.S. at 572, 62 S.Ct. at 769—*the ordinance in question withstands constitutional challenge.*[120]

As this passage makes clear, the Minnesota Supreme Court explicitly construed "anger, alarm, and resentment" narrowly to refer *only* to fighting words. It did not say, as Justice White supposed, that fighting words include any expression that " 'by its very utterance' causes 'anger, alarm, or resentment.' "[121] Nor was the state court under the illusion, as Justice White claimed, that "[t]he mere fact that expressive activity causes hurt feelings, offense, or resentment" is a sufficient basis for excluding speech from constitutional protection.

If there were any question about the Minnesota Supreme Court's intentions, inspection of the case it relied upon, *In re Welfare of S.L.J.*, should have resolved all doubts. *S.L.J.* considered the constitutionality of a state disorderly conduct statute that, like the St. Paul ordinance, prohibited speech that would tend "reasonably to arouse alarm, anger, or resentment in others."[122] *S.L.J.* explicitly recognized that the "vulgar, offensive, and insulting"[123] character of words does not alone make them constitutionally punishable even if the "overwhelming majority of citizens"[124] would condemn them. It therefore found that the statute as written did not satisfy the constitutional definition of fighting words and was unconstitutional on its face.

Nonetheless, the court in *S.L.J.* proceeded to construe narrowly the statute to apply only to fighting words. Moreover, the way it applied the doctrine made it clear that words causing resentment were not necessarily tantamount to fighting words. The facts before the court in *S.L.J.* involved a fourteen-year-old girl who had been questioned by police officers on the hunch that she may have been sniffing paint or stealing bicycles. After the questioning, she was told to go home because it was past her curfew. After starting down an alley to depart, S.L.J. and her friend turned around somewhere between fifteen and thirty feet from the squad car in which the officers were sitting and said: "Fuck you pigs."[125] Arrests for disorderly conduct quickly followed.

The petition against S.L.J. alleged that she had used language that she
knew or had reasonable grounds to know would "tend to arouse resentment in others."[126] One of the officers testified: " 'I was mad. I was upset.
They didn't have any right to say that to me.' "[127] At the same time, the
officer admitted that he did not even consider a violent response.

Although the Minnesota Supreme Court accepted the police officer's
testimony and seemed to appreciate his resentment,[128] applying the fighting words test, it ruled that S.L.J.'s speech was constitutionally protected:

> Under this test, appellant's conviction for disorderly conduct cannot stand.
> While it is true that no ordered society would condone the vulgar language used
> by this 14-year-old child, and as the court found, her words were intended to,
> and did, arouse resentment in the officers, the constitution requires more before
> a person can be convicted for mere speech. In this case, the words were directed
> at two police officers sitting in their squad car from a distance of 15 to 30 feet
> by a small, 14-year-old child who was on her way home when she turned to the
> officers and made her statement. With the words spoken in retreat from more
> than 15 feet away rather than eye-to-eye, there was no reasonable likelihood
> that they would tend to incite an immediate breach of the peace or to provoke
> violent reaction by an ordinary, reasonable person. Thus, the state has failed
> to prove that under these circumstances the words uttered by appellant were
> "fighting words," and both her conviction for disorderly conduct and the find-
> ing of delinquency based on the conviction must be reversed.[129]

The Minnesota Supreme Court's reliance on *S.L.J.* in construing the St.
Paul ordinance makes Justice White's reading deeply implausible. Clearly,
in *R.A.V.* the Minnesota Supreme Court understood that arousal to anger
or resentment is an insufficient reed on which to base criminal punishment. Clearly, the court understood the flag-burning case's doctrine that
"[i]f there is a bedrock principle underlying the First Amendment, it is
that the Government may not prohibit the expression of an idea simply
because society finds the idea itself offensive or disagreeable."[130] Justice
White's intimation to the contrary is flatly wrong.

This leads to a difficult question: How does one account for Justice
White's failure? One might not have expected him to go wrong here: he
championed a narrow conception of the overbreadth doctrine, and he has
been praised for his strong analytic power.[131] Is there anything about his
more general constitutional perspective that could explain his opinion?
Some might think that Justice White's hostility to affirmative action might
spill over to a case of this kind.[132] After all, Justice Blackmun complained
in his concurrence that the majority may have been influenced by "the
temptation to decide the issue over 'politically correct' speech."[133] But
Justice White's opinion exhibits no such purpose. It is sharply critical of

Justice Scalia's, observing, for example: "Any contribution of this [Court's] holding to First Amendment jurisprudence is surely a negative one, since it necessarily signals that expressions of violence, such as the message of intimidation and racial hatred conveyed by the burning of a cross on someone's lawn, are of sufficient value to outweigh the social interest in order and morality that has traditionally placed such fighting words outside the First Amendment."[134]

If Justice White's performance in *R.A.V.* cannot be traced to his attitudes about affirmative action, it is also difficult to attribute his performance to anything in his more general understanding of the judicial role. Granted, admirers of Justice White understood him to be a firm opponent of any form of results-oriented jurisprudence, including outsider jurisprudence.[135] From this perspective, the Constitution is best interpreted as by a thoroughly impartial judge committed to following the rule of law, and prepared to address the merits of each case as it is presented.[136]

But Justice White does not approach the Constitution as if it were a blank slate. His interpretation of the Constitution provides for a judicial role limited by the need for broad deference to state and federal governments even when they attempt to limit freedom of speech.[137] A judge armed with this understanding had no incentive to decide *R.A.V.* against the City of St. Paul, but Justice White did. I am inclined to think he just made a mistake.[138]

Nonetheless, a delicious irony accompanies that mistake. If Justice White was committed to impartiality (albeit with a background constitutional understanding), so was Justice Thurgood Marshall (albeit with a different background constitutional understanding). Justice Marshall understood the Constitution to favor the powerless in general and the racially disadvantaged in particular. Whether this form of outsider jurisprudence is described as results-oriented jurisprudence or as impartiality within a particular background understanding is of little moment. What is important is that Justice Marshall, unlike Justice White, would have been actively on the lookout for persuasive arguments that would have protected the victims of cross burning. It is hard to believe that Justice Marshall would have so blatantly misread the Minnesota opinion, and that Justice White would have persisted in his misreading once it had been called to his attention. Thus, the irony. Those who admire justices like White for their alleged impartiality need to recognize that attention to real-world results and the diversity of possible constitutional understandings can make a vital contribution to the *technical* proficiency of the Court. If a voice for outsider jurisprudence had been present on the Court, Justice White's error could have been corrected before its publication.

The Unhelpful Search for Injury

As I have argued, Justice White invalidated the St. Paul ordinance based on an incorrect reading of the Minnesota Supreme Court's opinion. In addition, his suggestions for what might constitute an acceptable ordinance need considerable refinement. In *R.A.V.*, the Minnesota Supreme Court followed *Chaplinsky v. New Hampshire*'s characterization of fighting words as those that "by their very utterance inflict *injury* or tend to incite an immediate breach of the peace."[139] The Minnesota Supreme Court did not specify the nature of the injury required other than to make it clear (albeit not to Justice White and his signatories) that anger, alarm, or resentment do not in and of themselves suffice. In fairness to the Minnesota Supreme Court, this is more than the U.S. Supreme Court did either in *Chaplinsky* or in any subsequent case. Thus, when Justice White observed that the Minnesota court was "far from clear in identifying the '[injuries]' inflicted by the expression St. Paul sought to regulate,"[140] he cast a stone from a glass house.

Lower courts trying to make sense of this aspect of Justice White's opinion may focus on the word *injury* directly and come up with awkward, awful-sounding formulations requiring extreme or "really extreme" emotional distress, or distress that requires psychiatric or medical mental care. This approach, if adopted, would be understandable. The injuries associated with fighting words are often underappreciated. Indeed, a major contribution of outsider jurisprudence is to highlight the nature and extent of the injuries caused by racist speech.[141] But a doctrinal focus on injury obscures an important point: injury should be neither a necessary nor a sufficient condition for the imposition of punitive sanctions.

Consider the question of whether injury should be a *sufficient* condition for the imposition of punitive (or other) sanctions. The tort of intentional infliction of emotional distress provides an apt analogy. Among other things, the tort requires showings not only (1) that severe injury was actually caused and (2) that an intent to cause emotional distress existed but also (3) that the activity offends generally accepted standards of decency or morality or is outrageous.[142] As Chief Justice Rehnquist observed for a unanimous Court: "Generally speaking the law does not regard the intent to inflict emotional distress as one which should receive much solicitude, and it is quite understandable that most if not all jurisdictions have chosen to make it civilly culpable where the conduct is sufficiently 'outrageous.'[143]

By omitting any discussion of the context in which the injury might occur, the language of Justice White's *R.A.V.* opinion seems to suggest that a showing *less* stringent than that required for the tort of intentional infliction of emotional distress might suffice. He seems to invite lower courts to specify the *type*[144] of injury that insulting utterances might bring about, but not to address the question of whether speech was sufficiently "outrageous." But this approach is surely wrong.

Suppose a person informs his or her betrothed that he or she plans to break off their engagement in a soliloquy packed with angry, emotional, and insulting language. Assume further that the speech results in severe emotional injury and that the angry speaker hoped to hurt the victim. I venture that this has occurred on millions of occasions.

Yet it would be surprising if our hypothetical victim could recover in tort. A court would be loath to conclude that the perpetrator's conduct was sufficiently outrageous. If mental injury alone cannot afford a sufficient basis for tort liability, certainly it cannot be the sole basis for criminal liability, for which penalties are harsher. Mental cruelty may be a sufficient ground for divorce in some states; it would be surprising if, without more, it could justify a jail sentence.

Injury, then, should not be a *sufficient* condition for criminal liability; neither should it be a *necessary* condition. Let us return to the facts of *R.A.V.* Assume that the family witnessed the burning cross but suffered no emotional distress. What if the family was angry or somewhat fearful but not distressed? What if they were so much in denial as to be blasé? It may make sense for tort liability to turn on the existence of emotional distress (particularly if compensation is a primary goal), but why should criminal liability in this kind of circumstance turn on the response of the victims?

Notice that the record in *R.A.V.* disclosed nothing about the reaction of the victims.[145] Of course, a Black family living on a residential street in a predominantly white neighborhood could reasonably interpret the appearance of a burning cross on its front lawn as a terroristic threat directed at the family as a whole or at one of its members. As the Sixth Circuit observed, "[A] black American would be particularly susceptible to the threat of cross burning because of the historical connotations of violence associated with the act."[146] Cross burning might reasonably prompt "fear, anxiety, and apprehension for safety."[147]

Neither punishment nor culpability should turn on whether the act induces a certain type of reaction from the victim. Victims should not be required to report their precise thoughts and emotions, nor should the perpetrator who intended to insult on the basis of race be exonerated simply because the victim turns out to be exceptionally hardy.[148]

Reconsider *Chaplinsky v. New Hampshire.* When Chaplinsky hurled insulting remarks at a police officer, the Court made no effort to determine the emotional reaction of the police officer or his inclination to fight under the particular circumstances. If that part of its approach is right, it makes no sense to probe the specific character of the injury to the members of the African-American family in *R.A.V.*

Is that part of the *Chaplinsky* approach right? As a principle, I would say so, but that is a far cry from affirming either its language or its result. As I have already suggested, an utterance's mere *propensity* to inflict an injury should not be *sufficient* to remove it from constitutional protection; such a rule would obviate consideration of the context of particular situations and would therefore lack a suitable constitutional foundation. People in the course of being arrested by police officers are likely to depart from the queen's English with great frequency; their rudeness does not deserve to be a criminal offense, and officers unable to respond coolly in such situations do not belong in law enforcement.[149]

The Bottom Line

If Justice White's focus on injury needs revision, another portion of his *R.A.V.* opinion is somewhat more helpful, even though it too needs refinement. In footnote four, citing the majority opinion in *Texas v. Johnson*, Justice White observed that the fighting words doctrine applies to a "direct personal insult or an invitation to exchange fisticuffs."[150] Drawing on this standard and on *Brandenburg v. Ohio*, he said that burning a cross would "almost certainly be protected expression."[151]

While imperfect, Justice White's formulation of the fighting words doctrine has the merit of avoiding a purely pugilistic analysis that would find *Chaplinsky*-type injury if, but only if, the utterance would cause both a reasonable (or average) person *and* the actual addressee to respond with immediate violence.

Both prongs of the pugilistic analysis are problematic. First, it seems wrong to protect the *actual* strong victim who is willing to fight *above* the weaker or less aggressive victim. As Thomas Shea argued almost twenty years ago, there is something deeply anomalous about a test that would "permit a state to penalize a speaker who insults a burly construction worker[152] while forbidding the punishment of the reviler of a wheelchair-bound quadraplegic."[153]

Focusing not on the person to whom remarks are addressed but on an abstract "reasonable" or "average person"[154] provides little help as long as we remain within the pugilistic analysis. Consider who this "reasonable person" will be. The definition will exclude most men and women in society even if we leave size and physical ability out of the equation; most men (maybe I am wrong; perhaps it is just millions of men) and women do not respond to insults with fists.[155] To administer this test and allow it to help the helpless, the "reasonable person" would have to be the *stereo-*

type of a man in a rowdy bar (who has yet to drink enough to lose the mantle of reasonableness). The symbolic impropriety of protecting women, for example, by using the stereotype of *any* man as a proxy—all under the label of reasonableness or the "average person"—ought to send analysts back to the drawing board.

Thus, Justice White is to be applauded for recognizing that the fighting words doctrine applies *either* to a direct personal insult or to an invitation to exchange fisticuffs. As the analogy with the tort of intentional infliction of emotional distress makes clear, however, the personal insult should be required to be particularly offensive or outrageous before sanctions are imposed lest the net capture too much. Second, as discussed previously, the direct personal insult approach need not concentrate on *all* direct personal insults; it could focus on, or offer greater penalties for, racial insults. Justice White's opinion strongly agrees with this approach.

Some commentators have argued that the fighting words doctrine has been used primarily against people of color,[156] for example, against Black defendants for cursing white police officers. If this were true, it would be important to confine the prohibition of racial insults to those directed against people of color. The evidence for the commentator's claim, however, seems extremely speculative. What it establishes persuasively is only that discrimination occurs when people of color insult white police officers, and the rule I have already suggested, that police officers should be required to withstand such insults without retaliating, regardless of the arrestee's race, would solve this problem.

Nonetheless, a related notion—that only racial or ethnic insults directed against members of groups that are historically oppressed because of their race, color, or national and ethnic origin[157] should be subject to prohibition—has considerable merit. Racial or ethnic insults directed at non-Jewish white Americans simply do not have the same capacity as insults directed against subordinated groups.[158]

Notice that, by this standard, the ordinance at issue in *R.A.V.* is defective because it appears to apply to racial insults across the board, regardless of whether they are directed at members of advantaged or disadvantaged groups. From the perspective of outsider jurisprudence, one would have to evaluate whether this defect in the St. Paul ordinance would be likely to lead to the selective, racially biased enforcement that some commentators claim has plagued the enforcement of other fighting words statutes.[159] From the perspective of outsider jurisprudence, the ordinance would be substantially improved if it were limited to speech harming victims from historically oppressed groups. For the Court, however, the introduction of a historical oppression requirement would be an indefensible form of content discrimination, despite the fact that the sting of epithets is greater when directed at members of disadvantaged groups.[160] From my perspective, outsider jurisprudence is correct to call for the prohibition of targeted racial insults. I will leave the particulars of my own somewhat complicated proposal about racial fighting words for the notes.[161]

The remaining question is whether racist speech that does not target any particular individual[162] but instead insults a racial group by means that are "persecutorial, hateful, and degrading"[163] is protected by the First Amendment. Should such racist speech, uttered in public or private, be subject to punitive sanctions? Justice White seems confident that it should be protected: practitioners of outsider jurisprudence are divided on the issue.

To approach the question, I need to return to my own story about the First Amendment and the meaning of America.

Dissent and the Meaning of America

My story is not Justice Scalia's tale about a content-neutral government, nor is it about the town hall meeting or even a robust marketplace of ideas; still less is it about liberty, equality, self-realization, respect, dignity, autonomy, or even tolerance. My story—my partial truth—supposes that the First Amendment protects the dissenters, the unorthodox, and the outcasts. On this understanding, the First Amendment's major purpose and function in the American polity is to protect and sometimes affirmatively to sponsor the individualism, the rebelliousness, the antiauthoritarianism, the spirit of nonconformity within us all.

But the purpose and function of the First Amendment goes beyond the protection of outsiders. For example, the First Amendment also has special regard for the press as an institution intended to operate as a check on corruption and other abuses in private and public life whether or not such abuses affect people on society's margin of power, and special regard for the speech of the powerful when it dissents from our existing customs, habits, institutions, and authorities. Nevertheless, it seems unlikely that the most important or effective criticism of abuse of power will come from the powerful; for one thing, they are unlikely to criticize those aspects of the system that benefit them as a class. In some respects, the dissent story combines an insider and an outsider perspective.

So understood, the dissent story is not only a practical story about checks and balances but also a story of a society symbolized in large part by its protection of dissenters. From this perspective, racist speech that is not targeted against a specific individual presents a difficult First Amendment issue. On the one hand, as David Cole writes, "proponents of racist speech—Klan members, Nazis and the like—are also a minority, and a particularly unpopular one at that."[164] Moreover, it seems likely that members of the Klan and similarly racist groups perceive themselves as beleaguered, stigmatized, and marginalized.[165]

On the other hand, nontargeted racist speech implicates dissenting values on both sides. Although vocal proponents of racism are a minority group despised by many, they also state aloud views that are widely though privately held in society.[166] Hate speakers may differ from their fellow citizens only in their willingness to voice, baldly and vociferously, what they think.[167] Moreover, expressions of racial vilification can create a repressive environment in which the speech of people of color is chilled or not heard.[168] A cross burning directed at the home of a particular Black family is not an act of dissent against a powerful status quo; it is a threatening act of power against a victim. In a society in which race has been and continues to be used as a means of perpetuating inequality, the initiator of racist speech further aggravates the position of the subordinated. Racist speech causes many well-documented harms:[169] it is an assult on the dignity of people of color; it humiliates and causes emotional distress, sometimes with physical manifestations; it helps spread racial prejudice, stigmatizing people of color not only in the eyes of the societally dominant race but also in the eyes of the victims themselves, inspiring self-hatred, isolation, and impairment of the capacity for interpersonal relationships; and, finally, it frequently creates the condition for violence.[170]

Because both aggressors and victims can be characterized, with some accuracy, as dissenters, the dissent story underscores the difficulty of the First Amendment status of racist speech. On the one hand, the dissent perspective seeks to protect those with popularly disdained views and, in an important respect, this includes those who publicly express racist views. On the other hand, the dissent perspective seeks to assure that those who are out of power or lower in a hierarchy have the means to protest their status and to combat the inevitable abuses of power by higher-ups. A regime that is blind to the importance of assuring that disadvantaged groups are not intimidated will contain, as its status quo, substantial corruption and abuse.

How does one resolve conflicts between, or within, different stories about the First Amendment? When values conflict, philosophers may debate abstractly about which course to follow, but I think the legal community tends to focus on the probable *consequences* of such stories (and the regulations that follow from them) for the flourishing of human beings, with a background understanding that all persons are entitled to respect and dignity.

Contribution to Public Dialogue

One could argue that racist speech makes a contribution to public dialogue. For the purposes of this discussion, I shall rely on Mari Matsuda's definition of racist speech, namely, that it is a message of racial inferiority, that it is directed against a historically oppressed group, and that it is persecutorial, hateful, and degrading.[171]

Racist speakers seek to persuade people that government (and others) should not treat all persons with equal concern and respect. If our legal system has even a prayer of claiming to be legitimate, however, it must start from the premise that all citizens are worthy of equal concern and respect.[172]

Racist speech, such as that of the Klan, therefore promotes governmental illegitimacy[173] and makes a negative "contribution" to public political dialogue.[174] In this limited context, the best test of truth is the system's foundational premise of equality, not whether racist speech can emerge triumphant in the marketplace of ideas.[175]

Contributions to dialogue might arise in other ways, however. Potentially, racist speech can be intertwined with an exposure of real evils that deserve to be remedied. More important, racist speech certainly stimulates *responses* that contribute to the democratic dialogue. It may contribute to "the clearer perception and livelier impression of truth produced by its collision with error."[176] Moreover, racist speech inadvertently adds a valuable fact to the marketplace of ideas: the rest of us learn that extreme racists are active in society.[177]

Although racist speech seems to have some minimal marketplace value, it is much more difficult to argue that this value *outweighs* the harm racist speech causes.[178] As an African-American father once said to me when I talked about the contribution of racist speech to the democratic dialogue, "Tell that to my seven-year-old daughter."[179]

The Right of the Speaker

An important feature of the First Amendment is its protection of the autonomy (or the self-expression or liberty) of the speaker.[180] Opponents of racist speech regulations can argue that such regulations unreasonably impinge on the right of the speaker to autonomy, liberty, or self-expression,[181] but this argument has substantial weaknesses. Recall that one of the minimum conditions of a legitimate system is that it assumes that all citizens are worthy of equal concern and respect. It is hard to understand why a polity governed by this assumption would regard it as vital to offer constitutional support for individual preferences that contradict the major premise on which the polity is constituted.[182] Moreover, the racist speaker is in a poor position to claim a right derived from the principle that all citizens deserve to be treated with equal respect or concern because the speaker wholeheartedly denies this principle.[183] The racist speaker, then, is practically estopped from using this First Amendment theory.[184]

Perhaps, however, principles of estoppel should play no role. Even if the speaker might be inconsistent in raising the right,[185] the system might not be inconsistent in respecting it.[186] Moreover, the system could condemn the content of the expression but nevertheless support the speech right. The argument would be that respect for speakers demands that they be permitted to autonomously choose good or evil, right or wrong. Autonomy of this sort is certainly important, but its value is not absolute; if respect for persons demanded absolute autonomous choice, persons would have the right to choose to murder. Of course, our system does not permit that, nor does it permit the use of heroin even when its use does not directly harm others. These examples are, of course, restrictions of conduct and not speech, but speech autonomy is not absolute. In the arena of speech, our system limits the autonomous choice to make defamatory statements in some circumstances.[187] The basic problem with the autonomy argument is that it cannot show that the value of individual autonomy outweighs the harm caused by racist speech.[188] Nor can it show that the idea of respect for persons demands any particular weighing of the competing values in this context.[189] Any confidence that the value of free speech in this context outweighs the harm requires placing a thumb on the scales.

Political Identity and the First Amendment

Many would claim, however, that the point of the First Amendment is that a thumb in favor of free speech *should* be placed on the balancing scales. I do not propose to retrace the question of whether balancing is itself desirable under the First Amendment. It is certainly the reigning paradigm of First Amendment law.[190] Similarly, but as is less frequently noted, it is *not* the case that free speech *invariably* gets privileged weight in balancing cases; speech is favored in most contexts, but it is not favored over all other values. In *Gertz v. Robert Welch, Inc.,*[191] for example, the Court fashioned a set of rules to resolve the conflict between preserving individual reputation and the freedoms of speech and press. Rather than supposing free speech was more important than reputation, the Court spoke of the need for rules that would come to a "proper accommodation"[192] of competing interests, both of which it obviously regarded as important[193] and neither of which it explicitly preferred in the abstract. Although the Court has often stated that free speech gets extraordinary weight in the balancing process, those statements must be read against a broader background which reveals that the weight afforded to speech in practice turns on context. Contrast, for example, the different weights afforded free speech values in the context of obscenity[194] and that of pornography.[195] The extent to which free speech rights get extra weight in the First Amendment balance, then, is context-sensitive.[196]

Why is this point so frequently missed? In part because of wishful thinking: people want to believe their country is just, and they also believe justice depends on a more robust First Amendment. For many, what is unique about this country is that it cherishes and protects free speech. Indeed, a major reason people seem to value free speech (beyond the instrumental reasons) is that their sense of political identity, of belonging, is bound up with the First Amendment. The protection of racist speech allows people to maintain a *symbolic* commitment to free speech and, more generally, to reaffirm the notion that we live in a free country. This symbolism is not entirely unattractive; it is important that citizens take pride in constitutional values. Thus, the powerful appeal of First Amendment rhetoric serves a significant purpose.

Nonetheless, free speech is often compromised (consider again the rules governing defamation and obscenity) without major loss to the First Amendment's symbolic importance. If free speech can be accommodated when it clashes with reputation or sexual mores, it is not easy to appreciate why it should stand absolute, or be privileged in the balance, in a contest with racial equality. As in these special cases, the sacrifice of First Amendment symbolism would be partial, not total. Also, while it is important to maintain the symbolism of free speech, it is also important to maintain the attractive symbolism of racial equality and an antiracist public morality.[197] Moreover, it seems difficult to justify tolerating real harm in the name of promoting symbolism.

The Effectiveness of Regulation Involving Nontargeted Hate Speech

The First Amendment contains many values, of which I have discussed a few of the more important ones. I have argued at length that the impact on free speech values of racist speech regulation should be considered palpable but nonetheless tolerable. This conclusion, however, depends on the assumption that racist speech regulation would be effective in achieving its goals, and that assumption, unfortunately, is open to serious question.

One important goal of the regulation of nontargeted racist speech is simply to prevent such speech and thereby eliminate its harms. Another goal of such regulation is to affirm an antiracist public morality that over the long term could persuade people (including the privately prejudiced) to abandon racism. There is substantial room for worry, however, that the imposition of punitive sanctions against nontargeted racist speech would *harm* people of color.[198]

No doubt, some, indeed much, racist speech would be deterred, and that is an important result. However, some racist speech will not be wholly deterred but rather transformed into an even more effective yet unprosecutable Willie Horton–like "code" speech. Even if all explicit racist vilification were eliminated in American society, racism and much unprosecutable implicitly racist speech would still remain. That speech is not only part of the basic fabric of social life but also quite harmful. Even if a program against the speech of racial vilification were entirely successful, then, only the tip of the iceberg would have been liquidated. Moreover, it is important to recognize that much explicit racist speech will *not* be deterred. Of particular concern in this connection is public racist speech. Self-styled "patriots" who think that racist speech sanctions violate the very meaning of America would be induced to defy the regulations;[199] they would act on the belief that whiteness is part of the core of America, and that the First Amendment necessarily protects expressions of white superiority.

Unfortunately, millions of Americans hold the view that the prohibition of such expression violates a precious constitutional freedom. As a consequence, public racists might become martyrs,[200] and governmental intervention might be resented. This resentment could aggravate existing racism or be transformed into new racism by demagogues.

The social science literature concerning racism contains a substantial debate about the extent to which animosity toward people of color fuels support for policies that negatively affect people of color. One group of theorists argues that a form of "symbolic racism" is of major explanatory value in understanding contemporary racial politics.[201] Symbolic racism "represents a form of resistance to change in the racial status quo based on moral feelings that Blacks violate such traditional American values as individualism and self-reliance, the work ethic, obedience and discipline."[202] As a consequence, these theorists argue, prejudice "remains in this century, as it was in the last, a potent influence in many political choices."[203] An important related claim of these theorists is that the opposition of millions of citizens to programs designed to benefit people of color frequently has little to do with their own self-interest and much to do with symbolic racism.[204]

Other theorists place less emphasis on the role of prejudice and more on the role of real group conflict over access to material or other goods, or status competition.[205] From this perspective, racism is a rational attempt to maintain an advantageous position even if what is at stake is not a material good but merely a racial status. From the perspective of these theorists, the symbolic race theorists define self-interest too narrowly.

Although the extent to which factors—prejudice, group conflict, or others—best explain race relations in this country remains the subject of serious debate, it seems clear that prejudice and realistic group conflict are both important and, in many circumstances, dynamically interrelated.[206] Moreover, there is considerable overlap between the two theories. It is well established, for example, that people who are relatively lower in the socioeconomic hierarchy (and who consequently feel deprived) are more likely to harbor resentment toward people of color than those who are higher.[207] Derrick Bell argues that it has been traditional for American politicians (either explicitly or through code words) to rally whites "on the basis of racial pride and patriotism to accept their often lowly lot in life, and encourage [them] to vent their frustration by opposing any serious advancements by blacks. Crucial to this situation is the unstated understanding by the mass of whites that they will accept large disparities in economic opportunity in respect to other whites as long as they have priority over Blacks and other people of color for access to the few opportunities available."[208]

Whether the racism of whites is fueled by prejudice, status competition, or both, it is empirically clear that whites in general do seem to resent special efforts to help people of color. Indeed, attitude studies regularly show that white Americans generally believe that government has done too much for Blacks.[209] Of course, millions of people who do not think people of color are inferior think that government has done too much for people of color at the expense of the white middle class. Although some would broadly label these millions "racists," in my view it is better to think in this context of racism—regarded as occurring on a continuum—rather than deciding in a binary fashion whether particular people are or are not racists. Thus, in my view, one can wrongly believe that government does too much for people of color without being a racist. Nonetheless, if one holds that belief, it becomes natural (but not inevitable) to resent not only the government that provides the benefits but also the "undeserving" beneficiaries. As I would characterize it, then, the more resentment, the more racism.

From the perspective of many millions of Americans, to enact racist speech regulations would be to pass yet another law exhibiting special favoritism for people of color. What makes this kind of law so potentially counterproductive is that its transformation of public racists into public martyrs would tap into widespread political traditions and understandings in our culture.[210] In short, the case of the martyr would be appealingly wrapped in the banner of the American flag.[211] Millions of white Americans already resent people of color to some degree. To fuse that resentment[212] with Americans' love for the First Amendment is risky business.[213]

I recognize that a substantial portion of this argument bears an uncomfortable resemblance to an argument frequently made, by the Court and by some commentators, against affirmative action programs; they "may in fact promote notions of racial inferiority and lead to a politics of racial hostility."[214] The problem with these arguments is not that they are false; affirmative action programs *do* create racial hostility,[215] which is further fueled by the perception of many that basic constitutional principles have been violated. Nonetheless, affirmative action programs provide benefits—such as access to jobs, contracts, and places at educational institutions—that (at least in my view and, more important, in the view of the *recipients)*[216] outweigh the disadvantages. The difficulty with regulations against nontargeted racist speech, I am suggesting, is that, unlike affirmative action programs, they are likely to promote racial hostility *without sufficient compensating advantages.*

Is this objection equally applicable to *targeted* racist speech? I do not think so. Applying racist speech sanctions to targeted racist speech does risk the same fanning of racial resentment,[217] but this effect is somewhat mitigated by the presence of a specific victim.[218] When government protects a specific victim from a personal remark, the public is much less likely to see the law as censorship.[219] Irrational as it may seem, a speaker who explicitly and obviously harms a single, particular person through speech is often less sympathetic than one whose speech hurts many more people. The harm is more concrete and less diffuse.

More important, the principle that the legal system should avoid the imposition of sanctions for particularized harm done to individual victims out of fear that the rendering of justice will fan racial resentment is a principle to be avoided (save perhaps in the most extreme of circumstances). The individual may wish to make that judgment (by refusing to cooperate in a proceeding against the perpetrator), but society should not. By contrast, when a group is generally victimized by racial slurs, the group should be fully entitled to decide that legal remedies will make things *worse* for the group and decide that legal remedies should not be made available despite the harm. Indeed, that is precisely what I argue people of color and the larger society should conclude.

Many practitioners of outsider jurisprudence would resist that conclusion. One reason for such resistance is the enormous symbolic value of a broad prohibition on racist speech, which could be thought to outweigh the harms associated with the increased racism that might follow. For those of us who are not persons of color, the question arises: Who are we to weigh the symbolic value against the harm, if we are neither the primary beneficiaries of the symbolic value nor the potential victims of the discrimination and abuse? I have little difficulty in being predominantly guided on this issue by what the majority of people of color think (recognizing, of course, that differences among people of color may be substantial).

Nevertheless, certain considerations ought to take some steam out of the symbolic value argument. First, it should be recognized that political struggles are *always* fraught with symbolism. If a general racist speech ban is passed, symbolic issues arise concerning what kinds of racist remarks are properly prosecuted and which are not. Any feelings of inclusiveness generated by the passage of hate speech legislation might quickly dissipate. Moreover, even if the implementation of a racist speech ban would be effortless, other political struggles of major symbolic importance would still recur, and for many people, if not most, the joy of last year's symbolic victory will be quickly eclipsed by the sadness of this year's defeat. Finally, there ought to be some concern that what is of important positive symbolic value for people of color may have negative symbolic value for millions of others. When so many crucial issues of poverty, violence, and other ills confront people of color,[220] it may be prudent to have the system give up chips in a different place.

There is an another unhappy aspect to my overall conclusion: it suggests compromising with racist preferences in the case of nontargeted racist speech. A practitioner of outsider jurisprudence might object to the argument precisely on the ground that compromises with racism are abhorrent.[221] The alternative, however, as I have argued, may only be to increase long-term racism by standing on principle. Still, practitioners of outsider jurisprudence may oppose compromising with racist preferences *even if* the alternative to compromise is increased racism; they may argue that the psychic benefit (or Kantian purity) of maintaining a simple political identity that *never* gives in to racism is so attractive and powerful and has so much integrity that it can ground counterproductive measures.

Ironically, ACLU liberalism takes similar pride in the uncompromising integrity with which it protects the First Amendment. Both ACLU liberalism and outsider jurisprudence of this stripe avoid compromise, to adhere to a well-defined, relatively uncomplicated political identity.

In a sense, this form of argument replays the sixties' rhetorical conflict between radicals and liberals. The radicals attacked the liberals, saying that they "sold out," lacked integrity, accepted short-term incremental gains at the expense of long-range radical change, and lacked "analysis" and vision.[222] The liberals, on the other hand, accused the radicals of being stubborn, unrealistic, utopian, and self-indulgent.

One of the interesting aspects of this dialogue and of other arguments about political identity is the extent to which political identity can affect the estimate of the probable consequences of particular political moves. Presumably, "hard-line" ACLU liberals would have an easy time concluding that racist speech regulation would increase racism. By contrast, "hard-line" practitioners of outsider jurisprudence have a stake in denying this. And the liberal, compromising pragmatists—who seek not to be marginalized, who appreciate their place in the dialectical dance, and who revel in the diversity and complications of political and social reality— may look for complexity of the right sort and find it (whether or not it is there). Hard proof about either the conclusion that racism would or would not in fact increase or the underlying psychology will be hard to come by.

In any event, my contention should be clear. I am not arguing that racist speech should be protected to safeguard the liberty of the speaker or because it is valuable. Nor do I think that counterspeech will cure the harm of public racist speech.[223] I am not worried about a chilling effect in the marketplace of ideas (though some marginally valuable speech could be lost); nor am I worried about the vagueness of working out standards case by case (though vagueness is of course not a virtue).[224]

The argument I raise is quite different. It suggests that American society may be so thoroughly racist that nontargeted racist speech regulations would be counterproductive. If I thought such regulation would be effective *on balance* in combating racism, I would presently support punitive measures against public instances of racial vilification even when not targeted against individuals.[225] Further, I want to make clear that I am doing no more than putting an argument on the table. Even if the choice were mine to make, I would not seek to impose my predictions and weighing of the potential effects of racist speech regulations on people of color. Were I a member of a legislature who made this argument only to find it rejected by people of color, I would vote, according to their preferences, for nontargeted racist speech regulation. It is their lives that will predominantly be affected by the legislation, and it is this effect that is the crux of my argument.[226] Similarly, as a contributor to academic dialogue, I believe that an argument of this sort carries considerably less weight if the people purportedly advantaged by it end up ultimately, after consideration, rejecting it.[227] People of color might think that the tangible benefits of deterrence and the symbolic importance of the legislation outweigh the speculative possibilities of nondeterrence, evasion, and increased racial hostility; that, in short, the advantages of taking a stand outweigh the costs.

They might. But they might not. Arguments never pressed are rarely adopted. So I suggest that attention be focused more on the empirical costs and benefits of racist speech regulation and less on the all-too-frequently exaggerated First Amendment values.

Conclusion

In the course of this discussion of *R.A.V.* and racist speech, I have discussed five major perspectives on the issue of racist speech. Justice Scalia seems moved by the image of a content-neutral government, although that image is deeply compromised in practice. Justice White appears to pursue the image of an impartial magistrate bound by the rule of law, although his reading of the law is badly skewed in the *R.A.V.* case. St. Paul's ordinance, as construed by the Minnesota Supreme Court, seems to reflect a conception that uninhibited public debate deserves protection but private racial epithets do not. St. Paul's ordinance is not ideal from the perspective of outsider jurisprudence because it punishes speech against historically advantaged groups as well as historically disadvantaged groups, drawing no distinction between them. It thus fails to appreciate the amplified character of the injuries such remarks cause minorities, and it leaves open the prospect of selective prosecution of exclusively minority speakers.

The dissent perspective I endorse is not an instance of outsider jurisprudence; for one thing, it is not built predominantly from the experience of people of color. It protects dissent by both the powerful press[228] and the marginalized. It freely employs an insider's perspective in defending dissent, contending that the system benefits from continued critique. Nonetheless, the dissent perspective shares much with the outsider perspective, and the conclusion I draw from it is one that I think outsider jurisprudence should also favor. Speech *targeted* at members of historically oppressed racial groups which insults on the basis of race ought to be punished;[229] individuals deserve redress[230] for what is intended and felt as particularized injury[231] even if racist speech regulations are symbolically ineffective or even counterproductive. But government intervention against *nontargeted* racist speech depends on a judgment that it will effectively promote—or even institute—an antiracist public morality in our culture. Public morality may perhaps be furthered through other forms of socialization,[232] but the combination of racism and of the purist stories we tell ourselves about the First Amendment (despite actual doctrine that is far from absolutist) makes it unlikely that racist speech regulation could ever serve as an effective source of antiracist public morality.

We tell ourselves many stories about the First Amendment, however, and America would still have a FIRST AMENDMENT and a strong First Amendment tradition even if it enacted general racist speech regulations. The problem is not the First Amendment; the problem is that racism is now and always has been a central part of the meaning of America.

Part Two ———————————————————

COMBATING INJUSTICE

IV

Dissent and Injustice

FREE SPEECH theory should be taken beyond protecting or tolerating dissent: the First Amendment should be taken to reflect a constitutional commitment to *promoting* dissent. Although much dissent is worthless or worse,[1] the institutional promotion of dissent is necessary to combat injustice.[2]

After tracing the assumptions supporting this position, first, I want to suggest that liberal theory underappreciates the importance or desirability of encouraging dissent. To the extent that this is so, however, that underappreciation has more to do with the focus of liberal theory than with the merits of the position. Second, far from encouraging dissent, dominant institutions in our society often make dissent more difficult. Despite undeniable contributions to the practice of dissent, the mass media in many important ways reinforces the status quo, produces insufficient information to ground intelligent dissent, and marginalizes the concerns of those outside the centers of power. Similarly, the Supreme Court in its recurrent interpretations of the First Amendment does not do nearly enough to protect or encourage dissent. Third, I hope to reflect on some of the changes that might be implemented if dissent were to be promoted in the United States.

The Social Value of Promoting Dissent

The case for the promotion of dissent in order to combat injustice rests on a number of reasonable assumptions. America is not a land of perfect equality. Hierarchies exist throughout the society, in both political and nonpolitical realms. It would be possible to assume that hierarchies are perfectly just, but any such assumption would be fantasy. Similarly improbable would be the suggestion that all hierarchy is inherently or mainly unjust. But hierarchies are often generally or partially unjust for many reasons.[3] People who exercise substantial power in hierarchies are prone to act in their own self-interest and are in a position to be effective. Even if they do not see themselves as acting in their own self-interest, they will often tend to see things in a biased way that operates to their advantage.[4] Moreover, power in one hierarchy has a tendency to spill over to other arenas in unjust ways.[5] Wealth should not enable one to buy political favors, but it often does. Even without blatant corruption, and regrettably there is much of that, people with prominent positions in hierarchies frequently enjoy privileges they do not deserve.

Injustice does not inevitably and invariably thrive, but substantial barriers to its recognition and to confronting it exist. In some cases the presence of injustice is not recognized. Elites have substantial power to make their systems of hierarchy attractive. With respect to national and international issues, elites control the mass media, and, I shall argue, that control makes it difficult for many issues to appear on the public agenda. Of course, there is disagreement among elites and much public controversy, but this does not belie the failure of many issues to be raised. To be sure, some indulge Holmes's assumption that the best test of truth is its ability to emerge in the marketplace of ideas. That particular beliefs have emerged in a particular society, however, may more likely be testimony to the power of habit, custom, tradition, or the interests of those in power than to their "truth." People in Paris, Moscow, London, Lima, and San Diego entertain quite different views on a wide range of issues. The people in those cities may hold strong views, but it is hard to deny that their views would be altogether different had they been raised in a different city. When countries go to war, typically the overwhelming majority of their citizens believe that justice is on their side. Again, had they been raised in the country of their enemy, they most likely would have believed exactly the opposite, and just as strongly.[6] Beyond the issue of war, there seems to be a strong psychological need for people to believe that their society's way is the right way.[7]

With respect to local issues, say, in a local workplace, even if the local spin doctors are ineffective and injustice is recognized, there is a tendency to go along to get along. There is the fear that dissent will not be effective and that reprisals might be taken. The impulse to conform or, alternatively, to quietly grumble, is strong.

To summarize, there is no such thing as a perfectly just society. In any large-scale society, powerful interest groups and self-seeking politicians and bureaucrats are unavoidable. It is not just that power corrupts. Persons in power also have the all-too-human tendency to believe in good faith that the "right" answers to moral and political issues just happen to be ones that consolidate and enhance their own power. Moreover, because these individuals have power, they possess a disproportionate ability to convert their answers into society's answers. Elements of injustice, therefore, pervade social hierarchies both within and outside of politics—from the economy to the academy. This is not a prescription for hopeless abdication; injustice may never be completely eradicated, but some societies are more just than others. It is always possible to move toward a better society.

Given this general perspective, an important contribution of free speech theory is its endorsement of a particular social practice, namely, dissent. Dissent attacks existing customs, habits, traditions, institutions, and authorities. It spies injustice and brings it to light. This does not mean that dissent is always effective; indeed, much dissent does little to bring about effective change.[8] Nor is dissent always fair. It may often be distorted by envy of those higher up in a particular hierarchy. Nonetheless, dissent is a part of the *daily* dialectic of power relations in the society.[9] For all its occasional faults, dissent is indispensable. Without it, unjust hierarchies would surely flourish with little possibility of constructive change. If the truth about the presence of injustice is to be spread, social institutions must be constructed in a way that nurtures critical speech.

In the end, the premises of the argument are quite simple. Injustice exists; the impulse to resist it is less than it should be; dissent should be encouraged.

The Place of the Argument in Liberal Theory

Many liberals might suppose that to move beyond tolerance toward encouraging dissent is to move beyond liberal theory. Indeed, I will argue that liberal theorists have for the most part underappreciated the importance of encouraging dissent. The argument, however, is more complicated than it might seem.

Political Liberalism and Autonomy-Prizing Liberals

One might interpret John Rawls, for example, as an apostle of toleration. For Rawls, on this interpretation, diversity of views and dissent are *problems* for political theory to solve, not occasions for celebration. Thus, in *A Theory of Justice*, Rawls employs the now-famous veil of ignorance as a vehicle to help generate a structure of society that people might be said to agree upon apart from their different conceptions of the good life.[10] Similarly, in *Political Liberalism*, Rawls argues for a structure of political society that he contends would be accepted as reasonable and rational to those holding a diversity of reasonable religious, philosophical, and moral doctrines.[11] Since Rawls's projects depend so heavily on overcoming difference, it would not be surprising if he failed to appreciate difference.

To interpret Rawls in this fashion, however, would be to misread him. Although Rawls's theory is designed to transcend difference, this is not out of a failure to appreciate it. As Rawls puts it: "A critical assumption of liberalism is that equal citizens have different and indeed incommensurable and irreconcilable conceptions of the good. . . . [L]iberalism accepts the plurality of conceptions of the good as a fact of modern life, provided, of course, these conceptions respect the limits specified by the appropriate principles of justice. *It tries to show both that a plurality of conceptions of the good is desirable and how a regime of liberty can accommodate this plurality so as to achieve the many benefits of human diversity.*"[12] Rawls clearly appreciates difference. In addition, he recognizes that contemporary society confers unjust privileges upon the powerful. Or, to adopt his terminology, the current system does not assure the fair value of political liberty:

> Historically one of the main defects of constitutional government has been the failure to establish the fair value of political liberty. . . . Disparities in the distribution of property and wealth that far exceed what is compatible with political equality have generally been tolerated by the legal system. . . . Political power rapidly accumulates and becomes unequal; and making use of the coercive apparatus of the state and its law, those who gain the advantage can often assure themselves of a favored position. . . . Universal suffrage is an insufficient counterpoise; for when parties and elections are financed not by public funds but by private contributions, the political forum is so constrained by the wishes of the dominant interests that the basic measures needed to establish constitutional rule are seldom properly presented.[13]

It would be a small step for Rawls to suggest that dissent should be encouraged in an unjust system. He stops short, however, stressing that the question of what measures are appropriate to establish "just constitutional rule . . . belong to political sociology"[14] or to a theory of the political system, not to a theory of justice.

I believe that if he were to step across the threshold, Rawls would encourage dissent on issues of political injustice, but there is a basis for believing that he might confine such encouragement to a narrow conception of political injustice. In order to create the minimum requisites to be "fully cooperating members of society,"[15] Rawls assumes that free and equal persons have a sense of justice.[16] Rawls seems to understand this to mean that citizens would be encouraged to act in ways that would protect the "basic liberties of democratic citizenship."[17] Encouraging much broader dissent not only is foreign to Rawls's project but also is contradicted by other parts of his theory. Most important, for example, Rawls would not permit the state to use its educational process or other means to promote citizens who prize autonomous decision making.[18] On Rawls's understanding, this would constitute endorsement of a comprehensive conception of the good, which a just and stable state is not permitted to do.[19] If one believes, however, that injustice is a permanent feature of even democratic societies, encouraging autonomous decision makers is a prescription for justice and its maintenance, not an endorsement of a comprehensive conception of the good.

Of course, liberalism of the Rawls vintage is not the only game in town, and other liberals have criticized him for his laissez-faire position on autonomy.[20] On their premises, however, autonomy is promoted not in order to encourage dissent and combat injustice but because of a position about the needs of personhood for human flourishing.[21]

I do not wish to explore the merits of the debate between Rawls and other autonomy-prizing liberals. My point is that the nature of their theoretical enterprise presents a form of political theory that obscures questions of power, and that theories of justice bereft of power analysis cannot do justice to the problems of injustice. Nor does it appear that the recognition of the recurring privileges assumed by people in power is too rich an assumption for theory. To put it another way, theories of justice need theories of injustice and notions of transition to a better society. The problem is not with theory but with the questions to which many liberal theoreticians restrict themselves.

Millian Liberals

John Stuart Mill's theory presents a partial exception to the critique I have offered.[22] Mill is concerned about the crushing effects of social customs inducing the mass of people to conform.[23] He exalts autonomy and individuality not only for their positive effects on the individual but also for their beneficial impact on society.[24] For Mill, not to exercise choice, but to acquiesce in custom without thought, is to be no better than an ape or a machine.[25] The richness of human life demands choice: choice leads to individuality, which strengthens the individual and the human race.[26] Mill does not argue that all contrary lives or positions are always better than those held by society at large. He does suggest somewhat optimistically that confronting false positions leads to a livelier impression of the truth in the society.[27]

Most interesting for the position I am advancing, Mill clearly favors the encouragement of dissent: "On any of the great open questions . . . , if either of the two opinions has a better claim than the other, not merely to be tolerated, but to be encouraged and countenanced, it is the one which happens at a particular time to be in a minority. That is the opinion, which for the time being represents the neglected interests, the side of human well-being which is in danger of obtaining less than its share."[28]

   Moreover, Mill's analysis is thoroughly compatible with an educational system that promotes autonomy. Mill believes government can assure that parents not deprive their children of education.[29] Indeed, he argues that the most important "point of excellence which any form of government can possess is to promote the virtue and intelligence of the people themselves."[30] That autonomous decision making is necessary for virtue seems at least implicit in his discussion of representative government[31] and is explicit in *On Liberty*.[32]

   My concern with Mill's theory is not with its sociology but with its politics. For the most part, Mill prizes dissent for its general enlightenment function. He exhibits little sense of the unjustified privileges of hierarchy or the role of dissent in combating injustice. His analysis seems faulty in two ways. In delineating the great open questions he refers to democracy versus aristocracy, suggesting that the idea that deserves to be encouraged is the one in the minority.[33] Implicit in this suggestion is a fear of the conformist masses and a respect for the "aristocracy" that are difficult to respect. Neither in his time nor in ours have we had too much democracy. To be sure, Mill endorsed education of the masses and greater participation. Nonetheless, his baseline respect for the aristocracy greatly exceeds ours, as witness his proposal that the educated should receive plural votes.[34]

   Deeper still, Mill has a shriveled sense of social change. Although he underscores the need for educating the masses in order to assure social progress, he seems to emphasize the kind of change inspired by breakthroughs of the geniuses.[35] Here Mill unreasonably slights the role of social movements in bringing about change. Why does he make this mistake? Not because social movements were foreign to human history when he wrote. Instead, the weakness is similar to that of Rawls. In addressing the appropriate scope of liberty, Mill picks a particular set of questions for theory to answer, and the problem of unjust hierarchy is not among them.

   To his credit, in his work on representative government, Mill refers in a brief passage to the general public as "the mainspring of the whole checking machinery" against administrative corruption or negligence.[36] Without addressing the relationship between social movements and the general public, together with their relative importance in combating corruption and negligence, suffice it to say that Mill at least recognizes the presence of unjust hierarchy in a part of government and a role for dissent in combating it. If he had focused on unjust hierarchy generally (within and without government), he could hardly have missed that dissent has a role to play in promoting progressive change and that such change is not typically occasioned by the prompting of geniuses. By focusing on how a culture might flower under a regime of liberty without focusing directly on the issue of injustice, Mill missed arguments in favor of liberty that I suspect he would have no reason to reject.

Prominent theorists will inevitably focus on some issues at the expense of others, and generations of scholarship will be affected. But there are limits to the scope of theory in any event. One would not expect political theory to evaluate the role of the media or the Supreme Court in promoting dissent. Yet the media and the Supreme Court are widely believed to be institutionalized expressions of our commitment to dissent. I will argue, however, that both institutions fall far short of what is needed to protect and promote dissent. In examining this contention, we move from political theory to political sociology, political economy, and legal analysis.

The Distorted Marketplace

Journalists routinely applaud the media as a powerful check on abusive government, a neutral reporter of all the news, or both.[37] Unquestionably, the media has served on many occasions to check abusive government and to report important information that can ground intelligent dissent by others.[38] The mass media is a complicated phenomenon, however, and I propose to reflect on the many ways in which it provides a distorted picture of social and political reality—reinforcing the status quo, providing inadequate information to ground intelligent dissent, and marginalizing those dissenters who stand outside the centers of power. In supporting the latter point, I will concentrate on the marginalization of perspectives on the left end of the political spectrum, but I do not suppose that the mass media discriminates only against the left. In my view, a strong case can be made for the view that the media discriminates, for example, against the Christian right.[39]

In discussing the overall weaknesses of the media, it will be helpful to emphasize entertainment programming and media structure; domestic affairs reporting; foreign policy reporting and the objectivity ethic; and, finally, depictions of corporations, whether in entertainment or public policy formats.

Entertainment Programming and Media Structure

Perhaps the most important feature of the mass media is its support by advertisers.[40] Commercial broadcasters, for example, receive virtually all of their revenue from advertisers. Newspapers receive the vast majority of their revenue from advertisers.[41]

The negative impact of this advertiser dependence is perhaps most severe in the broadcast media, whose commercial character exposes millions of citizens to a daily torrent of commercial messages. These messages encourage the view that self-fulfillment and happiness come not from our interaction with others but through our relationship with goods. They collectively encourage a hedonistic, selfish, materialistic culture. As the UNESCO International Commission for the Study of Human Problems stated, advertising "tends to promote attitudes and life-styles which extol acquisition and consumption at the expense of other values."[42] Moreover, it tends to promote a political atmosphere that exalts short-term economic growth over long-term ecological damage.

Advertising also promotes a sexist culture. The appeal of many commercials is explicitly sexual, and women are depicted as sex objects and subordinate creatures.[43] As the chief creative officer of a major advertising agency put it, "The old saying 'sex sells,' still prevails. But it has to be done with taste."[44] In other words, treating women as sex objects is considered an appropriate way to sell products,[45] but excessive nudity or violence may be offensive. The problem, of course, is *not* any puritanical judgment that sex is dirty, or even the antiegalitarian assumption that sex best flourishes in circumstances where women are subordinate—though that assumption eroticizes injustice.[46] The problem is that an enormous number of televised depictions of women focus on their sexual characteristics. Television thus encourages men to see women, and women to see themselves, as sexual creatures to the exclusion of other characteristics.[47] As Ronald Collins puts it, "When a single voice badgers or degrades women in the workplace because of their gender, we call it sexual harassment. When that voice is amplified for millions of people by millions of dollars, we call it advertising."[48]

These, of course, are not the only distortive effects of advertiser power in the mass media. Although some advertisers thrive on fearful messages,[49] most take advantage of upbeat themes and jingles.[50] The overall theme is that all is right with the world—so long as you have the advertiser's product. But that theme is a major source of anxiety and frustration. As Collins and Jacobson write: "Our system of advertising purposefully promotes envy, creates anxiety, and fosters insecurity. The tragic end-product of this is kids killing kids in Baltimore and elsewhere in order to walk in their playmates' $100 name-brand sneakers."[51]

The importance of advertiser power carries far beyond the content and emotional impact of the advertisements.[52] For the most part, advertisers insist that their product messages be placed in programs that create a sunny consumer atmosphere.[53] Messages that might be disturbing to a mainstream audience are discouraged.[54] Of course, mass audiences do not thrive on disturbing messages, but there is reason to believe that advertisers are more squeamish than audiences simply because they do not want their products to be associated with controversial programs.[55] For example, abortion is a subject that entertainment television will rarely consider. As the *New York Times* put it: "The subject of abortion makes networks and advertisers so uneasy that on the rare occasion it has been mentioned on a show characters twist themselves into elocutionary contortions rather than actually say the word. Even the razor-tongued Murphy Brown did not use the word during an episode about whether to continue her pregnancy."[56]

In explaining a decision by Home Box Office to carry a documentary about abortion, Bridget Potter, HBO's senior vice president for original programming, stated: "We're not any braver than the networks. It's just that our economic basis is different."[57] Or, as the *New York Times* puts it, "HBO, a viewer subscription service, does not have to assuage sponsors."[58]

In lieu of controversial programs, advertisers often insist on "action," fast-moving programming that keeps people glued to a screen without encouraging thought: "In pursuit of higher ratings that bring higher earnings, TV programmers have honed mesmerizing techniques—described by one critic as 'constant violence, gratuitous sex, and deliberate manipulation of split-second change of images and sounds to make an emotional and sensory impact that leaves no time for reflection.' More than ever, what's on the screen is in constant motion, with a style of eventfulness and a lack of substance—designed to minimize the risk that viewers will think long enough to tune out."[59] The violent programming is particularly noteworthy. As Sonia Shah observes:

> Every day, all across the land, behind tightly locked doors, millions of Americans are watching other Americans stalking, harassing, raping, and killing each other on TV. With growing alienation and creeping paranoia, we are engrossed with over fifteen acts of violence, including at least two murders, every evening. It has not made us more violent, necessarily. But it scares us. It makes us more likely to buy locks, watchdogs, and guns for protection; think that nuclear or biological annihilation will occur within our lifetimes; want more money spent on crime, drug abuse, and national defense; and, most ominously, consent to our own and others' repression in the name of security.[60]

Whatever the advertisers' needs might be to hold an audience, television programmers have been only too willing to accommodate. As Ben H. Bagdikian states, "The basic strategy in designing programs on commercial television and cable is not primarily what is perceived as the highest needs and wants of the audience, but what is perceived as the most likely to attract advertising."[61] Thus, television programming in general promotes an "all is right with the world"[62] atmosphere or, alternatively, exposes viewers to a frightening (yet titillating) world where violence is omnipresent, ironically, while desensitizing viewers to the effects of violence.

The desire to please advertisers also infects the print media. Chrysler's ad agency, for example, among others, has told magazines that it must "be alerted in advance of any and all editorial content that encompasses sexual, political, social issues or any editorial that might be construed as provocative or offensive."[63] Similarly, Ford takes the position with magazines that it is "very concerned about the environment it is part of" and observes that "[i]f you're a major company and you do business with a number of constituencies, it's in your best interest not to offend any group."[64] And the *Wall Street Journal* reports that these perspectives reflect the "sweeping new influence large advertisers are demanding, and receiving, from the nation's biggest magazines."[65]

Advertising has an undemocratic impact in the sense that some citizens are more equal than others. Substantial portions of the public are excluded from a broadcaster's conception of the target audience.[66] Advertisers, and therefore television programmers, want consumers, not just viewers. Accordingly, children (who have little money) and the aged (whose buying habits are thought to be fixed) are excluded from the target audiences of most television programming.[67] NBC, for example, has canceled a number of shows not because of poor ratings but because of poor demographics. From the advertiser's perspective, the wrong people were watching these shows. As one television critic explained, "What NBC was doing was what almost all the networks are doing these days—basically telling viewers over 50 years old to get lost. In fact, for advertisers, you're kind of suspect once you hit 35 or 40."[68]

CBS provided a particularly infamous example of discrimination against those over fifty. It moved *Murder She Wrote* from its highly ranked position on Sunday night—where it had been for many years the most highly ranked drama on television—to Thursday night as a counterprogramming alternative to *Friends*. The move was made because advertisers were not prepared to pay enough for the large, but old, audience on Sundays. They were prepared to pay substantially more for *Lois and Clark* despite its much smaller ratings. On Thursday night, the show could not compete against *Friends* and was moved back to Sunday night for a final run where the ratings boomeranged. In a protest against the network, the show's final title was "Death by Demographics."[69] CBS, of course, made the right decision for its shareholders. The profits of the network depend on pleasing advertisers, not audiences.

This phenomenon is not confined to television. As Bagdikian reports: "Otis Chandler, head of the Times Mirror Empire, owner of the *Los Angeles Times* and the fourth-largest newspaper chain said, 'The target class of the *Times* is . . . in the middle class and the upper class. . . . We are not trying to get mass circulation, but quality circulation.' On another occasion, he said, 'We arbitrarily cut back some of our low-income circulation. . . . The economics of American newspaper publishing is based on an advertising base, not a circulation base.' "[70]

And Columbia University sociologist Herbert Gans observes that the problem is not confined to broadcasting and newspapers: "[M]any magazines have tried to reduce their total circulation, hoping to discourage less affluent readers whom neither advertisers nor journalists want."[71] When *Ms.* magazine decided to drop advertising, the editors spoke of new freedom in editorial policy, including the freedom "to appeal to all readers, including elderly women, who are normally shunned by most advertisers."[72]

Domestic Affairs Reporting

Although the national news media aims at a target audience that is similar to the audience sought in network entertainment programming, its reporting to some extent offers a corrective to the misleading picture of the world afforded in entertainment television. Nonetheless, the presentations of the national news media are bounded in ways that serve to exclude questions and critique from the left end of the political spectrum.[73] These include questions about the structure of American society, such as "why wealth and power are so unevenly distributed in America, and between the developed and developing nations; why corporations have so much power, and citizens so little; why unemployment, inflation, and poverty remain; and why women and racial minorities continue to occupy an inferior position."[74]

Consider, first, the coverage of election campaigns, whether in the broadcast or the print media. From the outset, many would find election coverage inflated. From their perspective, the media wrongly assumes that the outcome of particular elections is very important rather than a choice between Tweedledum and Tweedledee.[75] Third-party candidates who frequently raise searching questions about the political system receive conspicuous inattention from the media.

The exclusion of any significant attention to such candidates or the issues raised by them is related to another standard criticism of the media, namely, that it focuses on the question of who will win (the "horse race") at the expense of the issues.[76] The media typically treats the audience as a group of prognosticators rather than as a group of citizens preparing to vote. Reporters tend not only to disregard the issues raised by minor party candidates (of whatever political persuasion unless they are billionaires with a chance in the horse race) but also to downplay the issues raised by the candidates of the major parties.[77] Although the press will usually explain that the audience is not "interested," there may be another factor.

Reporters are a cynical group. They tend to write about the horse race at the expense of the issues because they—*like many of the candidates*—perceive the programs and issue statements to be nothing more than a part of the horse race. If the candidates do not take issues seriously, and if political reporters continually mingle with the politicians and their "savvy" handlers, a tendency to look at how issues "sell" in various locales tends to trump serious consideration of the issues on their merits (of course, there is a chicken-and-egg problem here). Perhaps more important, the horse race is easier and less time-consuming than any attempt to master the issues would be. Indeed, it would be impossible for a reporter or a few reporters to master any but a fraction of the issues that might face important politicians and their staffs.[78]

Thus, the primary sources of election news are those that are easy to acquire—public speeches and debates by the candidates and interviews with sources in the opposing camps, typically about their strategy. We hear all about the horse race—who is winning so far, where, why, and speculation about whether and how the race could change. We often hear or read snippets of what the candidate said in a public speech or an "intimate" private interview. Yet the most revealing part of the horse race is the part that is virtually never covered. We do not hear what the candidate said in the balance of a campaign day—in between the speeches and after the speeches are over. Perhaps the candidate asked representatives of political action committees and special interests for money.[79] What happened in those conversations? What was promised? What did the candidate say about the issues there? Is there any difference between the candidate's public pronouncements and his or her statements to contributors?

Presumably the money trail should be of interest even to the cynical. Moreover, in many races it is relatively easy to gain access to databases that track contributions made to candidates.[80] Nonetheless, it is difficult for reporters to get information about what was said in private conversations between contributors and candidates. Although campaign disclosure laws often make it possible to draw differences between candidates by their financial supporters, the filing dates are sometimes too late to permit meaningful reporting during the election. For some of the most important contributions, it is too time-consuming and too expensive for reporters to follow the money trail. By contrast, it is convenient and easy to write the daily story or broadcast the nightly sound bite while following the candidate from place to place. Thus, the nightly sound bite becomes the regular fare, and the investigative story is a comparatively rare phenomenon.[81] This is not to deny that reporters will leap upon scandals when they appear. The postelection reporting about the campaign financ-

ing techniques of Bill Clinton, Al Gore, and Newt Gingrich is surely proof
of that. These apparent counterexamples, however, only serve to drama-
tize the extent to which the reporting of day-to-day fund-raising efforts by
ordinary state and congressional representatives is conspicuously absent.

The manner in which reporters cover elections is typical of their overall
patterns of public affairs coverage. Reporters do not have the time, the
resources, or, in many cases, the training to conduct primary investiga-
tions.[82] Moreover, to report on what sources in power say appears to
"mirror" reality in a way that is least likely to offend the mass audience.
The reliance on convenient, inexpensive, but powerful sources, therefore,
dominates the national news generally, not just in election seasons.[83] The
White House, the administrative agencies, and sources in the Congress
are major suppliers of "product" for the news industry. The role of the
press in dealing with this product is at once active and surprisingly passive. It is active in the sense that it decides what to report and what not
to report, and that exercise of discretion is notoriously influential. Despite
its frequent characterization as the fourth estate, however, the press, save
for the editorial pages, does not ordinarily speak with an independent
voice.[84] As Sam Donaldson puts it, "As a rule, we are, if not handmaidens
of the establishment, at least bloodbrothers to the establishment. . . . We
end up the day usually having some version of what the White House has
suggested as a story."[85] As Mark Hertsgaard states: "According to the old
journalistic truism, a reporter was only as good as his sources. For White
House reporters, this raised a troubling dilemma. Most news organizations' definition of proper White House coverage stressed reporting the
views and actions of the President and his aides above all else. Thus the
officials with whom reporters were, in theory, supposed to have an adversarial relationship were the very people upon whom they were most dependent for the information needed to produce their stories."[86]

In most of the years when Presidents Bush and Reagan occupied the
White House, the Congress was not a reliable adversarial source. As Les-
ley Stahl maintained, one reason press coverage of Reagan was not more
aggressive was that the Congress had "not been a source for the press in
the whole Reagan administration. They [did not] want to criticize this
beloved man."[87]

The causes of the Democratic failure to criticize the Republican White
House on many domestic economic issues during those years were complex, but campaign finance appeared to be especially important. In a real
sense, corporations have bought the congressional Democrats,[88] and the
difference between the two major parties has narrowed considerably. This
is important not merely from a legislative perspective but also from the
perspective of the national dialogue about policy issues. By and large,
reliance on these sources confines the agenda[89] for public discussion in

national politics.[90] If the conversation in Washington is narrowly confined, so, too, will be the press analysis. The phrase "Beltway mentality" did not appear from nowhere.[91]

During President Clinton's first two years in office, his occupancy of the White House shifted the national domestic dialogue in a somewhat less conservative direction than was the case in the prior administrations. Some of the negative criticism focused on his unwillingness to follow through on some of his moderately liberal policies.[92] Other criticism echoed the Republican complaint that he was too liberal. In the next two years of his first term, Clinton received much favorable press coverage for being "smart" enough to move to the right, making it difficult for the Republicans to criticize him.[93] In other words, the press implemented the horse race focus at the expense of serious examination of the issues.

The press continued to confine the national dialogue to a narrow spectrum. For example, the perspective of the left remained at the margin throughout President Clinton's first term. Congress has few leftists and a fair assortment of liberals. But pressures to support the president in most cases muffle liberal criticism, and criticism by a few representatives outside the leadership is frequently not regarded as newsworthy. There is no reasonable basis to expect congressional leftist criticism to occupy a substantial part of the media stage in Clinton's second term. Although the reelection of President Clinton could move the national domestic dialogue in a leftward direction, it is unlikely. The focus is likely to be on the relationship between the president and the Congress, not on the substantive issues. To the extent the focus is on substantive issues, the dialogue will continue to be framed in narrow terms.

Foreign Policy Reporting and the "Objectivity" Ethic

The room for criticism of American foreign policy is even narrower. Here, too, reporters are ordinarily forced to rely on sources from the executive branch.[94] Moreover, in most situations Congress will leave foreign policy decisions publicly unquestioned. Thus, America is routinely on the correct side in its foreign policy dealings—unless "responsible" members of the party not in the White House voice opposition. Then the press will report the "other side."[95] Only in rare cases would the point of view of other countries be fully and accurately reported.[96]

CBS Evening News Washington producer Susan Zirinsky sheds light on this point: "Even as an objective journalist, you're an American first and a journalist second. . . . You come from a framework to every story, and I'm an American, that's where I come from."[97] Foreign policy thus becomes a tale told through executive branch eyes, a tale about the war between good and evil rather than a struggle over competing interests. Thus, it is known that America is despised in many countries around the world, but little information is provided that would help a reasonable reader understand why.

Assume, for example, the United States conducts an imperialistic policy in a Latin American country ("country X") to make it safe for American business.[98] Assume the American press repeats the State Department or CIA perspective that the government's real purpose is to advance the cause of "democracy"—even though the policy is directed against a government whose real "crime" is nationalism. Why would the press wait for a public official to criticize the government action before it could contradict the State Department?

First, the reporter in country X might believe the State Department and know little of the particular business investment interests. Reporters who are assigned to a beat requiring regular reliance on the same sources tend to ally themselves with those sources (to see the world through their eyes).[99] Even if the reporter disbelieved the State Department, to contradict the State Department in this context would raise the risk of being excluded from the reporter's most consistent source of information about country X. This risk is not to be taken lightly.[100]

Even if the reporter submitted a report critical of the State Department, the particular media outlet could have a number of concerns in using the report. The mainstream press is particularly anxious to maintain an image of objectivity. If it is going to criticize government policy on its own in a context that could generate substantial controversy, it will demand substantial evidence.[101] On the other hand, if one of its competitors files a critical story, its standards might then be relaxed. In that circumstance, its objectivity could be questioned if it did not run a story about the controversy.

Although journalists think of objectivity as a professional consideration, there is also a powerful business justification for the appearance of objectivity in the mainstream media.[102] As Mitchell Stephens observes: "[A]s so many newspapers fell victim to competition with radio and television in the twentieth century[,][103] [it] would no longer make sense to tailor a newspaper for Republicans or Democrats or Progressives. Those newspapers that would survive—often the only papers in their towns—would seek to maintain a broadly based readership, which meant they could not afford to offend large groups of potential customers with overly partisan coverage. Corporate advertisers—concerned about the impact controversy might have on sales—would also prove more comfortable associating themselves with newspapers that maintained . . . this 'appearance of neutrality.' "[104]

Obviously, neutrality or objectivity is a relative term in a profession necessarily devoted to a process of editing. In a world of scarce resources, all sides cannot be presented, and the represented sides will tend to be those that could be expected to be widely held.[105] Douglas Kellner puts a radical spin on the point: "In general, television tends to reproduce the positions of the dominant hegemonic political forces of the era simply because, in its zeal to win good ratings and big profits, it gravitates toward what it believes is popular. As a consequence, it tends to reinforce and reproduce the dominant ethos. . . . [I]n the event of intra-ruling-class conflict, television will tend to reproduce it."[106]

According to Kellner, "The opinion spectrum that dominates television thus includes only those liberals and conservatives who tacitly agree that all discourse must take place within the framework of the existing system of production and representative democracy, from which more radical views are rigorously excluded."[107]

Whatever the explanation for the comparative absence of radical voices on American television, it seems obvious that they *are* comparatively absent. Indeed, during the Gulf War, of the 878 on-the-air sources on the network evening news shows, only 1 was a representative of a peace organization.[108] At no time during the first month of *Nightline*'s conversations about the war did a single U.S. guest argue against the decision to send American soldiers to the region.[109]

Even during calmer times, a study of forty months of *Nightline* shows found that representatives of "civic and community organizations, popular social movements, [and] minority communities [were] essentially absent."[110] The report concluded that "*Nightline* serves as an electronic soapbox from which white, male, elite representatives of the status quo can present their case. Minorities, women, and those with challenging views are generally excluded."[111]

The posture of the media is that of an overseer monitoring competing "responsible" antagonists.[112] This posture is itself ideologically charged. As Herbert Gans observes in his careful study of the news: "The political values in the news . . . are dominated by the same principle; in fact, insofar as the news has an ideology of its own, it is moderate."[113] Thus, journalists as a group tend to be moderate.[114] More precisely, journalists of the mainstream media do not think of themselves as ideological,[115] and they naturally tend to distrust idealogues of the far left and the far right.[116]

In describing the treatment of radicals by the mainstream media, Gans states: "All the major news media approve the moderate core, which includes liberals, moderates, and conservatives; adherents to other positions are treated less favorably, but generally those on the Right are labeled more politely than those on the Left."[117] From the perspective of the left, the situation Gans described at the outset of the 1980s is even bleaker today. Liberals are no longer part of the media's perceived moderate core[118] but are closer to the fringe of that core; radicals are virtually nonexistent.

Corporations

The failure of the fourth estate is perhaps most conspicuous when one considers the media's treatment of corporations, whether in entertainment programming or public affairs reporting. Recall that the media is dominated by advertising. Important advertisers have demanded a pro-business atmosphere: "Proctor & Gamble, which spends over a billion dollars a year on advertising once decreed in a memo on broadcast policy: 'There will be no material that will give offense, either directly or indirectly, to any commercial organization of any sort.' Ditto for Prudential Insurance: 'A positive image of business and finance is important to sustain on the air.' "[119]

Entertainment programming largely meets these requirements, but it is not an unmitigated corporate paradise. Business executives are frequently portrayed in derogatory terms on entertainment television. The legendary *Dallas* character, J. R. Ewing, for example, was something less than a goody-two-shoes. Even though powerful businessmen are frequently portrayed in derogatory ways, however, the social message is one of individual corruption rather than a radical indictment of the political structure. As Todd Gitlin observes, however, "Structures rarely exist; culprits do."[120] Moreover, the quest for riches is not called into question. Even if J. R. Ewing was morally impoverished, millions of viewers were encouraged to enjoy the sumptuous surroundings. We can hate the rich, but we want the riches.

Of course, business corporations might prefer that all such stereotypes be excised from the air, but television itself is a business. *Dallas* stayed on the air so long as audiences were willing to watch and advertisers were prepared to pay. Conflicts of corporate interest persist even in a structure that is largely hospitable to corporate interests.

The same is true of public affairs coverage of corporations.[121] Morton Mintz, a *Washington Post* reporter for twenty-nine years, complained of a "chronic tilt [that] distorts mainstream media coverage of grave, persisting, and pervasive abuses of corporate power."[122] Similarly, Frances Cerra, who for six years served as the consumer reporter for the *New York*

Times, observed, "The *Times* never wanted stories critical of consumer treatment by major corporations."[123] Of course, many critical stories have been published or broadcast.[124] Critical discussions of corporate activity are often triggered when public officials have focused attention on them,[125] but many of those same public officials rely on corporate campaign contributions in order to get reelected. In the absence of government attention of one sort or another, the national press will rarely press for reform of corporations.[126]

Nonetheless, if a government agency or a "responsible" researcher criticizes a corporation or its product, the media will frequently give substantial exposure to such a charge. And, during some periods, many such charges have created a negative impression of business as a whole. Little mystery should surround the question of why a corporate conglomerate would broadcast stories that might be detrimental to long-term corporate interests. Short-term profits explain much, and all corporations are not hurt alike. Indeed, when corporate interests collide, the competitors will often seek government assistance, and the news will not be far behind.

The question is what discourages more critical stories, what accounts for the "chronic tilt [that] distorts mainstream media coverage of corporate power"?[127] Some of the reasons are obvious. First, libel laws discourage aggressive media reporting. Corporations often have the resources and the will to bring a lawsuit. Even if the plaintiff ultimately loses, the press defendant will, despite insurance, spend substantial amounts defending the lawsuit and will have editors and reporters tied up in a grueling legal discovery process. Before publishing a hard-hitting story about a wealthy potential plaintiff, the media is encouraged to think hard. The so-called chilling effect of libel suits is a reality.

Second, corporate abuses are not easily unearthed by the press. In the absence of government sources or reports in scholarly journals, the press must turn to investigative reporting. Such reporting is expensive and, therefore, rare. More difficult to assess is the role that corporate ownership of and corporate advertising in the media plays in discouraging corporate criticism. Advertiser pressure, of course, runs to prevent criticism of its own products. As Bagdikian reports: "The mainstream news media postponed for more than fifty years full public awareness of the hidden dangers of the medically known threat to public health from tobacco. They did it by self-censorship and by deliberate obfuscation of authoritative medical reports. They did it to protect a major advertiser."[128] More recently, the reporting of the *New York Times* has been soft on the automobile industry because of the need for advertising by that industry.[129] Indeed, Arthur Sultzberger, then the publisher of the *New York Times*, "admitted that he had leaned on his editors to present the auto industry's position because it 'would affect advertising.' "[130] And Turner Catledge, the Times's former managing editor, has written that he frequently carried out Sultzberger's directives without indicating that the policy was emanating from the publisher.[131] Reporters thus may often be unaware that editorial policy is the product of the publisher's intervention.[132]

Why would publishers want to intervene—apart from wanting to avoid lawsuits and to secure a favorable atmosphere for advertisers? Some media critics speak in conspiratorial terms about the desire of corporate managers to maintain their position of class power in a capitalistic system. I doubt this is an important factor. But I do think it is relevant that the owners of the press are largely conservative, and I think it is natural for owners of the press, whether liberal or conservative, to want their paper to reflect their general view. Otis Chandler of the *Los Angeles Times* put it succinctly: "I'm the chief executive. I set policy and I'm not going to surround myself with people who disagree with me. . . . I surround myself with people who generally see the world the way I do."[133]

In the end, the news media tends to cover those arguments that divide corporate interests but not those arguments directed against that which unites them. Whether this is good or bad, the business climate created by the structure of the American communications media is as good as business could reasonably desire. The airwaves are organized as a medium to attract consumers, and criticism of corporate power is kept to a minimum.[134]

Even if the media were not financed by advertisers, even if it were not owned by powerful corporations, even if it did not depend on people in power for much of its product, the *mass* media is constrained by its financial need to appeal to a mass audience. This need itself constrains the issues discussed. Millions of Americans tend to value dissent in the abstract and recoil from it in the concrete. They prefer to avoid challenges to their deepest views. From a programming perspective, this is not trivial. No institution in the mass media can get rich offending a mass audience.[135]

The media is often characterized as a fourth estate functioning to *criticize* the status quo, yet if the picture I have painted is largely correct, the media, without engaging in a conspiracy, largely functions to *preserve* the status quo.[136] Criticisms from the left and parts of the right are marginalized. The power of the media to preserve the status quo is especially effective because formal censorship is rare, because the media often exposes corporate and government abuses, and because the press so frequently proclaims itself as free.[137] Hidden in each of these dimensions is a set of political, cultural, and economic factors that guide our free press away from the kind of informed debate that is symbolized by our national commitment to freedom of the press.

Legalizing the Marginalization of Dissent

It is often remarked that the current Supreme Court is greatly and surprisingly protective of free speech. Decisions protecting flag burning are the kinds of cases eliciting such reactions. Overall, however, the Court's record in protecting and encouraging dissent is checkered. In examining the positions taken by the Supreme Court affecting dissent, it is helpful to distinguish among (1) regulations limiting the content of government criticism; (2) regulations limiting the content of criticism of powerful figures outside of government; and (3) institutional barriers limiting the opportunities for effective dissent and privileging those in power.

The Court's record regarding regulations of the content of governmental criticism is admirable on the whole. Although decisions recognizing the constitutional right to burn flags are of substantial symbolic importance,[138] of even greater importance are decisions that greatly limit the power of public officials to win libel or slander judgments.[139] The doctrine that advocacy of illegal action is protected unless it is directed to inciting or producing imminent lawless action and is likely to incite or produce such action is also worth mentioning,[140] although the durability[141] and the scope[142] of this doctrine are open to some question. Less admirable are decisions that make it difficult for public employees to speak out, including the permissibility of overly strict confidentiality requirements,[143] and direct restrictions on employees' ability to criticize their bosses[144] and even actively to participate in political campaigns.[145]

The Court's record regarding criticism of people with power outside of government is nowhere near as good. To be sure, the Court has held that persons have as much freedom to criticize public figures as they do public officials.[146] In practice, however, the Court has narrowly construed the public figure category.[147] The people and the press, therefore, have substantial leeway to criticize "public figures" if they can identify them. The problem is not just that most people who occupy positions of power in local areas are not public figures. Even the chief executive officers of Mobil Oil and other major companies are not public figures except with regard to public controversies that they have attempted to influence.[148] Even the term *public controversy* is notoriously vague.[149] Clearly, under this doctrine, however, the reporting of corruption involving corporate executives involves far greater risks than the reporting of corruption by even relatively low-level public officials. These are not crazy distinctions if one is wedded to a politically centered conception of the First Amendment; they are unproductive if it is important to encourage criticism of unjustified exercises of power.

Most serious are the institutional barriers to effective dissent. Government and private centers of power are given substantial discretion to control the opportunities for dissent. The Court has prevented demonstrations or denied access for certain speech opportunities outside of prisons[150] and post offices,[151] in the park across the street from the White House,[152] in school mailboxes[153] and private mailboxes,[154] on utility poles[155] and outside polling booths,[156] and at airports,[157] county fairs,[158] and shopping centers.[159] Individually, these cases may not be important. Collectively, they make it quite difficult for dissenters who are unable to expend substantial sums. Indeed, the denial of access to shopping centers for speech opportunities alone is an especially harsh decision for dissenters who need access to the public.

The worst decisions, however, are those that deny access to the mass media. *CBS v. Democratic National Committee*[160] held that CBS could prevent the Democratic National Committee from even *buying* television time to protest the handling of the Vietnam War. Instead, with the exception of limited and often unenforced government regulations, corporate licensees are ceded untrammeled control over access to the broadcast media. These licensees resist further government regulations, such as requirements to present substantial children's programming, on the ground that such regulations impair their First Amendment rights. The outright scandal of the current system is that companies are granted the use of these extremely valuable broadcast frequencies without any charge on the theory that they are supposed to act as public trustees. Although the broadcasters are supposed to act as public trustees, the evidence is that they overwhelmingly operate as free market entrepreneurs. Despite abundant evidence to the contrary, for many years, the FCC sought to deregulate on the ground pressed by the broadcasters that the public trustee system would work best in a free market with little government regulation.

I will discuss alternatives shortly. For the moment, suffice it to say that Supreme Court interpretations of First Amendment law and FCC enforcement of the Communications Act make it easy for broadcasters to deny access to minority points of view to the mass media, and, as I discussed in the last section, broadcasters take advantage of this opportunity.

The other significant area from an institutional perspective is the treatment afforded by the Supreme Court in the elections area. *Buckley v. Valeo*[161] is the key case. Here the Court mauled an attempt by Congress to limit the spending of the wealthy in election campaigns.[162] The Court said, "[T]he concept that government may restrict the voice of some elements of our society in order to enhance the relative voice of others is wholly foreign to the First Amendment."[163] That is one way of putting it.

The lower court characterized the issue quite differently: Can "the wealthy few [claim] a constitutional guarantee to a stronger political voice than the unwealthy many because they are able to . . . spend more money, and because the amounts they . . . spend cannot be limited?"[164] To put it another way, why is it "wholly foreign to the First Amendment" for Congress to take measures limiting injustice in the democratic system? If free speech can be limited to protect reputations, morality, and order, why can't it be limited to combat injustice and promote equal citizenship? So long as the dollar sign dominates politics, politics will be inordinately corrupt.[165]

In sum, the mass media in its daily operations and the Supreme Court in its jurisprudence frequently marginalize dissent while privileging the powerful. This is not to say that the powerful write their own check at all times, nor that dissent is invariably smothered. It is to say that we are a long way off from a society that is committed to encouraging dissent in an effort to combat injustice.

Encouraging Dissent

What would a society committed to encouraging dissent begin to look like? That is a large question deserving of multivolume treatment.[166] I have too much respect for the difficulty and scope of the question to purport to provide a complete answer here. Instead I will confine myself to discussing the conditions such a society would have to meet and to sketching some of the kinds of proposals that I believe could help promote dissent. I do not claim that these proposal are original, although I am not aware of any attempt to group such proposals around the idea of promoting dissent. I do not claim that the proposals I mention would eliminate injustice, nor that they would revolutionize society. My claim is that they would encourage dissent and be a progressive force.

Of course, that contention is open to question. Moreover, the proposals themselves might or might not be disadvantageous for other reasons. My goal here is not to present arguments and counterarguments but to invite the reader to consider these proposals as part of a program to promote dissent and to challenge the reader to think of other proposals to add to the mix. In other words, I am trying to open a dialogue rather than provide the last word.

Any society that encouraged dissent would have to meet four conditions: (1) its system of education would need to promote attitudes and to teach skills that would assist in creating a substantial body of citizens with the talent and the will to challenge injustice in appropriate circumstances; (2) channels of communication for expressing dissent would need to be open; (3) legal barriers to dissent would need to be held to a minimum; and (4) social and government institutions would need to be designed to make information available to those who wish to dissent.

Education and Dissent

Any society committed to encouraging dissent must begin its encouragement in its system of education. Within limits, there is nothing wrong with teaching our students what society generally values.[167] Indeed, it is important to communicate the importance of constitutional values. If our citizens are not educated with a sense of justice, they are less likely to acquire it. Indeed, a sense of justice and of injustice is typically a prerequisite for progressive dissent. In addition, our educational system must educate not only autonomous thinkers prepared to reject the habits, customs, and traditions of the larger society but also citizens who generally regard dissent against injustice as virtuous behavior.

I have no pie-eyed expectations. Whatever the educational system does, most people will let others speak out against injustice for the reasons previously described. Still, an educational system committed to producing active citizens with a sense of justice can produce a more active citizenry. Little evidence supports the hypothesis that our educational system has such an agenda, however. Indeed, the widespread use of the pledge of allegiance, with its statement that we are a nation under God with liberty and justice for all, seems to communicate to our students a statement of national condition that is far from the truth. That our students are socially, but not legally, forced to make this statement signals a system out to induce loyal, conforming citizens. The practice seems more likely to induce docility than critical dissent.[168] Consider, further, a recent sixth-grade textbook that purports to teach the nature of citizenship.[169] The textbook states that a good citizen:

> plays by the rules
> obeys laws and respects authority
> does his or her share of the work
> stays informed
> votes
> pays taxes
> is charitable with money and time
> protects the environment and conserves natural resources[170]

The problem with this vision of citizenship is less with what it affirms than with what it leaves out. Good citizens respect authority when it is just. Good citizens not only are charitable with money and time but also actively participate to make our society better in substantial part by challenging injustice where it exists.

Of course, our schools at the very least give lip service to autonomous decision makers and critical thinking; many do more than that. Generally, however, in educating for democracy in public and private realms, our schools could do more to encourage dissent.

Courses in argument and debate should be more than extracurricular activities but regular, required features of the curriculum. Debate should be encouraged not just for debate's sake but as a necessary tool for responsible citizenship in moving all facets of society toward a more just condition. Critical thinking might embrace media education and a careful look at the positions of all candidates in political races, not just those who emerge in the "horse race." Even more important, schools need to be structured more democratically, and students need training in democratic processes. For example, students in large and small groups could be assigned projects of challenging injustices they collectively perceive within their local communities.[171] The practice of challenging injustice should not only instruct them in the present but also encourage them to do so in the future. On the other hand, injustice need not be challenged willy-nilly. We all pick our fights. Role playing or discussions concerning how one determines when and whether to "fight" and the rhetoric surrounding those decisions should be carefully considered.

Even more important, there is no reason not to give students a voice in many other issues that make up the daily life of classrooms and schools. Teachers make many decisions that need not be made by teachers, and if power is placed in the hands of students to democratically make decisions, they will learn how to participate. They will learn more than to do what the teacher says or else. Schools will be less training grounds for responding to authority and more training grounds in democratic process.[172]

I wholeheartedly agree with Chris Sperry and Dave Lehman, who write:

> The great majority of U.S. schools are autocratic institutions which try, albeit often unsuccessfully, to gain the obedience and compliance of young people. Schools teach our young people to follow rules, but not how to create them; to respect authority, but not how to take responsibility for it; to learn *about* democracy, but not to *practice* it. If we expect our young people to take their choices in life seriously, to take responsibility for themselves and ownership of a positive future, then our schools must help them develop as moral actors in a democratic society. We must give students practice in democratic decision-making, teach them to consider the perspectives of others, and offer them opportunities to take responsibility for the world around them.[173]

Ultimately, in my view, the goal of training people who recognize the virtue of combating injustice and who have the ability to dissent in an effective manner should be part of the mission statement of every school and school district. If it is recognized as a goal, administrators and teachers are more likely to internalize it as an important feature of the curriculum.

Finally, beyond education, we ironically might encourage dissent against injustice if we produce a more just society. People cannot be effective citizens if they lack adequate food, clothing, shelter, jobs, or medical care.[174] I believe the state should guarantee that no resident is denied such necessities without regard to the impact on dissent. But making good on such a guarantee might increase participation and dissent in society both because citizens with material assurances can afford the luxury of participation and because rising expectations might trigger demands for greater equality and justice.

Access to the Media

Our present system of broadcasting is an outright scandal. Although much attention is focused on the extent to which "public" broadcasting is subsidized, commercial broadcasters are given an even greater subsidy. They are given not only *free* use of the frequencies but also a far greater right to demand payment by advertisers for access to the media. In theory, commercial broadcasters are "public trustees,"[175] but when they are asked to act like public trustees, they claim the First Amendment protects them from doing so. For example, our students receive their education not only in school but also through their attending to the mass media. Commercial broadcasters have resisted programming for children because other programming is more lucrative. Howling and screaming against government regulation, they are now forced to offer but three hours of educational children's programming per week. Even those programs are presently dubious, for some broadcasters have insisted that programs like the *Jetsons* and *G.I. Joe* are educational.[176] In addition, the amount of violent content on television is enormous. The social science evidence powerfully indicates that children watch such programming and that it has negative social effects in terms of aggressive conduct.[177] Such programming rarely teaches that there are productive alternatives to violence. Of course, dissent is one such alternative in many circumstances.

In reacting to this aspect of the problem, it seems clear that more children's programming is desirable and that profit-seeking broadcasters are not the appropriate decision makers for educating the nation's children. In this connection, a group such as the National Education Association could be empowered to clear programming that the broadcasters claim is educational. Alternatively, educational groups could be empowered to provide programs. Nothing in a sensible system of constitutional law suggests that broadcasters be given a twenty-four-hour-a-day license. There could be multiple licensees in a single day, and educators could be licensed for a portion of the day.

Similarly, because licensees need not be given total control of the frequencies, groups might be afforded petition access to the media on a first come, first served basis, as Charles Firestone and Phil Jacklin have long proposed.[178] In addition, *CBS v. Democratic National Committee* should be reversed. Broadcasters should not be permitted to refuse access to those who wish to buy time for political messages. Some might object that the wealthy might be advantaged by this, but the wealthy already dominate the media. Moreover, there are many organized dissenting groups with the wherewithal to buy time. The idea that broadcasters have a monopoly on the judgment of what needs to be presented to the American public turns the public trustee concept into a fetish.

The *CBS* decision was at least partially influenced by the concern that broadcasters under the fairness doctrine would have to use airtime to provide the other side to the views of the wealthy who had bought time for political access. The fairness doctrine, however, seems to have been misconceived from the outset. As many commentators have observed, the requirement to be fair and to cover both sides seems to have dampened partisan debate. The fairness doctrine, however, makes more sense as applied to advertising. Application of the fairness doctrine to commercial advertising might permit free access for those who would respond to the rampant commercialism of the media or to the ubiquitous advertisements for alcoholic beverages.

Even more important is the question of free access for political candidates. In order to diversify debate, such access should be provided for all candidates on the ballot, not just major party candidates. Although broadcasters maintain that this would be too expensive, a significant step forward would be taken if the candidates merely replaced the spots in which the networks promote their own shows. Moreover, given the enormous subsidy already provided to the broadcasting media, the fact that such regulation would cost it money is a description, not a criticism. According to one FCC insider, interest from the sale of digital licenses alone could triple the budget of the Corporation for Public Broadcasting, fund the FCC, and give to political candidates an amount equal to twice what they typically spend.[179] Even if the frequencies were sold off, in a just constitutional regime, claims of access could be made to the commercial media without First Amendment violation because the educational, justice, and public health needs are pressing. Alternatively, claims of access could be justified by placing conditions on the sale of the frequencies, assuring a sort of easement for access purposes. I do not maintain that *any* conditions could be placed on such a sale. Conditions assuring access, however, ought to be regarded as less troublesome than those that would seek to keep material off the frequencies.

Of course, access to the media is not enough. As discussed previously, the Court has prevented demonstrations or denied access for speech opportunities in numerous places, including access to government and "private" property. Demonstrators and dissenters need access to the sites of injustice. They need to be able to talk with citizens face-to-face if democratic dialogue is to get off the ground. They need access to local channels of communication. The power relations regarding access need to be shifted from the bureaucrats to those confronting the centers of power.

Limiting Sanctions Against Dissent

Dissent cannot be encouraged if legal sanctions against it are not confined. As I suggested earlier, the Court's record regarding regulations of the content of governmental criticism is admirable on the whole. Nonetheless, some areas need to be improved. The power of public officials to win libel and slander judgments is rightly limited, but there are gaps.[180] Reporters ought to be able to print the charges of responsible individuals or organizations without fear of reprisals, whether or not they agree with those charges. Regrettably, many states have rejected that view even in circumstances where the reporter prints the response of the public official involved.

The Court has stated that advocacy of illegal action is protected unless it is directed to inciting or producing imminent lawless action and is likely to incite or produce such action.[181] Nonetheless, it has confused the situation by stating that advocacy of illegal action can be sanctioned when it is directed toward actions now or in the future. The Court needs to make it clear that sanctions are available only when the advocacy is limited to imminent lawless action.

Of more general importance are sanctions involving criticism of people with power outside of government. Our defamation laws need to be more hospitable to the criticism of powerful people, whether they exercise their power in local, state, or national nongovernmental hierarchies. The public figure category needs to be construed in a far broader way. People need not be nationally famous to be powerful. The focus of the public figure category should emphasize the extent to which the criticized individual exercises power. If it does, our society will encourage criticism of the powerful through its many manifestations, not just in governmental arenas.

Reconfiguring the power relations is particularly necessary in the workplace. Although workers spend much of their lives in the workplace, the importance of justice there is all too often underemphasized. It is singularly indefensible that workers are free to criticize their union but not their employers. Workers need to be free to criticize the way things are managed on the job without fear of dismissal or other forms of retaliation.[182] That corporations own the job site should not be regarded as critical; the point is that workplaces will function better if injustice can freely be brought to light.[183] They will function better if discussions about workplace justice are recognized to be part of the democratic dialogue.

Information and Dissent

Dissent will be encouraged if information is available that reveals problems or issues to be explored. Encouraging a responsible citizenry prepared to challenge injustice when appropriate, opening channels of communication, and keeping legal sanctions to a minimum should make more information and debate available to the relevant public. But more can be done. Government is already in the business of subsidizing speech in the hopes of producing information and debate. Subsidies for education and libraries are among the most important. Shortchanging these subsidies, as government frequently does, is indefensible. Indeed, the development of a new communications infrastructure makes it even more important that all citizens have equitable access.[184] Schools and public libraries presumably must play a central role if anything close to equity is to be assured. Other subsidies need to be considered as well. The federal government permits contributions to educational, charitable, and religious organizations to be tax deductible but will not permit these contributions to be used for substantial lobbying. Meanwhile, veterans organizations can use tax-deductible contributions for such purposes,[185] and businesses can deduct lobbying expenses in connection with local governments. If veterans organizations can use tax-deductible contributions for substantial lobbying, so should peace organizations. The issue ranges beyond war and peace. Legislatures should not make decisions in ignorance of the contributions that can be provided by a wide range of public interest organizations (recognizing that such organizations have diverse views of the good).

Similarly, government used to provide a substantially reduced postal rate for magazines and then raised the rates, putting many publications at risk. If a diverse marketplace of ideas is to be encouraged, government should be going out of its way to make it easy for publications to flourish. To be sure, not all magazines or nonprofit organizations challenge injustice, but ad hoc determinations of which do and which do not challenge injustice would be intolerable, and subsidies of a diverse marketplace support other important values.

In addition, taxes on the press seem quite difficult to justify unless they can be structured to make the press more independent of advertisers. C. Edwin Baker, for example, has proposed a tax on newspaper advertising revenue, combined with a subsidy redistributing the revenue to papers on the basis of their circulation revenue.[186] The proposal seeks to reduce the incentive of newspapers to respond to advertiser pressure and, instead, to provide newspapers of greater quality and responsiveness to readers. As presented by Baker, the proposal seems to be even more effective than would a proposal to outlaw advertiser influence.

Beyond tax proposals regarding the press,[187] some obvious approaches to the broadcast media need to be considered. In large part the public broadcasting system was designed to provide sources of programming that were free from the grip of national advertisers, but much has been lost along the way. Public broadcasters today rely too heavily on corporate sponsors, and the problems that permeate commercial broadcasting also plague public broadcasting. We need to return to the original design of public broadcasting in which commercial advertising of all kinds was prohibited. At the same time, public broadcasting needs to be put on a firm financial footing. Public broadcasters need not be public beggars. As I suggested previously, a way to assure generous funding for public broadcasters would be to stop giving commercial broadcasters free use of the spectrum or to sell off portions of the spectrum and use the moneys collected in a trust fund for public broadcasters.[188] Alternatively, we might tax broadcasters on the basis of their advertising revenue and distribute the money to public broadcasters.[189] In the end, we might have true public trustees instead of commercial trustees.

In addition, we could license particular kinds of programs that speak to the needs of the public. For example, licensees could be required to offer specified amounts of public affairs programming during election season (within months of the election) without coverage of the "horse race." (Horse race coverage could come in other programming.) But requiring licensees to provide particular kinds of programming or giving other access to the media to do so cannot be the main strategy. It seems crucial to assure that the media and the public have access to vital information. It is an open secret that the Freedom of Information Act is being widely circumvented by the overclassification of information.[190] Justifications of such classifications ought to be made to independent review boards within governmental agencies. But disclosure needs to be expanded outside of government. In the absence of publicly funded elections, for example, the source and amount of campaign contributions should be reported to a government Web site within twenty-four hours of their receipt. Reporters would then have easy access to information disclosing how our elections process really works.

Perhaps even more critical is the financing and structure of elections. Public funding of elections, preferably through vouchers,[191] with guaranteed free access to the media and restrictions on additional spending,[192] is crucial to secure the independence of our politicians from moneyed interests. Separating politicians from such interests not only would advance the cause of justice in and of itself but also would free them up to seek and provide more information to the public.

But in many respects politicians in a two-party system wish to address a narrow spectrum of issues. A proportional representation system would improve on the winner-take-all system.[193] It would assure that more voices would be heard in the political process;[194] it would stimulate fuller participation in the political process[195] while striking a dagger at Tweedledum Tweedledee politics;[196] and it would broaden the bases of power.[197] The reporting focus of the mass media on the utterances of the two parties would also be changed because, as power shifts, so do the eyes of the media. The result would be a broader spectrum with more challenges to the traditional wisdom.

As I have said, I am content to provide this sketch without further elaboration. Some readers might have preferred long discussions of these proposals, but most of them have been discussed pro and con by many others elsewhere. Many of those readers may nonetheless experience a sense of unease. There frequently is an unstated belief that if there is a problem, there must be a tidy solution. I wonder how much of that unease is prompted by a desire to believe that our society is more or less just, or could be with only a few changes. In the end, I return to basics. Even if we do all we can to encourage dissent, our society will be riddled with injustice because an unjust hierarchy is inevitable in a large-scale society. We can do better. We cannot do enough.

V

The Politics of Free Speech

CONSERVATIVES have recently discovered the First Amendment, and they are beginning to like what they see: a banner for corporations seeking to dominate election campaigns,[1] for tobacco companies to hawk their wares,[2] for shopping centers to exclude demonstrators,[3] and for media corporations to resist access,[4] and a club to use against those who seek to regulate racist speech[5] and pornography.[6]

Conservative victories are not yet monumental, and liberals themselves divide on some of these issues, but many believe it is time for progressives to reconsider their historic commitment to free speech and press. Many have begun to wonder whether the First Amendment is itself a barrier to justice. Although Mary Becker particularly focuses on the negative consequences of the First Amendment for women, she makes the more general argument that abstract rights like freedom of speech protect the powerful and work against other disadvantaged groups.[7] Richard Delgado and Jean Stefanic maintain that First Amendment doctrine is equipped to handle "small, clearly bounded disputes"[8] but is less able to deal with systemic social ills, such as racism and sexism, that are widespread and deeply woven into the fabric of society. They conclude that "free speech is least helpful when we need it most."[9] Morton J. Horwitz argues that rights discourse in free speech cases underlines its "continuing ability to preserve the privileges of the rich and powerful."[10] David Kairys argues that the Court "has narrowed and restricted the free-speech rights available to people of ordinary means [and] enlarged the free-speech rights of wealthy people and corporations."[11] And Mark Tushnet maintains that the First Amendment has replaced the due process clause as the "primary guarantor of the privileged."[12]

Of course, the general claim that rights rhetoric, including the right of free speech, does not serve the cause of justice has been much discussed in the academy. A number of critical theorists have pointed to the disadvantages of rights, though some have stopped short of recommending the abandonment of rights discourse. Recurring themes include the contention that rights are indeterminate, incoherent, contradictory, excessively abstract and subject to reification, excessively individualistic, dependent on an unmakable public-private distinction, and generally manipulated to serve the privileged classes.[13]

In a provocative essay, Frederick Schauer makes a related but ultimately quite different argument.[14] He suggests that the commitment to free speech itself tends to favor those in power and tilts against those out of power.[15] In support of this suggestion, he observes that conservative free speech arguments are increasingly being made by wealthy individuals and powerful corporations, and he notes that these arguments have frequently been successful. In attempting to account for this "rightward shift in the political center of gravity of free speech argumentation,"[16] Schauer resorts to a philosophical explanation buttressed by a technological observation. The observation is that entry into the intellectual marketplace is increasingly costly, and that any sustained effort to bring about attitudinal changes requires the kind of substantial resources enjoyed by powerful people. The philosophical explanation is that a market unregulated by government will be a market dominated by powerful social and economic forces. From these premises, he suggests that liberals should have second thoughts about their commitment to the free speech principle.[17]

What makes Schauer's argument provocative is that it does not depend on any of the much-debated claims about the indeterminate character of law. Rather, he puts forward what I will call the market capture thesis, which combines three assumptions: (1) the market is controlled by conservative sources; (2) the free speech principle is a laissez-faire principle; and (3) the free speech principle is harmful to the left. The market capture thesis should be contrasted with the conservative interpreters thesis, namely, that conservative justices convert a relatively indeterminate principle like free speech into a principle of protection for the privileged. By contrast, the market capture thesis regards the free speech principle as more determinate. According to the postulates of the thesis, the free speech principle is rightly interpreted in ways that are damaging to the left.

Although the proposition that the market is controlled by conservative sources deserves at least qualified support, the market capture thesis has two major flaws. First, the assumption that the free speech principle is harmful to the left deserves to be repudiated even if it were interpreted as a laissez-faire principle. The assumption does not take sufficient account of the multiplicity of power relations both in the mass media and without. Moreover, the assumption is too blasé about the kinds of interventions one might expect from government. If conservative forces can control the market, they also can control the government and repress dissident movements.

Second, the assumption that the free speech principle is laissez-faire deserves to be contested. Other interpretations of the free speech principle countenance a more active state, but a state nonetheless limited in its authority to squelch the less powerful. In other words, the free speech principle is susceptible to interpretations more sympathetic to the concerns of the less powerful.

Before addressing the preceding issues, I need to begin with a point about political definition and perspective. Schauer refers to liberals in a general way, specifying the array of people who actively supported Michael Dukakis and Bill Clinton in his first presidential election campaign, in contrast to those who actively supported Ronald Reagan and George Bush.[18] Surely, however, Schauer would agree that many of the active supporters of Clinton and Dukakis were not liberals (consider southern conservatives) or were not necessarily liberals (consider the Wall Street bankers). In addition, downtown real estate developers whose interests in some ways coincide with those of liberals need not themselves be liberals (they oppose defense spending to make room for projects that many believe will assist the disadvantaged). Given that the business interests that supported Clinton or Dukakis do not conventionally parade under the title of liberal, I take it that Schauer has in mind a picture of the liberal activist.

As to the content of what liberals believe, Schauer states that they are concerned with the less powerful and with equalization of opportunity.[19] I do not quarrel with this view (though the latter in particular is emphasized by conservatives), but a more precise account of liberalism would require an account of the many liberalisms, together with their situation on a larger political map. It would require discussions of autonomy, equality, toleration, diversity, welfare, and opportunity. Schauer merely suggests that concern with the less powerful and equality of opportunity are among the primary characteristics of contemporary liberalism, and for my purposes, that is acceptable except in one respect. What seems missing from Schauer's perspective on liberalism is the recognition that many liberals value freedom of speech as an end in itself or as flowing from notions of dignity or respect, not merely as a means to helping the less powerful. Some of these liberals are absolutists; some will balance free speech only against other rights. If they were convinced the free speech principle helped the powerful, they would regret it, but that demonstration would prompt them to press harder for change in the distribution of wealth in the society. They would not be prompted to reevaluate the free speech principle because their support for that principle is primarily based on nonconsequentialist reasoning.[20]

To be sure, many liberals are more enthusiastic about consequentialist arguments,[21] but the sting of the market capture thesis seems to attach most strongly to those on the left whose embrace of the free speech principle is more likely to be consciously strategic than the typical liberal[22] and whose political identity is even more closely tied to the concerns of the downtrodden than is the case with liberals.

I am unsure from Schauer's article, however, whether he means to exclude those supporters of Clinton and Dukakis who thought of themselves not as liberals but as progressives, radicals, or just members of the left. At one point he refers to radicals as "the term of choice for everyone who vigorously disagrees with you."[23] Nonetheless, progressives, radicals, or members of the left meet Schauer's working understanding of liberals, that is, they favor economic intervention but also favor the free speech principle. (Those radicals who do not favor the free speech principle would clearly be excluded from Schauer's analysis and are not necessary to mine.)

In any event, whether or not I am right about Schauer's meaning, I shall refer to the left (including progressives, left-liberals, and radicals) in my comments and will include those who identify with the left (assuming they support the free speech principle)[24] whether or not they made the strategic choice to support Clinton, Dukakis, or both. In so doing, I obviously do not suppose that the left is monolithic. Liberals disagree; radicals disagree; and the categories of liberal and radical do not fit all those who think of themselves as being on the left. I, for one, find most liberals to be insufficiently critical of the structure of the status quo and too sunny about the possibilities for change within it. At the same time, I believe that most radicals unduly romanticize the democratic possibilities associated with the People and mass movements, though I regard dissenting movements as critical to the progress of combating injustice. Perhaps I should be counted as a radical-liberal. In any event, I will discuss differences among the left where they become relevant to confronting the market capture thesis.

The Impact of the Free Speech Principle

Admittedly, the free market is not a fair market; indeed, it is a distorted market. Power sets the agenda and constructs the range of issues to be discussed. By preventing government intervention to correct or mitigate such market failures, the market capture thesis postulates that the free speech principle does not serve the interests of the left. But this begs an important question, which is whether government intervention would make the unfair market better or worse than it already is. If the powerful control the marketplace with iniquitous consequences for the left, why would not the powerful control the state and make matters worse? In his attempt to promote the market capture thesis, Schauer concedes the possibility that the powerful will do precisely that (though he is puzzled about why people on the left would not also have worries of similar depth in the economic market), but he also maintains that the "number of good interventions may still be sufficient to produce more good results than would have been the case with non-intervention."[25] The obvious tentativeness of that conclusion ("may still be sufficient"), however, forces Schauer to a final contention of the "there may be reason to believe" variety,[26] rather than a firmer thesis. In response, I argue that there is insufficient reason to suppose that the left acts against its interests in supporting the free speech principle even assuming that the principle were laissez-faire.

Part of my analysis proceeds from my earlier discussion of the mass media. The mass media is obviously quite influential,[27] and control of it is important. Moreover, it is reasonable to expect that the mainstream press will continue to discriminate against those outside the corridors of power so long as its present structure remains in place. But control of the mass media in its current structure is not monolithic,[28] and the mainstream press is not the only press. Even if mass media power were monolithic, power is not.[29] The content of the mass media is by no means a perfect predictor of what people will believe. As John B. Thompson writes, "[W]e cannot claim or pretend to read off the consequences of media messages by attending to the structure and content of these messages alone."[30] Progressive change, from the perspective of many on the left,[31] typically does not come from independent agitation from the mass media[32] or via gifts from political power brokers: progressive change is the culmination of grassroots agitation and organizing.[33] As James MacGregor Burns and Stewart Burns conclude in a book that traces centuries of rights organizing: "Advances in rights have been achieved far more by grass-roots protesters, movement activists, and bold leaders—such as Martin Luther King, Jr. . . .—than by even the most well-meaning political brokers of those days. Transactional leaders may be still less relevant in the years ahead."[34] To the extent that leftist politics depends on social movements and grassroots protests and activities, the free speech principle is vital.[35] Without this principle, government could squelch antiwar protesters and civil rights protestors. Of course, the government has frequently censored or vilified the left despite the free speech principle. Consider the treatment of antiwar protestors in World War I, the Palmer raids, the House Un-American Activities Committee, and the reign of Joseph McCarthy.[36] Consider also the continued media red-baiting, which now extends to all those on the left for committing a sin that ironically parades under the title of "political correctness," ironic because the only way to commit the sin is to express views that are to the left of that which is regarded as orthodox in the mainstream media.

The extent to which the free speech principle has actually protected the left in the past is a fair subject for debate;[37] nonetheless, it seems that the free speech principle is in many ways more solidly anchored in our culture today than it has been in prior times.[38] It is hard to imagine, for example, that a conservative Supreme Court would have upheld the right of a leftist to burn a flag during World War I or the McCarthy era. Indeed, the constituency for free speech is broader today than it has ever been, in part because vested business interests have a stake in its strength.

But the issue of the salience of free speech goes beyond that of *protecting* the left. When the government engages in repression, the free speech principle itself becomes a basis for organizing grassroots movements. The Free Speech Movement at Berkeley did not come from nothing.

If the free speech principle is important to the left in protecting and forming grassroots movements,[39] it also furthers the left's interests with respect to the media, despite the factors causing the media to incline in so many circumstances against the left. Whether or not government were equipped to deal with the antileftist biases of the press, solving this problem is not and has never been a primary mission of the government. The free speech principle has not interfered with any government initiatives plausibly addressing these problems in a major way. On the other hand, the free speech principle, if followed in a capacious way, would protect the press[40] from the government initiatives the left has reason to fear, such as prior restraints, defamation suits, interference with confidential sources, and searches and seizures of press materials. Of course, these governmental initiatives can damage other political perspectives as well in many circumstances, but the suggestion that liberals or the left should consider the free speech principle as an on balance detriment is more contestable than might initially appear.

On the other hand, a laissez-faire free speech principle could prevent a liberal government from enacting many forms of campaign reform, most forms of mass media access regulation,[41] and most forms of hate speech and pornography regulation. The left would generally regard the limits on campaign reform and mass media access regulation to be serious costs of the free speech principle (assuming they were not incumbent protection programs).[42] The left, of course, is divided about hate speech and pornography regulation and would be divided about the merits of the free speech principle in that context.

From my own perspective, a laissez-faire free speech principle has costs for the left, and estimating the relative seriousness of those costs depends on an assessment of the importance of the regulations envisioned, their likely impact, and their likely enforcement. It also depends on an assessment of how often liberals would be in power and the speech agenda they would likely follow.[43] Since I assume the free speech principle will apply in good times and in bad, and since conservatives are likely to control the executive branch at least as often as liberals, any abandonment of the free speech principle on the ground that such abandonment would bring substantial benefits smacks of a riverboat gamble. Although I admit the free speech principle has costs, I think the market capture thesis underestimates the benefits of retaining the free speech principle to the left and to those liberals who value social movements and a free press.[44]

The Free Speech Principle

The market capture thesis assumes that the free speech principle is libertarian (i.e., does not interfere with the market),[45] but that assumption is open to serious question. First, I would guess that the overwhelming majority of modern conservatives are not libertarian.[46] To be sure, they are less likely than the left to intervene in the marketplace (still, there is something to John Kenneth Galbraith's quip that conservatives practice socialism for the rich and capitalism for the poor). But conservatives have been prepared to intervene in the market to combat obscenity and perceived threats to order or national security. Of course, libertarians would not subscribe to any such intervention, but the "modern conservatives" who sit on the Court do not appear to include *any* libertarians. Thus modern conservatives exhibit the converse side of the problem Schauer associates with liberals: How does one justify laissez-faire in the economic marketplace (if we accept that assumption about modern conservatives) while proposing intervention in the intellectual marketplace?

Enough about modern conservatives. What about the left and the free speech principle? Is it true that liberals and others on the left resist intervention in the intellectual marketplace while accepting intervention in the economic marketplace? Unquestionably, some do, but many do not. Indeed, many liberals want to intervene in the intellectual marketplace, for example, to promote children's television, to stop the wealthy from dominating election campaigns, to bring greater fairness to broadcast coverage of issues in the mass media, or to enact hate speech regulations.

Liberals and others on the left who take these positions either accept the laissez-faire free speech principle, but think the importance of the principle is outweighed, or entertain a different interpretation of the free speech principle, or both. It is certainly not the case that liberals or those on the left need to confine themselves to a laissez-faire conception of the First Amendment. Owen M. Fiss, for example, arguing from a liberal perspective, maintains that the "first amendment does not supply considerations in favor of laissez faire, but rather points toward the necessity of the activist state."[47] On his view, the First Amendment embodies our commitment to robust public debate, and if that commitment is to be realized the state must stand on an "equal footing with other institutions and is allowed, encouraged, and sometimes required to enact measures or issue decrees that enrich public debate, even if that action entails an interference with the speech of some and thus a denial of autonomy."[48] Thus, Fiss argues that broadcasters, for example, should not have been permitted to deny access to those who sought to oppose the Vietnam War.[49] The interference with the broadcaster's institutional autonomy was justified by the free speech principle's interest in public debate. There is no necessary libertarian spin to the First Amendment principle.

Nor is Fiss's alternative the only rival to the principle of laissez-faire. As I have argued throughout this book, the free speech principle is not best interpreted by reference to a free marketplace of ideas or even a rich and robust public debate. A starting assumption might better be that truth does not easily emerge in the marketplace of ideas. Power contributes to the construction of knowledge, and the incentives to conform are great. If principles like separation of powers and federalism serve to combat concentrated power, the First Amendment serves to encourage and protect those who speak out against established customs, habit, institutions, and authorities—whether or not they inhabit the public sphere.

On this understanding, the First Amendment spotlights a different metaphor than the marketplace of ideas or the richness of public debate; instead, it supports the American ideal of protecting and supporting dissent by putting dissenters at the center of the First Amendment tradition. Of course, this conception protects both left-wing and right-wing dissenters. But it has a strong political tilt against the unjust exercise of power.

On the dissent model, business corporations and commercial speakers have less of a claim to be at the heart of the First Amendment than they would if the marketplace of ideas were our guiding metaphor. Flag burners would come to be understood as entitled to First Amendment protection not so much because there is an "idea" that needs to be protected but because their expression is at the heart of American dissent. So, too, on this model speakers have strong claims of access to government property, to shopping centers, and to the mass media. In short, the dissent model provides for the negative liberty of protecting dissent but also illuminates the areas where government intervention is justifiable,[50] indeed, in many instances required.[51] Of course, the deconstructionists who maintain that concepts like dissent can be distorted are correct. But concepts cannot always be flipped to mean their opposite. A court that tries to maintain that antiwar speakers or those who criticize authorities are not dissenters would not have an easy opinion to write. Ambiguities can exist in some contexts (such as racist speech), but much speech is clearly within the core of dissent and much is not.

Presumably, I have said enough to indicate that some principles are better for the left than others. Nonetheless, as I have suggested, even the laissez-faire principle serves the left more than the market capture thesis allows. Though I have argued that a dissent theory, or, to a lesser extent, a laissez-faire theory, serves the left, I have not supposed that a dissent-based theory, let alone a laissez-faire theory, serves only the left. To be sure, some might accuse my analysis of tracking my political preferences too closely, so that left-wing dissenters get protected while people I do not like (corporations and right-wingers) do not. In an important sense, however, this accusation is wrongheaded. Rules under my approach are fashioned to protect dissent without regard to the politics of the dissenters. The overwhelming majority of right-wing dissent is fully protected under my theory.[52] The political bias of a dissent-centered conception of the First Amendment is for those who wish to challenge the status quo and for those who believe that society stagnates and furthers injustice when it is not open to challenge. People with these beliefs sit at many points on the political spectrum. Those who wish to preserve the status quo, of course, should oppose a dissent-centered theory (though their own speech remains protected in the overwhelming majority of circumstances). In my view, apart from those who are concerned about preservation of the status quo, centrists and others across the spectrum also gain from a society that tolerates and encourages dissent.

Finally, I do not believe the rightward drift of arguments surrounding the free speech principle has much to do with the free speech principle. The principle does not interpret itself. The rightward drift of argument cannot be understood by searching for an inherent meaning of the free speech principle or even by seeking to assess its political tilt. We would make more progress if we recalled the name of the chief justice of the United States: William H. Rehnquist.

I have not sought to argue that the free speech principle serves the left in its interpretation by a conservative Court. But the First Amendment is an important cultural and political force of its own wholly apart from the Court. Moreover, despite conservative control of the Court, the rights of business corporations in election campaigns are sharply limited,[53] tobacco companies do not yet have a free speech right to hawk their wares,[54] shopping centers have no First Amendment right to exclude demonstrators,[55] broadcasters have no First Amendment right to exclude access to the airwaves,[56] and the jury is still out on hate speech issues.[57] Indeed, Chief Justice Rehnquist has carried the banner on some of these issues. Power is complicated; so are conservatives; so is law.

But some things are simple. Like it or not, the free speech principle is here to stay. 'Tis better political strategy to claim it than to hold out oneself as an enemy of a cherished right. It is one thing to recognize that free speech interests conflict with other important values in a variety of important contexts, and that in some of those contexts, free speech values are outweighed or best interpreted not to apply. It is quite another to attack the free speech principle itself. Some version of the former is necessary for anyone who *thinks* about free speech. The latter promises to guide the left into outer darkness.

Notes

Introduction

1. For a historical perspective on the rhetoric surrounding the concept of America and related notions, see Michael Kammen, "The Problem of American Exceptionalism: A Reconsideration," 45 *American Quarterly* 1 (1993).

2. See U.S. Department of Health and Human Services, *Substance Abuse and Mental Health Statistics Sourcebook*, ed. Beatrice A. Rouse (Rockville, Md.: U.S. Department of Public Health, 1995), 9 (*Substance Abuse*); Daniel Lowenstein, " 'Too Much Puff': Persuasion, Paternalism, and Commercial Speech," 56 *U. Cin. L. Rev.*1205, 1210–11 (1988); cf. Note, "Cigarette Advertising and Freedom of Expression," 48 *U. Toronto Fac. L. Rev.* 304, 306 (1990) (reviewing Canadian situation). Alcohol is also a major cause of preventable deaths, accounting for more preventable deaths than firearms, sexual behavior, and motor vehicles put together. *Substance Abuse, supra*, at 9. In addition to preventable deaths, alcohol is a major cause of unmeasurable suffering among the living. Indeed, 43 percent of Americans over the age of eighteen have been exposed to alcoholism within their family. George A. Hacker and Tara L. Siegman, "Alcohol Consumption," in The Coalition for Consumer Health and Safety, *The Nation's Health and Safety: A Status Report* 52 (Washington, D.C.: Coalition for Consumer Health and Safety, 1997).

3. Steven H. Shiffrin, *The First Amendment, Democracy, and Romance* (Cambridge, Mass.: Harvard University Press, 1990).

Chapter I
The First Amendment and the Meaning of America

1. Patrick Buchanan, "This Is the Battle for America's Soul," *L.A. Times,* March 25, 1990, at M5.

2. Tex. Penal Code Ann. §42.09 (1989).

3. 491 U.S. 397 (1989).

4. 496 U.S. 310 (1990).

5. *Johnson,* 491 U.S. at 414; *Eichman,* 496 U.S. at 319.

6. *Johnson,* 491 U.S. at 417–18.

7. In fact, he has driven this truck before. See *FCC v. Pacifica Foundation,* 438 U.S. 726 (1978); Stevens, J., joined by Burger, C.J., and Rehnquist, J.

8. *Eichman,* 496 U.S. at 322; Stevens, J., joined by Rehnquist, C.J., White and O'Connor, JJ.

9. 250 U.S. 616, 624 (1919).

10. *Id.* at 630.

11. See *Paris Adult Theatre I v. Slaton,* 413 U.S. 49 (1973); Brennan, J., joined by Stewart and Marshall, JJ., dissenting.

12. *Johnson,* 491 U.S. at 418.

13. It is also possible to argue that foreclosing the method of expression in the flag-burning cases is not justified by a sufficiently substantial interest. But once the idea is separated from the method, the outcome is not obvious, particularly in light of the many other possible modes of communication.

14. According to standard legal doctrine, the First Amendment is not confined to the protection of ideas. In certain circumstances, it protects the publication of drug prices, the names of rape victims, true factual statements that harm the character of individuals, and in some cases false factual statements that damage the character of individuals.

15. *Johnson,* 491 U.S. at 400.

16. Geoffrey R. Stone, "Flag Burning and the Constitution," 75 *Iowa L. Rev.* 116 (1989) (first emphasis in original; second emphasis added).

17. There is substantial room both to doubt that he did and to doubt that he was convicted for any such act. See Steven H. Shiffrin and Jesse H. Choper, *The First Amendment: Cases, Comments, Questions* (St. Paul, Minn.: West Publishing, 1991), 232.

18. *Id.* at 411.

19. I assume that the communication of an *attitude* is the communication of a *message.*

20. *Johnson,* 491 U.S. at 412. Getting to that stage was a touch more complicated in *Eichman.* Indeed, the legislation had been crafted with the hope that it might appear to be unconcerned with the content of any message. The Flag Protection Act of 1989 provided that whoever "knowingly mutilates, defaces, physically defiles, burns, maintains on the floor or ground, or tramples upon any flag of the United States shall be" fined or imprisoned. 18 U.S.C.A. §700 (a)(1) (Supp. 1990). Notice that the act prohibited the burning of a flag whether or not the actor intended to communicate anything by doing so and whether or not one or more persons were offended or were likely to be offended by the burning.

Thus, in defending the statute, the government maintained that its interest was in " 'protect[ing] the physical integrity of the flag under all circumstances' in order to safeguard the flag's identity 'as the unique and unalloyed symbol of the nation.' " *Eichman,* 496 U.S. at 315, quoting Brief for United States 28, 29. So, if a tired person burned a flag to light a campfire without any intent to communicate a message, and even without an audience to witness the destruction, the statute would apply. Kent Greenawalt, "O'er the Land of the Free: Flag Burning as Speech," 37 *UCLA L. Rev.* 925, 932 (1990).

But from the Court's perspective in *Eichman,* this counted against the statute, not for it. As Justice Brennan stated: "[T]he mere destruction or disfigurement of a particular physical manifestation of the symbol, without more, does not diminish or otherwise affect the symbol itself in any way. For example, the secret destruction of a flag in one's own basement would not threaten the flag's recognized meaning. Rather, the Government's desire to preserve the flag as a symbol for certain national ideals is 'implicated only when a person's treatment of the flag communicates [a] message' to others that is inconsistent with those ideals." *Eichman,* 496 U.S. at 316. Thus, Justice Brennan was back to asserting that "exacting scrutiny" was called for.

21. 413 U.S. 49 (1973).

22. *Id.* at 60–61 (emphasis added).

23. *Id.* at 59, quoting Alexander Bickel, 22 *The Public Interest* 25–26 (Winter 1971).

24. Geoffrey R. Stone, "Content Regulation and the First Amendment," 25 *Wm. & Mary L. Rev.* 189 (1983).

25. To take just one example, the advocacy of illegal action is restricted in certain circumstances not because it has little value but because its value is outweighed by the harm it is feared might be caused in those circumstances. See generally Steven H. Shiffrin, *The First Amendment, Democracy, and Romance*, (Cambridge, Mass.: Harvard University Press, 1990), 35–44.

26. Subliminal speech might be considered of low value because of its insidious method of persuasion.

27. As a decision-making methodology this problem is importantly mitigated if the question of content neutrality is looked at from the perspective of the speaker and the audience. See Susan H. Williams, "Content Discrimination and the First Amendment," 139 *U. Pa. L. Rev.* 615 (1991). Our methodology for decision making, however, will ordinarily range beyond the metaphors that capture our strongest sense of First Amendment meaning.

28. See Frank I. Michelman, "Saving Old Glory: On Constitutional Iconography," 42 *Stan. L. Rev.* 1337, 1348 (1990).

29. *Id.* See also Harry Kalven, Jr., *A Worthy Tradition* (New York: Harper and Row, 1988) 63: "A society may or may not treat obscenity or contempt by publication as legal offenses without altering its basic nature. If, however, it makes seditious libel an offense, it is not a free society, no matter what its other characteristics."

30. Vincent Blasi's brilliant article on the checking value combines a politicially centered conception of the First Amendment, particularly of the press clause, with a variation of the dissent model. See Vincent A. Blasi, "The Checking Value and First Amendment Theory," 1977 *Am. B. Found. Res. J.* 521.

31. Notice that the politically centered conceptions of speech ordinarily offered are focused on democracy and government. The feminist conception of the political, as I understand it, focuses on power. That starting point has more in common with a dissent model. I return to a critique of the standard politically centered conception of the First Amendment in the next chapter.

32. House Committee on the Judiciary, *Statutory and Constitutional Responses to the Supreme Court Decision in Texas v. Johnson: Hearings Before the Subcommittee on Civil and Constitutional Rights of the House Committee on the Judiciary,* 101st Cong., 1st sess., 225, 231–32 (1989).

33. Fried, of course, is a strange bedfellow for a progressive.

34. See, e.g., Senate Committee on the Judiciary, *Measures to Protect the Physical Integrity of the American Flag: Hearings Before the Senate Committee on the Judiciary,* 101st Cong., 1st sess., 100 (1989) (testimony of Robert H. Bork).

35. Michelman, *supra* note 28, at 1359.

36. *Id.* at 1339.

37. *Id.* at 1340.

38. *Id.*

39. *Id.* at 1343.

40. *Id.* at 1357, quoting House Committee, *Measures to Protect the Physical Integrity of the American Flag: Hearings Before the Senate Committee on the Judiciary*, 101st Cong., 1st sess., 553 (1989) (testimony of Walter Dellinger).

41. *Id.* at 1358–59.

42. *Id.* at 1357.

43. *Id.* at 1358.

44. *Id.* at 1357.

45. *Id.* at 1354.

46. *Id.* at 1361, quoting Dellinger, *supra* note 40, at 557.

47. *Id.* at 1362.

48. *Id.*

49. *Id.*

50. Of course, a flag burner might not believe that the country has ideals to betray. The flag burner might affirmatively hate the political community. A dissent model would protect the speech. Michelman's formulation suggests that a communitarian model might not. Of course, a communitarian might be reluctant to formulate a standard requiring ad hoc exploration of the speaker's stance toward the political community. This same division in philosophy (if not the result) between the dissent model and the communitarian model suggested by Michelman's brief remarks also has implications for the contexts in which speakers advocate overthrow of the government.

51. Michelman, *supra* note 28, at 1362–63.

52. Perhaps not for some radicals, however.

53. See Michelman, *supra* note 28, at 1364, citing Hanna Fenichel Pitkin, "The Idea of the Constitution," 37 *J. Legal Ed.* 167, 168 (1987); Charles R. Lawrence, "Promises to Keep: We Are the Constitution's Framers," 30 *How. L.J.* 937, 942–43 (1987).

54. See Michelman, *supra* note 28, at 1358–59. Cf. Bruce A. Ackerman, *We the People: Foundations* (Cambridge, Mass.: Belknap Press of Harvard University Press, 1991), 16, 320–21 ("would be a good idea to entrench the Bill of Rights against subsequent revision by some future American majority") with Mary E. Becker, "The Politics of Women's Wrongs and the Bill of 'Rights': A Bicentennial Perspective," 59 *U. Chi. L. Rev.* 453 (1992) (suggesting that changes to the Bill of Rights could make it more "responsive to the needs of women and other outsider groups and should produce a more democratic structure").

55. Michelman, *supra* note 28, at 1359.

56. Frank I. Michelman, "Law's Republic," 97 *Yale L.J.* 1493 (1988).

57. Michelman, *supra* note 28, at 1359.

58. See generally Shiffrin, *supra* note 25.

59. See Yale Kamisar, "Keeping Up with the Gregory Johnsons," *Baltimore Sun*, July 22, 1989, at 9A.

60. But see Donald W. Hawthorne, "Subversive Subsidization: How NEA Art Funding Abridges Private Speech," 40 *Kansas L. Rev.* 437 (1992) (NEA plays a pervasive role in the art world, and its intervention dries up or controls sources of private support).

61. Owen M. Fiss, *The Irony of Free Speech* (Cambridge, Mass.: Harvard University Press, 1966), 41.

62. *Id.* at 42.

63. *Id.* at 44.

64. *Id.*

65. *Id.* Fiss would count it against an unorthodox project if it has a silencing potential against the unorthodox. On this criterion he would favor gay projects over Nazi projects. *Id.* at 45.

66. *Id.* at 38.

67. I return to this issue in chapter four.

68. *Id.* at 38.

69. Robert C. Post, "Between Governance and Management: The History and Theory of the Public Forum," 34 *UCLA L. Rev.* 1713, 1767–74 (1987).

70. *Id.* at 25–26.

71. Robert C. Post, "Subsidized Speech," 106 *Yale L.J.* 151, 176–93 (1996).

72. For our purposes, it is unnecessary to determine whether a free speech interest is balanced away by the superior government interest in achieving its goals within the bureaucracy (my view) or whether no free speech issue is present in the first place.

73. *Id.* at 172–74.

74. 500 U.S. 173 (1991).

75. I do not maintain that Post does that. He maintains that professors acquiesce in the "instrumental logic of education" (Post, *supra* note 71 at 170), though this need not commit him to the view that professors are bureaucrats in every respect. He has also suggested that the ends of education may be open to First Amendment challenge, though he has not taken a final position.

76. My position does not assume that professional standards are invariably worth deference. Often they are the self-serving prescriptions of a monopoly. Moreover, I do not pretend that the case law endorses my position.

77. Doctors should have standing to raise the rights of patients. Absent a right to abortion, however, patients' rights could be satisfied by informing them that the clinic does not advise about abortions.

78. I discuss limits on the discretion of broadcasters in chapter four. At the time of this writing, the Supreme Court is scheduled to hear oral arguments on March 31, 1998, in the case of *National Endowment for the Arts v. Finley,* a case that could reach the issues discussed in the text. If the Court reaches these issues, I have great confidence that they will be wrongly decided, and I regret that I will not be able to take potshots at the case in this book.

79. Post would agree that government ought not to be able to use subsidies to dominate public discourse, but he apparently would make ad hoc decisions whether general subsidy programs did that. I believe it is better to have a clearer line.

80. The situation should get worse before it gets better—if it ever does. Consider: "What we have seen in the last several years is the virtual takeover of art by big corporate interests. . . . Corporations have become the major patrons of art in every respect." David Harvey, *The Condition of Postmodernity: An Enquiry into the Conditions of Cultural Change* (Cambridge, Mass.: Basil Blackwell, 1989), 62, quoting Crimp, "Art in the 1980's: The Myth of Autonomy," 6 *PRECIS* 83, 85 (1987).

81. See, e.g., James Davison Hunter, *Culture Wars: The Struggle to Define America* (New York: Basic Books, 1991), 237.

82. See *id.* at 238–39.

83. John Stuart Mill, *On Liberty*, ed. David Spitz (New York: Norton, 1975), 6.

84. Many liberals would protect dissent but would not necessarily seek to promote it. I return to this point in chapter four.

85. Clearly, many liberals have fought courageously against tyranny in other countries and, for example, many ACLU liberals have been courageous in this country.

86. Liberals in dictatorships either stick with their principles and exalt freedom over community—at the risk of their lives—or adjust to the existing community and attempt to compromise from within. My claims, therefore, do not apply to all liberals, nor do they make claims about what those who compromise in this context might do in a different context.

87. For an insightful development of this point, see Charles Taylor, "Cross-Purposes: The Liberal Communitarian Debate," in *Liberalism and the Moral Life*, ed. Nancy L. Rosenblum (Cambridge, Mass.: Harvard University Press, 1989), 174–75.

88. Henry Louis Gates, Jr., "Patriotism," *The Nation*, July 15/22, 1991, 91.

89. See generally Bernard Yack, "Nationalism and Individualism: Odd or Happy Couple?" (paper delivered at the annual meeting of the American Political Science Association, September 1992).

90. See Taylor, *supra* note 87, at 280–81.

91. Many radicals have championed this view as well.

92. The need to operate within such frames exposes social movement organizations to the threat that they will be "outbid" by more radical groups. See Sidney G. Tarrow, "Mentalities, Political Cultures, and Collective Action Frames," in *Frontiers in Social Movement Theory*, ed. Aldon D. Morris and Carol McLurg Mueller (New Haven, Conn.: Yale University Press, 1992), 174, 190, 196.

93. In addition, to succeed in opposing a particular practice frequently takes the energy out of a broader movement. See, e.g., Kimberle Crenshaw, "Race, Reform, and Retrenchment: Transformation and Legitimation in Antidiscrimination Law," 101 *Harv. L. Rev.* 1331, 1385 (1988): "As long as race consciousness thrives, Blacks will often have to rely on rights rhetoric when it is necessary to protect Black interests. The very reforms brought about by appeals to legal ideology, however, seem to undermine the ability to move forward toward a broader vision of racial equality. In the quest for racial justice, winning and losing have been part of the same experience." James MacGregor Burns and Stewart Burns argue that this phenomenon is generally true in rights movements. See generally *A People's Charter: The Pursuit of Rights in America* (New York: Knopf, 1991).

94. Substantial evidence supports the view that some such framing is a necessary but not sufficient feature of successful social movements in the United States. See, e.g., Tarrow, *supra* note 92 (suggesting, among other things, that McCarthyism and other political activity has largely destroyed oppositional subcultures as an effective force in the United States, while resort to oppositional subcultures is a livelier option in many European countries). For the suggestion that the use

of the metaphor of America has served to co-opt oppositional forces, see Myra Jehlen, "The Novel and the American Middle Class," in *Ideology and Classic American Literature*, ed. Sacvan Bercovitch and Myra Jehlen (Cambridge: Cambridge University Press, 1986), 127–28.

95. See, e.g., Bercovitch, "Afterword," in *Ideology and Classic American Literature, supra* note 94, at 434 (emphasis in original): "Having adopted their country's *controlling* metaphor—'America' as synonym for human possibility—and having made this the ground of radical dissent, they effectively redefine radicalism as an affirmation of cultural values."

96. See, e.g., *Perry Educ. Ass'n v. Perry Local Educators' Ass'n*, 460 U.S. 37 (1983) (Court adopts set of rules making it extremely difficult for dissenters to gain access to property controlled by government except for streets and parks); *Clark v. Community for Creative Non-Violence*, 468 U.S. 288 (1984) (demonstration in Lafayette Park and the Mall concerning homelessness stifled by Park Service's time, place, and manner regulations); *Hudgens v. NLRB*, 424 U.S. 507 (1976) (dissenters have no constitutional right of access to shopping centers). I return to this problem and to the problems discussed in the next paragraph in chapter four.

97. See, e.g., James Boyle, "Is Subjectivity Possible: The Postmodern Subject in Legal Theory," 62 *U. Colo. L. Rev.* 489 (1991).

98. As Kobena Mercer puts it in a related context, "no one has a monopoly on oppositional identity." " '1968': Periodizing Politics and Identity," in *Cultural Studies*, ed. Lawrence Grossberg, Cary Nelson, and Paula A. Treichler (New York: Routledge, 1992), 424, 426.

99. I believe, however, that truth is vastly overrated as a political weapon. See Jane Flax, "The End of Innocence," in *Feminists Theorize the Political*, ed. Judith Butler and Joan Wallach Scott (New York: Routledge, 1992), 445, 448 (articulate and appreciative discussion of postmodernism as a political strategy).

100. Indeed, in some respects the strategy is counterproductive. Postmodernism in many of its forms tends to form an alliance with the crassest forms of commercialism. See Harvey, *supra* note , at 59–65; Frederic Jameson, "Postmodernism and Consumer Society," in *Postmodernism and Its Discontents: Theories, Practices*, ed. E. Ann Kaplan (London: Verso, 1988). By making "truth" an enemy rather than an ally, many postmoderns have no ground for criticizing the status quo and foreclose possibilities for a constructive politics. See generally David McGowan, *Postmodernism and Its Critics* (Ithaca, N.Y.: Cornell University Press, 1991).

101. At the same time, however, those who adhere to a postmodern perspective have produced much significant political commentary, and the postmodern perspective may have been vital in producing that commentary. Moreover, many of the same writers are political activists. Ironically, grassroots political culture frequently induces postmodernists to use the language of the culture, and that language assumes the existence of truth, morals, and, to a lesser extent, rights. Indeed, many postmodernists engage in a form of "strategic essentialism." See generally Gayatri Chavkravorty Spivak, *In Other Worlds: Essays in Cultural Politics* (New York: Routledge, 1988), 197–221, in which rights and humanism are denied in theory but adopted in practice. This move is sometimes described as the

"double gesture." Amanda Anderson, "Cryptonormativism and Double Gestures: The Politics of Post-Structuralism" 21 *Cultural Critique* 63, 65 (1992) (criticizing the practice and turning to a revision of Habermas' as a way out of the problems posed by poststructuralism).

William E. Connolly uses different terminology in his brilliant book *Identity/ Difference: Democratic Negotiations of Political Paradox* (Ithaca, N.Y.: Cornell University Press, 1991, 60: "While modernists univocally apply the code of interrogation and coherence to discourse on the implicit faith that only this code can save us, the postmodernist thinks within the code of paradox, because only attentiveness to ambiguity can loosen the hold monotonic standards of identity have over life in the late-modern age." But Connolly is careful to observe that *the postmodernists do not and cannot avoid the code of coherence.* That is why self-irony permeates much postmodern discourse.

102. Linda J. Nicholson, "Introduction" in *Feminism/Postmodernism*, ed. Linda J. Nicholson (New York: Routledge, 1990), 1, 11.

103. Harvey, *supra* note , at 117. On the other hand, postmodernists come in many varieties. See Judith Butler, "Contingent Foundations: Feminism and the Question of 'Postmodernism,' " in *Feminists Theorize the Political, supra* note 99; Jennifer Wicke, "Postmodern Identity and the Legal Subject," 62 *U. Colo. L. Rev.* 455, 456–57 (1991). Although others read him differently, I think the kind of analysis Harvey would press for is not inconsistent with Foucault's recommendations for studying power. See Michel Foucault, *The History of Sexuality: Volume I* (New York: Pantheon, 1978), ch. 5. Nonetheless, the emphasis on starting with the local is there, and, as Anthony E. Cook observes, that followers of Foucault emphasize thick descriptions of power relations in local situations frequently leads to an insularity that discourages more general theory. See Anthony E. Cook, "Reflections on Postmodernism," 26 *New Eng. L. Rev.* 751, 759 (1992).

104. Although I believe that some rights are prepolitical, I do not deny that my belief has been socially constructed. I mean that those rights do not depend on political arrangements.

105. I leave to the side whether torture can be justified in some rare and usually quite hypothetical circumstances.

106. Postmodernists can and do divide over this issue. The question of whether rights exist in an abstract way is separate from the question of whether it is strategically desirable to invoke the language of rights discourse. See *supra* note 101.

107. See, e.g., Patricia J. Williams, *The Alchemy of Race and Rights* (Cambridge, Mass.: Harvard University Press, 1991), 148–61; Crenshaw, *supra* note 93.

108. See, e.g., James T. Kloppenberg, *Uncertain Victory: Social Democracy and Progressivism in European and American Thought, 1870–1920* (New York: Oxford University Press, 1986).

109. Burns and Burns, *supra* note 93, at 12–13.

110. See, e.g., Mark Tushnet, "An Essay on Rights" 62 *Tex. L. Rev.* 1363 (1984).

111. See, e.g., Crenshaw, *supra* note 93.

112. I return to this issue in chapter five.

113. See generally Mary Ann Glendon, *Rights Talk: The Impoverishment of Political Discourse* (New York: Free Press, 1991), ch. 2.

114. Connolly, *supra* note 101, at 61.

115. Shiffrin, *supra* note 25, at 128; Lee C. Bollinger, *The Tolerant Society: Freedom of Speech and Extremist Speech in America* (New York: Oxford University Press, 1986), ch. 3.

116. Flax, *supra* note 99, at 447.

117. Cornel West, "The Postmodern Crisis of Black Intellectuals," in *Cultural Studies, supra* note 98, at 699.

118. See, e.g., Catharine MacKinnon, *Feminism Unmodified: Discourses on Life and Law* (Cambridge, Mass.: Harvard University Press, 1987), 164.

Chapter II
Cigarettes, Alcohol, and Advertising

1. Nonetheless, the book is too windy for my tastes. Although I do not recommend it, students of American literature have found much to praise. See, e.g., Wayne Franklin, *The New World of James Fenimore Cooper* (Chicago: University of Chicago Press, 1982), 75–118; Geoffrey Rans, *Cooper's Leather-Stocking Novels: A Secular Reading* (Chapel Hill: University of North Carolina Press, 1991), 46–101.

2. James Fenimore Cooper, *The Pioneers* (New York: Bantam, 1993), 223 (first emphasis in original; second emphasis added).

3. See generally *Tobacco Issues (Part 2): Hearings Before the Senate Subcommittee on Transportation and Hazardous Materials of the Committee on Energy and Commerce, House of Representatives*, 101st Cong., 1st and 2d sess., 1–172 (1989–1990).

4. The chief stumbling block for the commercial speech advocates was *Posadas de Puerto Rico Associates v. Tourism Co.*, 478 U.S. 328 (1986). *Posadas* upheld a body of regulations that prohibited advertising of casino gambling to Puerto Rican residents while permitting such advertising to tourists. Thus, advertisements were permitted in the *New York Times* but prohibited in the *San Juan Star*. If it is constitutional to outlaw casino gambling advertising in this somewhat bizarre way, it was hard to argue persuasively that advertisements for tobacco and alcoholic beverage advertising could not be outlawed as well.

5. 116 Sup. Ct. 1495 (1996).

6. Among other things, the Court rejected the deferential mode of analysis employed in *Posadas*, discussed *supra* note 4, although it did not decide whether the result in *Posadas* was justifiable.

7. See, e.g., Richard Blatt, "A Look at . . . Selling Tobacco," *Washington Post*, September 8, 1996, CO3; Bruce Fein, "Trip Wire for Anti-tobacco Forces," *Washington Times*, May 21, 1996, at A12; Linda Greenhouse, "High Court Says Liquor Ads Can't Be Banned," *New York Times*, May 14, 1996, at A1, col. 6; Jane Kirtley, "Letting People Decide for Themselves," *American Journalism Review* 54 (July/August 1996); Martin H. Redish, "Tobacco Advertising and the First Amendment," 81 *Ia. L. Rev.* 589, 617 n.139 (1996); David Savage, "High Court Calls Ads Protected Free Speech," *The Record*, May 14, 1996; Ira Teinowitz, "Supreme Court Ruling Bolsters Advertiser Rights," *Advertising Age*, May 20, 1996, at 3; Kathleen M. Sullivan, "Muzzle Joe Camel? It May Be Illegal," *News-*

day, Nassau ed., May 30, 1996, at A51; Jerome Wilson, "A Toast to Commercial Speech," *Legal Times*, July 29, 1996, at S39.

8. The most prominent of these efforts is the initiative of the Food and Drug Administration. See *Regulations Restricting the Sale and Distribution of Cigarettes and Smokeless Tobacco to Protect Children and Adolescents,* 61 Fed. Reg. 44,396 (Aug. 28, 1996).

9. See *infra* note 30.

10. 425 U.S. 748 (1976).

11. 447 U.S. 557 (1980).

12. *Id.* at 566.

13. *Liquormart,* 116 Sup. Ct. at 1515. He argued that the Court should look to the traditions of the country regarding advertising (particularly after the adoption of the fourteenth amendment) to determine whether it merited coverage. *Id.* In the end he did not reach the issue because it was not briefed. *Id.* As Vincent Blasi, "The Pathological Perspective and the First Amendment," 85 *Colum. L. Rev.* 449, 485 (1985) has observed: "There is a strong tradition of government regulation of advertising and, in the federal government and most states, an administrative regulatory apparatus in place. These considerations suggest that no first amendment doctrine protecting commercial speech could be either uncomplicated or historically grounded."

14. *Rubin v. Coors Brewing Co.,* 115 Sup. Ct. 1585 (1995) dispatched two other arguments for rejecting the applicability of *Central Hudson.* It refused to accept the argument that the "greater" governmental power to regulate the possession and sale of alcoholic beverages included the "lesser" power to regulate advertising of alcoholic beverages. It also rejected the argument that *Central Hudson* did not apply to advertising of products that could be labeled vices. For criticism of the vices argument, see Philip B. Kurland, "Posadas de Puerto Rico v. Tourism Company," 1986 *Sup. Ct. Rev.* 1, 15.

15. Justice Stevens argued that there is little basis for distinguishing between commercial speech and noncommercial speech when the state seeks to ban the dissemination of truthful, nonmisleading commercial messages (not involving aggressive sales practices). *Id.* at 1506. He maintained that in such cases there is "far less basis to depart from the rigorous review that the First Amendment generally demands" (*id.*), and he suggested that such bans "usually rest solely on the offensive assumption that the public will respond 'irrationally' to the truth." Thus, from Justice Stevens's perspective, the commercial speech doctrine does not apply when total bans are being considered, and he believes that such bans usually rest on illegitimate assumptions. For even broader perspectives, see Kathleen M. Sullivan, "Cheap Spirits, Cigarettes, and Free Speech: The Implications of Liquormart," 1996 *Sup. Ct. Rev.* 123; Howard K. Jeruchimowitz, "Tobacco Advertisements and Commercial Speech Balancing," 82 *Cornell L. Rev.* 432, 473 (1997); "Leading Cases," 110 *Harv. L. Rev.* 135, 216, 223–26 (1996).

16. *Liquormart,* 116 Sup. Ct. at 1507.

17. No difference in the Supreme Court, that is. The lower courts would have to decide who had won the wrestling match. As will become clear, the right answer might be neither.

18. This is a charitable description of the status quo. In fact, the status quo has teetered between wildly divergent degrees of scrutiny, all parading under the name of *Central Hudson*. Cf. cases cited in notes 4 *supra* and 22 *infra*. *Liquormart* is distinctive in that four justices maintain that certain bans of commercial speech should be treated as if they were bans of noncommercial speech. In addition to Justice Thomas's opinion, see *supra* note 15.

19. In particular, Justice Souter signed a portion of Justice Stevens's opinion that summarized *Central Hudson* as requiring "special care" in the review of blanket bans of commercial speech, together with the observation that blanket bans on commercial speech had not been met in the absence of deceptive speech or speech that was related to unlawful activity. *Liquormart*, 116 Sup. Ct. at 1506. Moreover, he signed a section of his opinion that reviewed Rhode Island's price advertising ban with considerable rigor. *Id.* at 1508–10.

20. But see Felix H. Kent, "A Significant First Amendment Decision," *N.Y.L.J.* 3 (July 21, 1996) (leaving Souter off the list of those who have called for "special care" or strict scrutiny without discussion, however, of Justice Souter's peculiar approach to the case). *Accord,* Sullivan, *supra* note 15.

21. In reading the tea leaves, something might be made of his unwillingness to sign a portion of Justice Stevens's opinion finding little basis for distinguishing commercial speech from noncommercial speech cases when a total ban is at issue. *Liquormart*, 116 Sup. Ct. at 1506–8. For discussion of that portion of the opinion, see *supra* note 15. See also Justice Souter's dissenting opinion in *Glickman v. Wileman Brothers & Elliot, Inc.*, 117 Sup. Ct. 2130, 2149 n.6 (1997) (referring to the commercial speech test as requiring less than strict scrutiny).

22. Cf., e.g., *Florida Bar v. Went for It, Inc.*, (1995; O'Connor, J.) with *City of Cincinnati v. Discovery Network*, 113 S.Ct. 1505 (1993; Stevens, J.).

23. 509 U.S. 418 (1993).

24. Indeed, North Carolina prohibited the advertising of lotteries "whether within or without" the state. Criminal Law, ch. 14, xi, art. 37, section 14–289. That provision was not before the Court.

25. *Id.* at 434.

26. *Id.* at 429, citing *Board of Trustees of State Univ. of New York v. Fox*, 492 U.S. 469 (1989). The Court stated that the federal interest was accommodating the divergent policies of North Carolina and Virginia, but this phrasing of the interest does not circumvent the paternalism problem. However phrased, the federal government is assisting North Carolina in its desire to keep its citizens from being encouraged to gamble.

27. As discussed previously, the justices are Rehnquist, C.J., together with Kennedy, O'Connor, Souter, Scalia, and Thomas, JJ. Although they did not sign the same sections of Justice White's opinion, the sections they did sign are inconsistent with the rhetoric of *Liquormart*. Justice Thomas acknowledged that the "outcome in *Edge* may well be in conflict with the principles . . . ratified by me today" (*Liquormart,* 116 Sup. Ct. at 1495 n.7). Justices Breyer and Ginsburg were not on the Court when *Edge* was decided. Justice Stevens's dissent was joined by Justice Blackmun (509 U.S. at 436).

28. "In *Edge* . . . [t]he statute was designed to regulate advertising about an activity that had been deemed illegal in the jurisdiction in which the broadcaster

was located" (*Liquormart,* 116 Sup. Ct. at 1510). In support of this claim, Justice Stevens cites to pages that refer to North Carolina's policy against gambling. Nothing in those pages claims that North Carolina had tried to prohibit its residents from gambling in other states. See *Edge Broadcasting,* 509 U.S. at 433–35.

29. *Edge Broadcasting,* 509 U.S. at 437 n.1.

30. The holdings in *Liquormart* and *Edge* are not inconsistent. The regulation in *Liquormart* was a clumsy attempt to regulate prices. If the goal were to regulate prices, the solution might be to regulate prices, not advertising of prices. The alternative in *Edge,* however, would have been to outlaw all lotteries, including state-run lotteries. But this alternative would deprive states of a significant source of revenue at a time of high needs and limited resources. It would be easy to conclude, therefore, that the available alternative in *Edge* was unacceptable, but the available alternative in *Liquormart* was acceptable. In this connection, it is sometimes argued that a ban on advertising of alcoholic beverages or tobacco would only make sense if the sale, distribution, and/or consumption of the product were made illegal. The argument assumes, however, that prohibitions of sales, distribution, and/or consumption are practical policies. But this assumption is dubious. The nation's experience with Prohibition and the resultant crime and black markets was less than happy. See also *infra* note 41.

31. As Richard Moon observes, "The only example ever given of an informational ad [involving tobacco] is one that informs smokers about the tar levels of particular cigarette brands. But as many have pointed out, this sort of advertisement could be seen as deceptive inasmuch as it suggests that smoking lower tar cigarettes is not unhealthy." Richard Moon, "RJR-McDonald v. Canada on the Freedom to Advertise," 7 *Constitutional Forum* 1, 3 (1995).

32. Although the Canadian Supreme Court struck down a ban on advertising of cigarettes by a 5 to 4 vote, two members of the majority, Lamer, C.J.C., and Iacobucci, J., would uphold a ban of "life style" advertising or of advertising directed at adolescents. *R. J. R. MacDonald Inc. v. Attorney General* [1995] 100 C.C.C. 3d 449. For commentary, suggesting that the former type of advertising should not be protected, see Daniel Hays Lowenstein, " 'Too Much Puff': Persuasion, Paternalism, and Commercial Speech," 56 *U. Cin. L. Rev.* 1205 (1988) (non-informational tobacco advertising should not be protected); R. Moon, "Lifestyle Advertising and Freedom of Expression Doctrine," 36 *McGill L. Rev.* 76 (1991) (lifestyle advertising should not be protected). See also Moon, *supra* note 31 (informational advertising for tobacco should not be protected). But cf. Sylvia Law, "Addiction, Autonomy, and Advertising," 77 *Iowa L. Rev.* 909 (1992) (tobacco advertising should not be protected because of the addictive qualities of tobacco, not because such advertising bypasses rational thinking processes). For a defense of image advertising, see Rodney A. Smolla, "Information, Imagery, and the First Amendment: A Case for Expansive Protection of Commercial Speech," 71 *Texas L. Rev.* 777 (1993).

33. With respect to tobacco advertising and alcoholic beverage advertising, the products cannot legally be sold to minors; therefore, advertising directed at minors fails the first prong of the *Central Hudson* test: "At the outset, we must determine whether the expression is protected by the First Amendment. For com-

mercial speech to come within that provision, it at least must concern lawful activity" (447 U.S. at 566). In addition, although many justices are concerned about
state paternalism regarding adults, paternalism regarding children is far less suspect. It would be ironic if the state could protect children from vulgar language
(see, e.g., *Bethel School Dist. No. 403 v. Frazier,* 478 U.S. 675 (1986); *F.C.C. v.
Pacifica Foundation,* 438 U.S. 726 (1978)) but could not protect them from messages that encourage the consumption of harmful products. For powerful arguments in support of the constitutionality of efforts to protect children and adolescents from tobacco advertisers, see the case put forward by the Food and Drug
Administration, *supra* note 8.

34. 425 U.S. at 766–70.

35. *Id.* at 770.

36. *Id.*

37. Some might argue that commercial speech received protection for the first
time in *Bigelow v. Virginia,* 421 U.S. 809 (1975). See, e.g., *Liquormart,* 116 Sup.
Ct. at 1504. Even if true, it would be the case that the First Amendment made
this decision for us rather late in the day. *Bigelow* dealt with advertising for abortions, a constitutionally protected activity. It would be difficult to support the
view that the choice to have an abortion was constitutionally protected, but that
the state could prevent people from learning about them. But cf. Rust v. Sullivan,
500 U.S. 173 (1991) (limitation on persons acting in federal programs providing
preconceptional services that they ordinarily may not even advise of the abortion
option does not violate the First Amendment). The *Bigelow* Court recognized the
narrow character of its holding: "We need not decide . . . the precise extent to
which the First Amendment permits regulation of advertising that is related to
activities the State may legitimately regulate or even prohibit" (421 U.S. at 825).

38. For complaints about governmental paternalism regarding misleading advertising, see Sullivan, *supra* note 15, at 152–56.

39. See Larry Alexander, "Speech in the Local Marketplace," 14 *San Diego L.
Rev.* 357, 376 (1977) (asking why government can "be paternalistic regarding the
purchase of goods but may not be paternalistic regarding information about those
goods").

40. Cf. Vincent Blasi, "The Pathological Perspective and the First Amendment," 85 *Colum. L. Rev.* 449, 487 (1985) (case to stop promotional advertising
for electricity not paternalistic in the same sense as that in drug advertising; assumption is, however, that consumers will not act as "public-spirited citizens").

41. *Liquormart,* 116 Sup. Ct. at 1510. Martin Redish, *supra* note 7, at 604–5
(1996) (emphasis added) suggests that it is a part of democratic theory that "individual citizens can be trusted to make *legally valid* life-affecting choices on the
basis of an open marketplace of ideas of information and opinion." This argument
would seem to prove too much. If democratic theory assumes citizens can be
trusted to make such choices in an open marketplace, one would imagine government would be foreclosed not only from fixing prices to discourage consumption
but also from regulating false and misleading advertising. In addition, it would
be unclear why government should be permitted to make products illegal for paternalistic reasons—if citizens can truly be trusted. Assuming it were consistent

with this version of democratic theory for government to ban products, it would be unclear why its paternalism could not extend to product advertising of legal products. It would not do, for example, to claim that products not made illegal have been certified as safe. To outlaw cigarettes, for example, might create black markets and enormous attendant enforcement problems. The failure to outlaw cigarettes need not suggest that government thinks of them as any less of a public health problem than numerous other drugs that are currently outlawed. Whether individual citizens can be "trusted" seems to bear no relationship to the legal status of the product. In addition, one could argue that the notion of democracy makes no claims about the quality of *individual* decision making but makes some relative claims about the quality of *public* decision making.

42. It does not always trouble the Court. See *Ohralik v. Ohio State Bar Ass'n,* 436 U.S. 447 (1978) (upholding ban on in-person solicitation by lawyers in part on paternalistic). Redish, *supra* note 7, at 601, however, suggests that a ban on tobacco advertising, unlike regulations of conduct, involves mind control, and that control offends First Amendment values. There is something to this objection after it is stripped of its overblown rhetoric. First, if a ban on cigarette advertising really represented a form of mind *control*, it would be so effective that everyone would stop smoking. A ban on cigarette advertising, however, would simply prevent cigarette companies from encouraging the use of their product. Any "control" is indirect. Contrast the addictive impact of nicotine. One could argue that the objective of tobacco companies is a form of mind control. In this connection, see generally, Law, *supra* note 32, and Lowenstein, *supra* note 32, at 1211–13. To be sure, there is First Amendment value in people making their own decisions on the basis of all the available information, and a ban on tobacco advertising would compromise that. First, however, one might ask how serious the compromise might be. To what extent is the "information" in tobacco advertising important to a reasonable decision? Is the loss in information worth the public health gain? To put it another way, must the country continue to tolerate needless death and suffering for First Amendment benefits that can be grandly phrased but deliver little in the concrete? As Lowenstein, *supra* note 32, at 1222–23, explains, the rhetoric of the tobacco industry:

> is utterly detached from the reality of cigarette advertising. It is not the government that will be manipulating consumers if it bans cigarette advertising. The manipulation occurs on the part of those who create and disseminate these advertisements, with their illusory associations of cigarette smoking with vigorous activity, sexiness, sociability, chicness, good health, and other desirable attributes. It is not the supporters of the ban who treat consumers like "rats in a laboratory maze," but the advertisers, whose messages make no pretense of appealing to rational deliberation and whose messages are imbued with the most manipulative techniques contemporary social science makes possible. The "flow of information" is now largely controlled through the cigarette industry, overtly through its purchase each year of $2 billion worth of . . . messages, but also . . . through "covert manipulation," by using its very considerable economic leverage to suppress the publication of genuinely informative discussion of the consequences of smoking. To ban cigarette advertising is not to control information on this critical issue in a manipulative manner but to prevent the tobacco industry, understandably motivated by enormous profits rather

than by concern for truth or the public welfare, from obstructing the flow of information and replacing it with noninformational manipulative messages, with disastrous consequences for the public.

43. 425 U.S. at 762.

44. *Id.* at 763. But cf. William Van Alstyne, "Remembering Melville Nimmer: Some Cautionary Notes on Commercial Speech," 43 *UCLA L. Rev.* 1635, 1657 n.10 (1996): "After all, as the National Enquirer likes to observe, 'Inquiring Minds Want to Know.' They 'want to know' about the kind of creme rinse Cyndi Lauper uses as much as, perhaps even more than, they want to know whether the CIA may have helped bring down the government in South Vietnam."

45. *Ohralik v. Ohio State Bar Ass'n,* 436 U.S. 447, 456 (1978).

46. *Id.*

47. See, e.g., *McIntyre v. Ohio Election Comm'n,* 115 Sup. Ct. 1511, 1518–19 (1995); *Boos v. Barry,* 485 U.S. 312, 318 (1988); *Garrison v. Louisiana,* 379 U.S. 64, 74–75 (1964); *New York Times Co. v. Sullivan,* 376 U.S. 254, 270 (1964); *Winters v. New York,* 333 U.S. 507, 510 (1948).

48. 425 U.S. at 765.

49. See *supra* text accompanying note 48.

50. Democracy might well be improved, however, if its editorial page were to take a thirty-year vacation.

51. Alexander Meiklejohn, *Political Freedom* (New York: Harper, 1960), 20–27.

52. *Id.* at 79.

53. Alexander Meiklejohn, *The First Amendment Is an Absolute,* 1961 *Sup. Ct. Rev.* 245, 256.

54. Cass R. Sunstein, *Democracy and the Problem of Free Speech* (New York: Free Press, 1993). For stimulating criticism of Sunstein's general position, see J. M. Balkin, Book Review, "Populism and Progressivism as Constitutional Categories," 104 *Yale L.J.* 2313 (1995); Robert Justin Lipkin, "The Quest for the Common Good: Neutrality and Deliberative Democracy in Sunstein's Conception of American Constitutionalism," 26 *Conn. L. Rev.* 1039 (1994); William Marshall, Book Review, "Free Speech and the 'Problem' of Democracy," 89 *Nw. U.L. Rev.* 191 (1994).

55. *Id.* at 154–65.

56. *Id.* at 53–119.

57. *Id.* at 18–19. Although Sunstein refers to the need for government by the People, he, for the most part, does not engage in the kind of populist rhetoric that obscures the diversity of the views held by the citizenry. See James A. Morone, *The Democratic Wish: Popular Participation and the Limits of American Government* (New York: Basic Books, 1990) (" '[T]he people' is a reification, a powerful political fiction. . . . [A] less grandiose democratic conception might offer more real power to real people" [7]); Michael Kazin, *The Populist Persuasion: An American History* (New York: Basic Books, 1995) (not clear " 'the people' share anything beyond a geographic space" [282]). Many of Sunstein's proposals are designed to assure that diverse viewpoints get into the political process.

58. Sunstein, *supra,* note 54, at 53–92.

59. *Id.* at 130 (italics removed).

60. *Id.* at 20–22.

61. Joseph Schumpeter, *Capitalism, Socialism, and Democracy* (New York: Harper, 1942), 269. Schumpeter's thesis has been extraordinarily influential, though Samuel Huntington may overstate the case: "For some while after World War II a debate went on between those determined, in the classical vein to define democracy by source ['the will of the people'] or purpose [the 'common good'], and the growing number of theorists adhering to a procedural concept of democracy in the Schumpterian mode. By the 1970's the debate was over, and Schumpeter had won." Samuel P. Huntington, *The Third Wave: Democratization in the Late Twentieth Century* (Norman: University of Oklahoma Press, 1991), 5. Sunstein, however, is hardly alone among normative democratic theorists who either explicitly or implicitly reject Schumpeter's approach. See, e.g., William E. Connolly, ed., *The Bias of Pluralism* (New York: Atherton Press, 1969); Benjamin R. Barber, *Strong Democracy: Participatory Politics for a New Age* (Berkeley: University of California Press, 1984); Amy Gutmann and Dennis Thompson, *Democracy and Disagreement* (Cambridge, Mass.: Belknap Press, 1988); Carole Pateman, *Participation and Democratic Theory* (New York: Cambridge University Press, 1977); Michael Sandel, *Democracy's Discontent: America in Search of a Public Philosophy* (Cambridge, Mass.: Belknap Press of Harvard University Press, 1996); Michael Walzer, *Radical Principles: Reflections of an Unreconstructed Democrat* (New York: Basic Books, 1980).

62. From his perspective, the exceptions are quite limited. Schumpeter, *supra* note 61, at 280–83.

63. Sunstein, *supra,* note 54, at 22.

64. *Id.*

65. *Id.* at xvi.

66. Robert D. Putnam, "The Strange Disappearance of Civic America," *The American Prospect* 34 (Winter 1996).

67. Michael Schudson, "What If Civic Life Didn't Die?" *The American Prospect* 17 (March–April 1996).

68. Andrew Greeley, "The Other Civic America," *The American Prospect* 68 (May–June 1997). On the other hand, participation is particularly skewed toward the wealthy and the well educated in the United States. Sidney Verba, Kay Lehman Schlozman, and Henry E. Brady, *Voice and Equality: Civic Voluntarism in American Politics* (Cambridge, Mass.: Harvard University Press, 1995).

69. Debra C. Minkoff, "Civil Society and National Mobilization in the United States," 40 *American Behavioral Scientist* 606 (1997); Theda Skocpol, "Unravelling from Above," *The American Prospect* 20, 24 (March–April 1996).

70. Sidney Verba, Kay Lehman Schlozman, and Henry E. Brady, "The Big Tilt: Participatory Inequality in America," *The American Prospect*, May–June 1997 at 74.

71. Seymour Martin Lipset, "America Today: Malaise and Resiliency," *Current*, December 1, 1995, at 3.

72. Sheri Berman, "Civil Society and Political Institutionalization," 40 *American Behavioral Scientist* 562 (1997); Bob Edwards and Michael Foley, "Social

Capital and the Political Capital of Our Discontent," 40 *American Behavioral Scientist* 669 (1997).

73. See, e.g., Bruce A. Ackerman, *We the People* (Cambridge, Mass.: Belknap Press of Harvard University Press, 1991), 234–35, 241–42.

74. Sunstein, *supra* note 54, at 73, 89–91. To the extent one has a duty to devote deep attention to public affairs, on Sunstein's premises it becomes problematic for an individual to devote attention to research in medicine or to charitable work at the expense of public affairs. Some people who might otherwise be considered saints, therefore, might be considered shirkers under the public affairs obligations put forward by Professor Sunstein.

75. *Id.* at 89–91. Although he suggests citizens might change their viewing habits, Sunstein does not make grand claims in that regard or about the likelihood of citizens turning to the public sphere. There are many reasons why attention to the public sphere might be substantially less than in classical times. Consider Will Kymlicka and Wayne Norman, "Return of the Citizen: A Survey of Recent Work on Citizenship Theory," in *Theorizing Citizenship*, ed. Ronald Beiner (Albany: State University of New York Press, 1995), 294: "[I]t is more plausible to view our attachment to private life as a result not of the impoverishment of public life but of the enrichment of private life. We no longer seek gratification in politics because our personal and social life is so much richer than the Greeks'. There are many reasons for this historical change, including the rise of romantic love and the nuclear family (and its emphasis on intimacy and privacy), increased prosperity (and hence richer forms of leisure and consumption), the Christian commitment to the dignity of labor (which the Greeks despised) and the growing dislike for war (which the Greeks esteemed). Those passive citizens who prefer the joys of family and career to the duties of politics are not necessarily misguided."

See also M. B. E. Smith, "The Value of Participation," in 16 *Nomos*, ed. J. Roland Pennock and John W. Chapman (New York: Lieber-Atherton, 1975), 126–35 (questioning the value of participation); Ackerman, *supra* note 73, at 311–12. But see Arnold S. Kaufman, "Human Nature and Participatory Democracy," in *The Bias of Pluralism*, ed. William E. Connolly (New York: Atherton Press, 1969), 178 (political participation valuable for personal development); Adrian Oldfield, "Citizenship: An Unnatural Practice?" 61 *Political Quarterly* 177 (1990) (accord).

76. Even if people spent all of their time studying political issues, they would run into what might be called the paradox of political understanding. Given the complexity of social and political life and the scarcity of time, deep study of some issues precludes deep study of others in a twenty-four-hour day. Cf. Carmen Sirianni, "Learning Pluralism: Democracy and Diversity in Feminist Organizations," in *Nomos*, ed. John Chapman and Ian Shapiro (New York: Atherton Press, 1993), 283–312 (referring to the "paradox of participatory pluralism"). Scholars aware of the motivation and time problems have suggested that it is enough that there be "a critical mass of well-informed citizens large enough and active enough to anchor the process." See Robert A. Dahl, *Democracy and Its Critics* (New Haven, Conn.: Yale University Press, 1989), 339, citing Gabriel Almond, *The American People and Foreign Policy* (New York: Praeger, 1950), 139, 228, 233. Dahl recognizes, however, that ordinarily such a group would be "very much smaller" than

the demos, and he worries that the group might not be representative of the public. *Id.* at 340. He suggests that a democratic country might select at random a group of a thousand to deliberate via electronic media on an issue for a year and announce its findings. *Id.* See also James Fishkin, *Democracy and Deliberation: New Directions for Democratic Reform* (New Haven, Conn.: Yale University Press, 1991) (recommending citizen juries to debate public issues).

77. See *supra* note 74.

78. It is also a prescription for ignorance. One can recognize that the "people" are not well informed without making the mistake of assuming that governing elites have the knowledge that counts. Ian Shapiro, "A Comment on John Harsanyi's 'Democracy, Equality, and Popular Consent,' " in *Power, Inequality, and Democratic Politics*, ed. Ian Shapiro and Grant Reeher (Boulder, Colo.: Westview Press, 1988), 284, 288. Dissent is a powerful antidote to ignorance. Nothing helps more to cure a public official's lack of knowledge than to read about it in the newspaper. The "public" may or may not remember what was said a day or two later, but the public official will. Sometimes ignorance is a cover for self-serving behavior, but, cynics to the contrary, public officials sometimes want to serve the public interest and have the power to do so. Steven Kelman, *Making Public Policy: A Hopeful View of American Government* (New York: Basic Books, 1987).

79. See generally Steven Shiffrin, *The First Amendment, Democracy, and Romance* (Cambridge, Mass.: Harvard University Press, 1990), 56–85; cf. Ian Shapiro, *Democracy's Place* (Ithaca, N.Y.: Cornell University Press, 1996), 224:

> Although this is less often commented on in the academic literature, democracy is as much about opposition to the arbitrary exercise of power as it is about collective self-government. . . . In the modern world at least, democratic movements have derived much of their energy and purpose from opposition to socioeconomic, legal, and political hierarchies that seemed capricious from a democratic point of view. Rooted in the remnants of feudal and absolutist regimes and shaped by the vicissitudes of conquest and chance, the political orders of eighteenth- and nineteenth-century Europe and North America seem to the dispossessed to personify arbitrary hierarchy and domination. This reality, as much as anything else, motivated working-class and other democratic movements. The English philosophic radicals, the French and American revolutionaries, the nineteenth-century Chartists, and the anticolonial movements in the Third World after World War II all wanted to free themselves from hierarchical orders for which they could see no rationale or justification.

80. Sunstein, *supra* note 54, at 264 n.5.

81. *Id.* See also *id.* at 58: "In a Madisonian regime, dissenting views are to be encouraged even if many people would prefer not to hear them."

82. *Id.* at 152.

83. Although Sunstein mentions offense, disagreement, self-interest, and fear that people will be persuaded as causes of censorship (*id.* at 155, 164), I believe he would agree that offense is the most significant cause of censorship. Disagreement is ordinarily insufficient to motivate censorship of literature in the absence of offense. Governmental self-interest usually derives from pressure of a constituency that is offended. The fear of persuasion is a rare reason for censorship of literature except for situations like pornography, where Sunstein favors regulation because of the harm associated with it.

84. *Id.* at 163.

85. See, e.g., Diane L. Zimmerman, "Requiem for a Heavyweight: A Farewell to Warren Brandeis," 68 *Cornell L. Rev.* 291 (1983).

86. *Id.* at 235.

87. 424 U.S. 1 (1976).

88. 110 Sup. Ct. 1391 (1990).

89. *Id.* at 238–39.

90. *Id.*

91. *Id.* at 94–101.

92. *Id.* at 99–101.

93. For quite different outlooks on commercial speech from perspectives emphasizing liberty, cf. Redish, *supra* note 7, with C. Edwin Baker, *Human Liberty and Freedom of Speech* (New York: Oxford University Press, 1989), 194–224.

Chapter III
Racist Speech, Outsider Jurisprudence, and the Meaning of America

1. Harry Kalven, Jr., *The Negro and the First Amendment* (Columbus: Ohio State University Press, 1965).

2. *Id.* at 10–11.

3. *Id.* at 11.

4. One of every two Black children lives in poverty. Cornel West, *Race Matters* (Boston: Beacon Press 1993), 7. Consider also Jonathan Kozol, *Savage Inequalities: Children in America's Schools* (New York: Crown, 1992), 4: "Liberal critics of the Reagan era sometimes note that social policy in the United States, to the extent that it concerns Black children and poor children, has been turned back several decades. But this assertion, which is accurate as a description of some setbacks in housing, health, and welfare, is not adequate to speak about the present-day reality in public education. In public schooling, social policy has been turned back almost one hundred years."

On the presence of continuing discrimination, see generally Ellis Cose, *The Rage of a Privileged Class* (New York: HarperCollins, 1993); Joe R. Feagin and Melvin P. Sikes, *Living with Racism: The Black Middle-Class Experience* (Boston: Beacon Press, 1994); and T. Alexander Aleinikoff, "The Constitution in Context," 63 *U. Colo. L. Rev.* 325, 325–50 (1992).

5. So far as I am aware, however, no one proposes the prohibition of all speech that might be labeled "racist." Unless the context makes it otherwise clear, I use the term *racist speech* in this chapter to refer to a universe of speech that is narrower than many would deem to be racist in ordinary circumstances. Within the term *racist speech* I include fighting words and other forms of speech that have triggered serious proposals for the imposition of sanctions.

6. Some of the most influential writings in this school include Richard Delgado, "Words That Wound: A Tort Action of Emotional Distress," 17 *Harv. C.R.-C.L. L. Rev.* 133 (1982) ("Words That Wound"); Charles R. Lawrence III, "If He Hollers Let Him Go: Regulating Racist Speech on Campus," 1990 *Duke L.J.* 431, 458–66 ("Campus"); and Mari J. Matsuda, "Public Response to Racist Speech: Considering the Victim's Story," 87 *Mich. L. Rev.* 2320 (1989). Beyond these

writings the literature, including the contributions of "outsiders" and "insiders," is voluminous. See, e.g., Lee C. Bollinger, *The Tolerant Society: Freedom of Speech and Extremist Speech in Society* (New York: Oxford University Press, 1986); Catharine A. Mackinnon, *Only Words* (Cambride, Mass.: Harvard University Press, 1993), 45–110; see generally Symposium, "Campus Hate Speech and the Constitution in the Aftermath of *Doe v. University of Michigan*," 37 *Wayne L. Rev.* 1309 (1991); Symposium, "Free Speech & Religious, Racial & Sexual Harassment," 32 *Wm. & Mary L. Rev.* 207 (1991); Symposium, "Frontiers of Legal Thought: The New First Amendment," 1990 *Duke L.J.* 375; Symposium, "Hate Speech After R.A.V.: More Conflict Between Free Speech and Equality," 18 *Wm. Mitchell L. Rev.* 889 (1992); Akhil Amar, "The Case of the Missing Amendments," 106 *Harv. L. Rev.* 124 (1992); Alan E. Brownstein, "Regulating Hate Speech at Public Universities: Are First Amendment Values Fundamentally Incompatible with Equal Protection Principles?" 39 *Buffalo L. Rev.* 1 (1991); David Cole, "Neutral Standards and Racist Speech," 2 *Reconstruction* 65 (1992); Richard Delgado, "Campus Antiracism Rules: Constitutional Narratives in Collision," 85 *Nw. U.L. Rev.* 343 (1991) ("Campus Antiracism"); Richard Delgado and Jean Stefanic, "Images of the Outsider in American Law and Culture," 77 *Cornell L. Rev.* 1258 (1992) ("Images"); Donald A. Downs, "Skokie Revisited: Hate Group Speech and the First Amendment," 60 *Notre Dame L. Rev.* 629 (1985); Mary Ellen Gale, "Reimagining the First Amendment: Racist Speech and Equal Liberty," 65 *St. John's L. Rev.* 119 (1991); Henry Louis Gates, Jr., "Let Them Talk: Why Civil Liberties Pose No Threat to Civil Rights," 209 *New Republic*, September 20, 1993, 37; Susan Gellman, "Sticks and Stones Can Put You in Jail, But Can Words Increase Your Sentence?" 39 *UCLA L. Rev.* 333 (1991); Kent Greenawalt, "Insults and Epithets: Are They Protected Speech?" 42 *Rutgers L. Rev.* 287 (1990); Thomas C. Grey, "Civil Rights vs. Civil Liberties: The Case of Discriminatory Verbal Harassment," 8 *Social Philosophy and Policy* 81 (1991); Alon Harel, "Bigotry, Pornography, and the First Amendment," 65 *S. Cal. L. Rev.* 1887 (1992); Kenneth L. Karst, "Boundaries and Reasons: Freedom of Expression and the Subordination of Groups," 1990 *Univ. Ill. L. Rev.* 95; David Kretzmer, "Freedom of Speech and Racism," 8 *Cardozo L. Rev.* 445 (1987); Kenneth Lasson, "Racial Defamation as Free Speech," 17 *Colum. Hum. Rts. L. Rev.* 11 (1985); Frederick M. Lawrence, "Resolving the Hate Crimes/Hate Speech Paradox: Punishing Bias Crimes and Protecting Racist Speech," 68 *Notre Dame L. Rev.* 673 (1993) ("Hate Crimes"); Peter Linzer, "White Liberal Looks at Racist Speech," 65 *St. John's L. Rev.* 187 (1991); Frank Michelman, "Universities, Racist Speech, and Democracy in America: An Essay for the ACLU," 27 *Harv. C.R.-C.L. L. Rev.* 339 (1992); Martha Minow, "Speaking and Writing Against Hate," 11 *Cardozo L. Rev.* 1393 (1990); Calvin R. Massey, "Hate Speech, Cultural Diversity, and the Foundational Paradigms of Free Expression," 40 *UCLA L. Rev.* 103 (1992); Burt Neuborne, "Ghosts in the Attic: Idealized Pluralism, Community and Hate Speech," 27 *Harv. C.R.-C.L. L. Rev.* 371 (1992); Robert C. Post, "Racist Speech, Democracy, and the First Amendment," 32 *Wm. & Mary L. Rev.* 267 (1991); Ronald J. Rychlak, "Civil Rights, Confederate Flags, and Political Correctness: Free Speech and Race Relations on Campus," 66 *Tul. L. Rev.* 1411 (1992); Suzanna Sherry, "Speaking of Virtue: A Republican Approach to University Regulation of Free Speech," 75 *Minn. L. Rev.* 933 (1991); Rodney A. Smolla, "Rethinking First Amendment Assumptions About Racist and Sexist Speech," 47 *Wash. & Lee L. Rev.* 171 (1990); Jean Stefanic and Richard Delgado, "A Shifting Balance: Freedom of Expression and Hate Speech Restriction," 78 *Iowa L. Rev.* 737 (1993); James Weinstein, "A Constitutional Road Map to the Regulation of Campus Hate Speech," 38 *Wayne L. Rev.* 163 (1991); Patricia Williams, "The Obliging Shell: An Informal Essay on Formal Equal Opportunity," 87 *Mich. L. Rev.* 2128, 2133–37 (1989); Patricia Williams, "Spirit-Murdering the Messenger: The Discourse of Fingerprinting as the Law's Response to Racism," 42 *U. Miami L. Rev.* 127 (1987) ("Spirit-Murdering"); R. George Wright, "Racist Speech and the First Amendment," 9 *Miss. C. L. Rev.* 1 (1988); Darryl Brown, Note, "Racism and Race Relations in the University," 76 *Va. L. Rev.* 295 (1990); and Eric J. Grannis, Note, "Fighting Words and Fighting Freestyle: The Constitutionality of Penalty Enhancement for Bias Crimes," 93 *Colum. L. Rev.* 178 (1993).

7. My description borrows heavily from Matsuda, *supra* note 6, at 2323–26. For a bibliography of the related concept of critical race theory, see Richard Delgado and Jean Stefanic, "Critical Race Theory: An Annotated Bibliography," 79 *Va. L. Rev.* 461 (1993) ("Bibliography").

8. The general subject of hate speech involves a variety of issues that go beyond the issue of racist speech. I am, however, confining this chapter to racist speech (although I will refer to some other forms of hate speech at a few points). Accordingly, I use the term *outsider jurisprudence* here to refer *only* to the perspectives of people of color regarding racial issues (but not to all such perspectives; see *infra* note 11). Ordinarily, that term would include many other perspectives that (because of the scope of my topic) are not included here, for example, that of feminist writing.

9. This aspect of outsider jurisprudence makes it narrower than the conception of critical race theory employed in Delgado and Stefanic, "Bibliography," *supra* note 7 (classifying many writings as critical race theory that are neither written by people of color nor derived from the experience of people of color). In other contexts, some might well equate the part of outsider jurisprudence discussed here with critical race theory. I have no quarrel with the approach of Delgado and Stefanic; my purposes here, however, are not bibliographic, and limiting the term to the writings of people of color serves a useful purpose in this chapter.

Despite having made this terminological choice, I do not believe I need enter into the debates about the scholarly value to place on the experience and perspectives of being a person of color in American society (except to indicate that outsider jurisprudence, in my judgment, has contributed significantly to the discussions of the hate speech question, among others). For general debate about the outsider perspective, see, e.g., Duncan Kennedy, *Sexy Dressing Etc.* (Cambridge, Mass.: Harvard University Press, 1993), ch. 2; Stephen L. Carter, "Academic Tenure and White Male Standards: Some Lessons from the Patent Law," 100 *Yale L.J.* 2065 (1991); Richard Delgado, "When a Story Is Just a Story: Does Voice Really Matter?" 76 *Va. L. Rev.* 95 (1990); Alex M. Johnson, Jr., "The New Voice of Color," 100 *Yale L.J.* 2007 (1991); Alex M. Johnson, Jr., "Racial Critiques of Academia: A Reply in Favor of Context," 43 *Stan. L. Rev.* 137 (1990); Randall Kennedy, "Racial Critiques of Legal Academia," 102 *Harv. L. Rev.* 1745 (1989);

"Colloquy: Responses to Randall Kennedy's Racial Critiques of Legal Academia," 103 *Harv. L. Rev.* 1844, 1844–86 (1990) (responses by Scott Brewer, Milner Ball, Robin Barnes, Richard Delgado, and Leslie Espinoza). For a brilliant exploration of the problems connected with generalizing about race and blackness in general and Africa in particular (among other things), see Kwame Anthony Appiah, *In My Father's House: Africa in the Philosophy of Culture* (New York: Oxford University Press, 1992).

10. Of course, such pretensions have been attacked not only by outsider jurisprudence but also by critical theorists, feminists, pragmatists, and legal realists. Critical race theory differs by emphasizing the extent to which claims of neutrality and universality are in reality proxies for racist political and cultural assumptions. In the same vein, feminist jurisprudence emphasizes the gendered character of the claims to neutrality and universality.

11. I do not maintain that people of color or people on the left uniformly support hate speech regulation. See, e.g., Gates, *supra* note 6. For the purposes of this chapter, from this point forward, I will use the term *outsider jurisprudence* to refer exclusively to the work of those scholars of color who favor hate speech regulation. In other contexts, however, that limitation would serve no useful purpose.

12. 112 Sup. Ct. 2538 (1992).

13. Prior to *R.A.V.*, the most significant case involving racist speech was *Beauharnais v. Illinois,* 343 U.S. 250 (1952) (group libel of racial groups is not constitutionally protected).

14. On the diversity of conservative judicial thought about the First Amendment, see Vincent Blasi, "Six Conservatives in Search of the First Amendment: The Revealing Case of Nude Dancing," 33 *Wm. & Mary L. Rev.* 611 (1992).

15. I have different views regarding speech by *government* that could be reasonably viewed as racist by subordinated groups. For example, on my reading of the Constitution, southern states would not be able to fly Confederate flags except in museums or other historical displays. But see Sanford Levinson, "They Whisper: Reflections on Flags, Monuments, and State Holidays, and the Construction of Social Meaning in a Multicultural Society," 70 *Chi.-Kent L. Rev.* 1079 (1995) (arguing that it is constitutional for southern states to fly Confederate flags, though it is wrong to do so except in historical displays and the like). In any event, I exclude racist speech by government from this discussion.

16. *Matter of Welfare of R.A.V.,* 464 N.W. 2d 507, 507 (Minn. 1991); Tom Foley, "An Analysis of the View from Above," 18 *Wm. Mitchell L. Rev.* 903, 905 (1992).

17. "Whoever places on public or private property a symbol, object, appellation, characterization or graffiti, including, but not limited to, a burning cross or Nazi swastika, which one knows or has reasonable grounds to know arouses anger, alarm, or resentment in others on the basis of race, color, creed, religion or gender commits disorderly conduct and shall be guilty of a misdemeanor" (112 Sup. Ct. at 2541).

18. 464 N.W. 2d at 509–11.

19. "Fighting words" is a category of speech that has long been declared to be beneath the protection of the First Amendment. See *Chaplinsky v. New Hampshire,* 315 U.S. 568, 572 (1942) (no First Amendment protection for "conduct

that itself inflicts injury or tends to incite immediate violence); *R.A.V.*, 112 Sup. Ct. at 2541. Despite the fact that *Chaplinsky* is routinely cited with approval by the Court, it is often suggested that *Chaplinsky* is no longer good law on the ground that the Court has not since upheld a single fighting words conviction. See, e.g., Nadine Strossen, "Regulating Racist Speech on Campus: A Modest Proposal," 1990 *Duke L. Rev.* 484, 510. The suggestion is itself technically inaccurate. See *Lucas v. Arkansas,* 423 U.S. 807 (1975) (dismissing for lack of a substantial federal question, after a prior remand, an attack on a fighting words conviction under a statute that prohibited "profane, violent, vulgar, or abusive [language that] in its common accept[ance] be calculated to arouse to anger the person about whom or to whom it is spoken or addressed, or to cause a breach of the peace or assault," *Lucas v. State,* 520 S.W. 2d 224, 225 (1975)). More important, the lower courts have frequently upheld post-Chaplinsky convictions under the fighting words doctrine. See Strossen, *supra,* at 512. That the few Supreme Court fighting words cases have been decided in favor of defendants does not speak to the overall standing of the *Chaplinsky* doctrine. For better or worse, the doctrine is alive and well.

20. *Id.* at 2547.

21. A statute forbidding false statements would involve content discrimination, but not subject matter discrimination, on its face.

22. 112 Sup. Ct. at 2548.

23. *Id.*

24. *Id.* He also stated that the ordinance "can be said to promote" the compelling state interests. *Id.* It is surprising that Justice Scalia was apparently prepared to accept this meager showing ("can be said to") under his strict scrutiny standard. Even the showings required in commercial speech for time, place, or manner restrictions are somewhat more demanding. *Board of Trustees v. Fox,* 492 U.S. 469, 476–81 (1989).

25. 112 Sup. Ct. at 2549.

26. *Id.* at 2550.

27. It makes little difference whether this result is described as violating equal protection, the equality dimension of the First Amendment, or both.

28. 478 U.S. 328 (1986).

29. *Id.* at 335. The Puerto Rican scheme also discriminates on the basis of audience, but that discrimination is not relevant for present purposes.

30. See *Ohralik v. Ohio State Bar Ass'n,* 436 U.S. 447, 455–456 (1978).

31. 112 Sup. Ct. at 2545.

32. *Id.*

33. *Id.* at 2546.

34. *Virginia State Bd. of Pharmacy v. Virginia Citizens Consumer Council,* 425 U.S. 748, 771 n.24 (1976).

35. *Ohralik v. Ohio State Bar Ass'n,* 436 U.S. 447, 456 (1978).

36. *Id.* at 455–56.

37. *Id.* at 456.

38. I do not mean to question the Court's conclusion, merely its justificatory prowess.

39. 478 U.S. at 341.

40. For discussion, see *Board of Trustees v. Fox*, 492 U.S. 469, 476–81.

41. 112 Sup. Ct. at 2546 (ellipsis in original).

42. 475 U.S. 41 (1986).

43. *Id.* at 48.

44. As Justice Brennan pointed out in dissent, the findings initially put forth by the City of Renton exhibited hostility to the messages emanating from adult theaters. 475 U.S. at 59. E.g., one finding was that the "[l]ocation of adult entertainment land uses on the main commercial thoroughfares of the City gives an impression of legitimacy to, and causes a loss of sensitivity to the adverse effect of pornography upon children, established family relations, respect for marital relationship and for the sanctity of marriage relations of others, and the concept of non-aggressive, consensual sexual relations" (*Id.* at 59 n.3).

Additionally, the city determined that the "[l]ocation of adult land uses in close proximity to residential uses, churches, parks, and other public facilities, and schools, will cause a degradation of the community standard of morality. Pornographic material has a degrading effect upon the relationship between spouses." *Id.*

Significantly, the findings involving "secondary effects" were added *after* the litigation was filed. *Id.* at 56–57. Despite the prelitigation findings of the Renton City Council, the Court determined that the postlitigation findings represented the predominant intent of the city council. *Id.* at 47–48. The Court reasoned in part that if the city " 'had been concerned with restricting the message purveyed by adult theaters, it would have tried to close them or restrict their number rather than circumscribe their choice as to location.' " *Id.* at 48, quoting *Young v. American Mini Theatres, Inc.,* 427 U.S. 50, 82 n.4 (1976; Powell, J., concurring). Of course, it would have done no such thing. To outlaw adult theaters or to limit the number of adult theaters would be to outlaw or set quantitative limitations on nonobscene *protected* speech. If the city were hostile to the content of adult movies, it would have been ill advised to enact legislation so obviously vulnerable to constitutional challenge. Its failure to enact such legislation sheds no light on its motivation.

Moreover, the emphasis on motivation is itself questionable. See, e.g., William E. Lee, "Lonely Pamphleteers, Little People, and the Supreme Court: The Doctrine of Time, Place, and Manner Regulations of Expression," 54 *Geo. Wash. L. Rev.* 757 (1986); Martin H. Redish, "The Content Distinction in First Amendment Analysis," 34 *Stan. L. Rev.* 113 (1981); Susan H. Williams, "Content Discrimination and the First Amendment," 139 *U. Pa. L. Rev.* 615 (1991); but see Frederick Schauer, *Free Speech: A Philosophical Enquiry* (Cambridge: Cambridge University Press, 1982). Whatever the motivation of the Renton City Council, the impact of the ordinance would be the same. See Geoffrey R. Stone, "Restrictions of Speech Because of Its Content: The Peculiar Case of Subject-Matter Restrictions," 46 *U. Chi. L. Rev.* 81, 111–112 (1978) (arguing that the impact is not viewpoint-neutral in that such restrictions operated against speech that encourages relaxed sexual mores).

It seems clear that justification of the result in *Renton* must turn to some degree on the character of the speech involved. See *Renton*, 475 U.S. at 49 (suggesting that *Young v. American Mini Theatres, Inc.,* 427 U.S. 50 (1976), may be confined to businesses that sell sexually explicit materials and opening the door to the argument that *Renton* is limited in the same way). It also seems likely that the impact of the ordinance is to suppress speech that successfully encourages the subordination of women. Having argued that *Renton*'s method is difficult to justify, I have not argued for or against its result.

45. This would not put the two on a par either because in the proposed hypothetical, the advertisement is for a constitutionally protected film; casino gambling, on the other hand, is not constitutionally protected.

46. See *Boos v. Barry*, 485 U.S. 312, 320–321 (1988; O'Connor, J., joined by Stevens and Scalia, JJ.): "So long as the justifications for regulation have nothing to do with the actual films being shown inside adult movie theaters, we concluded that the regulation was properly analyzed as content neutral. Regulations that focus on the direct impact of speech on its hearers present a different situation. Listener's reactions to speech are not the type of 'secondary effects' we referred to in *Renton*."

47. 478 U.S. at 341. Of course, the Court could ignore directly content-based interests as it did in *Renton*. See *supra* note 44.

48. 112 Sup. Ct. at 2546.

49. *Id.* This does not mean that no First Amendment test applies. See *Barnes v. Glen Theatre, Inc.*, 111 Sup. Ct. 2546 (1991); *United States v. O'Brien*, 391 U.S. 367 (1968). It does mean that the purportedly stricter tests ordinarily applied when content discrimination is present are not employed. But cf. Steven H. Shiffrin, *The First Amendment, Democracy, and Romance* (Cambridge, Mass.: Harvard University Press, 1991), ch. 1 (warning that the distinction between content-based regulation and regulation directed at conduct is not as important as many commentators believe).

50. 112 Sup. Ct. at 2546. For the suggestion that Justice Scalia could not mean to go that far, see Richard H. Fallon, Jr., "Sexual Harassment, Content Neutrality, and the First Amendment Dog That Didn't Bark," 1995 *Sup. Ct. Rev.*

51. 112 Sup. Ct. at 2547.

52. 116 Sup. Ct. at 1510–14 (Stevens, J., joined by Kennedy, Thomas, and Ginsburg, JJ.); *id.* at 1522–23 (O'Connor, J., joined by Rehnquist, C.J., Souter and Breyer, JJ.).

53. Even Justice Stevens concedes that. *Id.* at 1510.

54. 112 Sup. Ct. at 2547, quoting *Metromedia, Inc. v. San Diego*, 453 U.S. 490 (1981; Stevens, J., dissenting; citation omitted).

55. *Id.* at 2547.

56. *Watts v. United States*, 394 U.S. 705 (1969).

57. *Posadas*, 478 U.S. 328.

58. *Edge*, 509 U.S. 418.

59. *United States v. O'Brien*, 391 U.S. 367 (1968). For commentary suggesting that the government's purpose was to suppress dissent, see Laurence H. Tribe, *American Constitutional Law*, 2d, ed. (Mineola, N.Y.: Foundation Press, 1988), 824–25; Thomas I. Emerson, *The System of Freedom of Expression* (New York: Random House, 1970), Dean Alfange, Jr., "Free Speech and Symbolic Conduct," 1968 *Sup. Ct. L. Rev.* 1; and Melville B. Nimmer, "The Meaning of Symbolic Speech Under the First Amendment," 21 *UCLA L. Rev.* 29, 41 (1973).

60. *Renton,* 475 U.S. 41.

61. 112 Sup. Ct. at 2547.

62. *Id.* at 2545.

63. *Id.* at 2549 n.7.

64. *Id.*

65. *Beauharnais v. Illinois,* 343 U.S. 250, 258–59 (1952).

66. *Chaplinsky,* 315 U.S. at 572. See *supra,* note 19.

67. 112 Sup. Ct. at 2548.

68. *Id.* at 2549 (emphasis added).

69. *Id.* (emphasis added).

70. Harry Kalven, Jr., "The New York Times Case: A Note on the 'Central Meaning of the First Amendment,' " 1964 *Sup. Ct. Rev.* 191, 221 n.125 (quoting Alexander Meiklejohn's comment about *New York Times Co. v. Sullivan,* 376 U.S. 254 (1964)).

71. 112 Sup. Ct. at 2549.

72. *Chicago Police Dep't. v. Mosley,* 408 U.S. 92 (1972).

73. 413 U.S. 49 (1973).

74. *Id.* at 61 n.12.

75. *Miller v. California,* 413 U.S. 15 (1973).

76. *Brockett v. Spokane Arcades, Inc.,* 472 U.S 491, 498, 504 (1985).

77. *Id.* at 499.

78. *Id.*

79. *Id.* The treatment of such appeals thus discriminates on the basis of point of view. For examples of other exercises of legally permissible point-of-view discrimination, together with a perceptive discussion of what should count as such discrimination, see Cass R. Sunstein, "Pornography and the First Amendment," 1986 *Duke L.J.* 589, 609–17.

80. 413 U.S. at 69.

81. Denying that obscenity communicates ideas also has disturbing implications for the First Amendment status of art and music. Consider Harry Kalven, Jr., "The Metaphysics of the Law of Obscenity," 1960 *Sup. Ct. Rev.* 1, 16: "[B]eauty has constitutional status too, [and] the life of the imagination is as important to the human adult as the life of the intellect. I do not think the Court would find it difficult to protect Shakespeare even though it is hard to enumerate the important ideas in the plays and poems. I am only suggesting that Mr. Justice Brennan might not have found it so easy to dismiss obscenity because it lacked socially useful ideas if he had recognized at this point, at least, obscenity is in the same position as all art and literature."

82. See *supra* text accompanying note 67.

83. On the latter two themes, see Irving Kristol, *Reflections of a Neoconservative* (New York: Basic Books, 1983), 45, 47.

84. Harry M. Clor, *Obscenity and Public Morality* (Chicago: University of Chicago Press, 1969). Clor regards the interest in preventing women from being treated as sex objects as justifying the prohibition of too narrow a class of material. See *id.* at 222.

85. In particular, see *FW/PBS v. Dallas,* 110 Sup. Ct. 596, 617 (1990; Scalia, J., concurring in part, dissenting in part) (arguing that a business devoted

to the sale of highly explicit sexual material can be closed down, not merely zoned to a particular area of the community).

86. See generally Judith Butler and Joan Scott, eds., *Feminists Theorize the Political* (New York: Routledge, 1992).

87. *Gertz v. Robert Welch, Inc.,* 418 U.S. 323 (1974).

88. E.g., public officials and public figures must show that defamatory statements were published as a knowing or reckless falsehood in order to recover; private persons must show negligence in order to recover against media defendants. See *id.* Private persons may recover presumed and punitive damages against nonmedia defendants, at least when the matter is of private interest, without a showing that the statement was published as a knowing or reckless falsehood (see *Dun and Bradstreet, Inc. v Greenmoss Builders, Inc.,* 472 U.S. 749 (1985)), but may or may not be able to do so against media defendants with similar publications. Cf. *Gertz* with *Greenmoss.*

89. See generally Norman L. Rosenberg, *Protecting the Best Men: An Interpretive History of the Law of Libel* (Chapel Hill: University of North Carolina Press, 1986).

90. Cf. *Gertz,* 413 U.S. at 339–40 (ideas absolutely protected under the First Amendment) with *Milkovich v. Lorain Journal Co.,* 110 Sup. Ct. 2695, 2705 (1990) (denying that there is any "wholesale defamation exception for anything that might be labeled opinion").

91. See e.g., Marc A. Franklin and Daniel J. Bussell, "The Plaintiff's Burden in Defamation: Awareness and Falsity," 25 *Wm. & Mary L. Rev.* 825, 879 (1984) (opinions should be equated with nondisprovable assertions); Note, "Statements of Fact, Statements of Opinion, and the First Amendment," 74 *Calif. L. Rev.* 1001 (1986) (contending that the distinction between facts and opinions in the case law is rooted in verifiability).

92. 112 Sup. Ct. at 2545, quoting *Simon & Schuster, Inc. v. Members of N.Y. State Crime Victims Bd.,* 112 Sup. Ct. 501, 508 (1991). See generally Grannis, *supra* note 6, at 205.

93. *Chaplinsky, supra,* 315 U.S. at 572, quoted in *R.A.V.,* 112 Sup. Ct. at 2543.

94. 112 Sup. Ct. at 2545.

95. *Id.* at 2550. Leave aside that if the interest is protecting groups that have historically been subject to fighting words, this alternative would not be "narrowly tailored" even under the rather relaxed standards currently employed by the Court.

96. I do not contend, of course, that this concern is prompted by any sympathy for a person who burns a cross on the lawn of a Black family in the dead of night. Nor do I think Justice Scalia had any sympathy for the flag-burning defendant in *Texas v. Johnson,* 491 U. S. 397 (1989).

97. For criticism of this aspect of his perspective, see, e.g., Kimberle Crenshaw, "Race, Reform, and Retrenchment: Transformation and Legitimation in Antidiscrimination Law," 101 *Harv. L. Rev.* 1331 (1988).

98. See *Rust v. Sullivan,* 111 Sup. Ct. 1759 (1991).

99. As Geoffrey R. Stone, "Content Regulation and the First Amendment," 25 *Wm. & Mary L. Rev.* 189, 212 (1983): "The Court has long embraced an 'antipaternalistic' understanding of the first amendment." For a particularly strong

statement by the Court, see *Virginia St. Bd. of Pharmacy v. Virginia Citizens Consumer Council,* 425 U.S. 748, 770 (1976). But see the paternalism discussion in chapter two.

100. As Stone, *supra* note 99, at 216, writes: " 'Intolerance-based' justifications for restricting expression, like paternalistic justifications, are constitutionally disfavored, even if the restriction does not substantially prevent the communication of a particular idea, viewpoint, or item of information." On the relationship between the First Amendment and tolerance, see generally Bollinger, *supra* note 6.

101. See *infra* text accompanying note 171.

102. To the contrary, see MacKinnon, *supra* note 6, at 106 (emphasis added): "When equality is recognized as a constitutional value and mandate, the idea that some people are inferior to others on the basis of group membership is authoritatively rejected as the basis for public policy. *This does not mean that ideas to the contrary cannot be debated or expressed.* It should mean, however, that social inferiority cannot be imposed through any means, including expressive ones."

103. Matsuda, *supra* note 6, at 2321, 2348–56

104. *Id.* at 2550.

105. Justice Scalia seems to make this precise assumption when he objects that one side is licensed to speak one way in "debate," but the other side is precluded from doing do. See *supra* text accompanying note 22.

106. 112 Sup. Ct. at 2550.

107. See *supra* text accompanying note 19.

108. *New York Times Co. v. Sullivan,* 376 U.S. 255, 270 (1964).

109. See generally *Broadrick v. Oklahoma,* 413 U.S. 601 (1973) (unconstitutional overbreadth must be "substantial"); New York v. Ferber, 458 U.S. 747 (1982) (extending substantial overbreadth to books and films).

110. *Broadrick v. Oklahoma,* 413 U.S. at 616.

111. Sup. Ct. at 2541.

112. See, e.g., *Terminiello v. City of Chicago,* 337 U.S. 1 (1949) (stirring people to anger protected under the First Amendment).

113. For commentary on limiting constructions, see Richard H. Fallon, Jr., "Making Sense of Overbreadth," 100 *Yale L.J.* 853 (1991).

114. See *Marks v. United States,* 430 U.S. 188 (1977).

115. *Wainwright v. Stone,* 414 U.S. 21 (1973).

116. 112 Sup. Ct. at 2558–59.

117. *Id.* at 2559.

118. *Id.*

119. 464 N.W. 2d 507, 510 (1991) (emphasis added).

120. *Id.* (emphasis added; citations italics in original).

121. 112 Sup. Ct. at 2559.

122. Minn. St. §609.72 (1)(3)(1992).

123. 263 N.W. 2d at 416.

124. *Id.*

125. *Id.*

126. *Id.* (emphasis deleted).

127. *Id.*

128. "[N]o ordered society would condone the vulgar language used by this 14-year-old child. . . ." *Id.* at 419.

129. *Id.* at 419–20.

130. *Texas v. Johnson,* 109 Sup. Ct. 2533, 2544 (1989). Indeed, the Minnesota Supreme Court quoted that passage from the *Johnson* opinion shortly after it adopted its limiting construction. 464 N.W. 2d at 511.

131. Kenneth Jost, "The Courtship of Justice White," *A.B.A. J.* 63 (October 1993). Cf. Blasi, *supra* note 14, at 659 (tough-minded conservative who values analytic precision).

132. E.g., Jost, *supra* note 131, at 66.

133. 112 Sup. Ct. at 2561.

134. *Id.* at 2553. The emphasis on violence in the quoted paragraph leaves open the possibility that Justice White might strike down campus speech codes prohibiting speech that did not involve threats. But see *infra* text accompanying note 150. For language suggesting that "fighting words" might be limited to threats or intimidation when people approach patients of abortion clinics, see *Madsen v. Women's Health Center,* 114 Sup. Ct. 2516, 2529 (1994).

135. Dennis J. Hutchinson et al., "Perspectives on White: A Roundtable," *A.B.A. J.* 69 (October 1993). Cf. Blasi, *supra* note 14, at 660 (contending that Justice White is apparently opposed to ideology).

136. Hutchinson, *supra* note 135, at 69–70.

137. Jost, *supra* note 131, at 64.

138. Among other things, I very much doubt that he or his clerks read *S.L.J.*

139. 315 U.S. 568, 572 (1942) (emphasis added).

140. 112 Sup. Ct. at 2559.

141. See, e.g., Delgado, "Words That Wound," *supra* note 6; Lawrence, "Campus," *supra* note 6, at 452–56, 457–66, 482–83; Matsuda, *supra* note 6, at 2326–41.

142. *Restatement (Second) of Torts* §46 cmt. d (1966).

143. *Hustler Magazine v. Falwell,* 485 U.S. 46 (1988). Of course, the tort has limits. *Hustler* imposed limits on the ability of public figures and public persons to recover for a mass media parody even when it is regarded as offensive and is intended to inflict emotional distress. One might also argue that the language of the chief justice's opinion extends only to civil liability, but I do not think such an argument is persuasive. First, his statement may simply be describing the fact that the states generally do not impose criminal liability to the intentional infliction of emotional distress per se. Second, his statement may be an accommodation to someone like Justice Stevens who might want to make such a distinction here. Whatever Justice Steven's views might be, it seems unlikely that the Court would balk at a formulation of the *Chaplinsky* rule that tracked the tort of intentional infliction of emotional distress.

144. 112 Sup. Ct. at 2559.

145. For discussion of their reaction, see Charles H. Jones, "Proscribing Hate: Distinctions Between Criminal Harm and Protected Expression," 18 *Wm. Mitchell L. Rev.* 935, 948 (1992).

146. *U.S. v. Salyer,* 893 F. 2d 113, 116 (1989).

147. *Ford v. Hollowell,* 385 F. Supp. 1392, 1397 (N.D. Miss. 1974).

160

NOTES TO CHAPTER III

148. Cf. *Harris v. Forklift Systems, Inc.* 114 Sup. Ct. 367 (1993) (psychological injury need not be shown for "hostile environment" sexual harassment claim); 18 U.S.C. §871 (1988) (defining federal crime of threatening president without regard to whether president was afraid, emotionally distressed, or impaired in his duties). Similarly, the law of attempts does not require success or a showing of injury as a prerequisite for the imposition of punishment; for reasons similar to those provided in the text, I would not require a showing that the victim understood the perpetrator's remarks to insult on the basis of belonging to a group historically oppressed because of its race, color, or national and ethic origin, but I regard that as a closer question. Certainly, in a tort context it should be required. See Delgado, "Words That Wound," *supra* note 6, at 179 (tort action for racial insult should require plaintiff to show, inter alia, that he or she understood that the insult was intended to demean through reference to race and that a reasonable person would recognize it as an insult).

149. Cf. *Lewis v. New Orleans,* 408 U.S. 913 (1972; Powell, J., concurring): "If these words had been addressed by one citizen to another, face to face and in a hostile manner, I would have no doubt that they would be 'fighting words.' But the situation may be different where such words are addressed to a police officer trained to exercise a higher degree of restraint than the average citizen." Most of the fighting words cases involve language directed against police officers, and the arrests are quite difficult to justify. See Stephen W. Gard, "Fighting Words as Free Speech," 58 *Wash. U.L.Q.* 531, 566–69 (1980). The lower courts are sharply divided on the question whether such "fighting words" can support a criminal conviction. Michael G. Walsh, Annot., *Insulting Words Addressed Directly to Police Officer as Breach of Peace or Disorderly Conduct,* 14 A.L.R. 4th 1252 (1982).

150. 112 Sup. Ct. at 2553.

151. *Id.*

152. On this view, the state could arguably not punish such statements if they were made on the telephone. See *Anniskette v. State,* 489 P. 2d 1012 (Alaska 1971) (referring to the available cooling-off period).

153. Thomas F. Shea, " 'Don't Bother to Smile When You Call Me That':— Fighting Words and the First Amendment," 63 *Kentucky L.J.* 1, 2 (1975). Nonetheless, that seems to be the implication of *Gooding v. Wilson,* 405 U.S. 518, 523 (1972) (requiring that fighting words convictions be based on circumstances in which the actual addressee was likely to fight). But cf. *Ashton v. Kentucky,* 384 U.S. 195 (1966) (use of subjective standard is erroneous because it "involves calculations as to the boiling point of a particular person or a particular group").

154. See generally Shea, *supra* note 153 (recommending a focus on the average person).

155. Gard, *supra* note 149, at 580. Cf. Kent Greenawalt, *Speech, Crime and the Uses of Language* 295–98 (New York: Oxford University Press, 1989) (fighting words standard is gendered); Lawrence, "Campus," *supra* note 6, at 454 (paradigm is based on a white male point of view); Lawrence, "Hate Crimes," *supra* note 6, at 710 (probably gendered); Kathleen M. Sullivan, "Foreword: The Justices of Rules and Standards," 106 *Harv. L. Rev.* 22, 42 (1992) (fighting words

exception open to "criticism as a hopeless anachronism that canonizes the macho code of barroom brawls").

156. Gard, *supra* note 149, at 566, 571; Strossen, *supra* note 19, at 512; cf. *id.* at 556–58 (hate speech rules primarily enforced against people of color). The evidence put forward by these commentators is quite thin, but their conclusion may be correct.

157. See Matsuda, *supra* note 6, at 2357; see also Lawrence, "Campus," *supra* note 6, at 450 n.82 (would not protect persons vilified on the basis of their membership in dominant majority groups).

158. See Matsuda, *supra* note 6, at 2361–63. Of course, if the verbal insult were delivered in a way that might be reasonably interpreted as a threat, it ought not be protected regardless of the racial or ethnic character content. Moreover, if the proposal were designed for a college campus and the objective were to promote civility, one might regulate a broader class of racial and ethnic insults. See also *infra* note 219.

159. Even if there were selective enforcement in other jurisdictions, the problem might not exist in St. Paul. On the other hand, the failure to make clear in the ordinance that insults directed against non-Jewish white Americans are not punishable gives courts discretion they may be better off without.

160. See bell hooks, *Black Looks: Race and Representation* (Boston: South End Press, 1992), 15 ("The prejudicial feelings some blacks may express about whites are in no way linked to a system of domination that affords us any power to coercively control the lives and well-being of white folks").

161. My proposal is somewhat different than those given elsewhere, though (apart from what appears in the text) my defense of it against First Amendment objections would not go much beyond what already appears in the large literature.

Speech or other expression should be punishable if it (1) is intended to insult and stigmatize an individual (except for public officials, including police officers or their private counterparts, and public figures) on the basis of his or her belonging to a group historically oppressed because of its race, color, or national origin; and (2) is either addressed directly to the individual whom it insults and stigmatizes, or addressed or distributed in a way that is ultimately communicated to the individual; and (3) makes use of words or symbols that insult and stigmatize an individual on the basis of his or her belonging to a group historically oppressed because of its race, color, ethnicity, or national origin; unless (4) the speech or other expression is provoked by fighting words, threats, or violent conduct.

The same rules should apply when the insults are directed at families or, in some cases, small groups of individuals. See *infra* note 219. Approaches to the problem, e.g., of gender insults should be somewhat different. Developing that notion is beyond the scope of this chapter.

This proposal is designed for all contexts, including high school and college campuses, in which the question is whether sanctions, criminal or otherwise, are appropriate. If a campus is private, the First Amendment does not apply, and the policy can be evaluated on its merits without any need to follow the often slapdash First Amendment doctrine of the Rehnquist Court.

If the context, however, is that of a public university or a criminal statute, the Court's decisions must be respected. In those contexts, my proposal provides a criticism rather than a practical proposal for action because it diverges from the Court's ultimate understanding of fighting words. Some similarities will remain, of course.

First, the Court will insist on words or other symbolic conduct of an insulting and outrageous character. Second, the Court will presumably also impose an intent requirement. A person who uses insulting and stigmatizing words in a bad joke will not be subject to punishment. On the other hand, under the proposal, the words themselves or the symbolic conduct would be sufficient evidence of intent in a wide variety of circumstances, even in the face of denials by the perpetrator. Burning a cross on a Black family's lawn would be punishable even if the defendant insisted that he had believed it was all in good fun.

Of course, that is an easy case. From my perspective, the question of whether intent should be required is a close one. On the one hand, I do not think people should be punished for insensitivity without accompanying malice. On the other hand, I fear the intent requirement could be used to exonerate too many people undeservedly. In forging a compromise, I would recommend that the use of words or symbols that insult and stigmatize an individual on the basis of his or her belonging to a group historically oppressed because of its race, color, or national and ethnic origin should create a strong presumption of bad intent. This presumption, however, may violate due process in the criminal context. See, e.g., *Yates v. Evatt*, 111 Sup. Ct. 1884 (1991); *Francis v. Franklin*, 471 U.S. 307 (1985).

Third, some racial insults directed, for example, by one member of a historically disadvantaged group at another member of the same group may insult, *but not stigmatize*, within the meaning of my proposal. My sense is that a racial insult directed by a European American against an African American or a Latino or Latina usually functions differently than do racial insults hurled by members of the same racial group at each other.

Fourth, face-to-face insults would certainly be covered. But there are a range of other possible situations. Public stigmatization of an individual without his or her presence, in circumstances where the individual would likely learn of it, is also likely to be covered. I do not think it should matter, for example, whether the victim of a racial slur happens to be present when a speaker includes the slur in a public speech or if a Black family happens to be home when perpetrators burn a cross on the lawn across the street; perhaps it would matter to the Court.

More controversial still would be a circumstance in which an individual distributes a leaflet to a small group of friends containing a racist epithet directed at a particular individual, but with a directive not to republish the statement. If the statement is republished and the victim learns of it, is the perpetrator responsible? I would say yes, by analogy to defamation law. If you plan to defame someone, you are responsible for the damage caused by republication of the defamation whether or not it was anticipated. To be sure, a direct stigmatizing insult may be more injurious, but the delivery of the insult is foreseeably likely to cause injury one way or another, and the perpetrator who intentionally insults and stigmatizes on the basis of race deserves little inquiry into the particular context and circumstances. Nonetheless, the Court may require a more direct communication. A middle ground position would require that it be reasonably foreseeable that the offending statement would be communicated to the victim.

The Court would not permit punishment for oral statements made by one friend to another that ultimately get back to the victim no matter how outrageous the statement, though my proposal would permit punishment in such circumstances.

Finally, as discussed in the text, a showing of injury should not be required, and only stigmatizing insults directed at members of historically disadvantaged groups should be subject to sanctions. In my view, the Court would permit the former but not the latter.

162. The line between targeted and nontargeted racist speech is not self-defining. I mean the distinction to be substantive and not formal. Therefore, a perpetrator who addressed a general insult about Asian Americans to an Asian American in a way that insulted and stigmatized that person would have engaged in targeted speech even though the victim's name was not used. *See also* note 219 *infra*.

163. See Matsuda, *supra* note 6, at 2357.

164. Cole, *supra* note 6, at 67. See also Karst, *supra* note 6.

165. There is an important difference between organizations like the Klan and individual perpetrators of racist speech. The Klan has a history of violence. One wonders if the Federal Bureau of Investigation has infiltrated the Klan with the same ferocity it infiltrated the communists. There remains the possibility that a conspiracy to advocate violence is treated differently than individual advocacy. The former may not require a showing of imminent lawless action. *Communist Party of Indiana v. Whitcomb,* 414 U.S. 441 (1974) (dictum that urging others to engage in violence now or in the future satisfies constitutional standard).

166. Gale, *supra* note 6, at 141. The National Opinion Research Center reports that three of four Whites believe that Black and Latino/a people are more likely than whites to prefer living on welfare and that they are less hardworking, less intelligent, and less patriotic. "Poll Finds Whites Use Sterotypes," *New York Times*, January 10, 1991, at B10, col. 6.

167. See Sheri Lynn Johnson, "The Language and Culture (Not to Say Race) of Peremptory Challenges," 35 *Wm. & Mary L. Rev.* 21, 75 (1993): "While 'dominative racists,' persons who express bigotry and hatred openly, are less common than they were twenty-five years ago, they have been replaced, in substantial measure, by closet or 'aversive' racists, persons who continue to hold negative sterotypes of minorities and wish to avoid them." See also Sheri Lynn Johnson, "Unconscious Racism and the Criminal Law," 73 *Cornell L. Rev.* 1016, 1027–28 (1988) (citing literature from Freudians, cognitive psychologists, and sociologists); Sheri Lynn Johnson, "Racial Imagery in Criminal Cases," 67 *Tul. Rev.* 1739 (1993). See also sources cited *infra* note 201.

168. See Delgado, "Words That Wound," *supra* note 6, at 144–46, 179; Delgado, "Campus Antiracism," *supra* note 6, at 379, 385; Gale, *supra* note 6, at 148; Lawrence, "Campus," *supra* note 6, at 452–56, 468. See generally Peggy C. Davis, "Law as Microaggression," 98 *Yale L.J.* 1559 (1989).

169. See, e.g., Delgado, "Words That Wound," *supra* note 6; Kretzmer *supra*, note 6, at 462–67; Lawrence, "Campus," at *supra* note 6, at 452–56, 457–66, 482–83; Matsuda, *supra* note 6, at 2326–41.

170. See sources cited *supra* note 168. I do not suggest that the harms mentioned in the text are exhaustive.

171. Matsuda, *supra* note 6, at 2357. I am sensitive to Karst's powerful argument, *supra* note 6, that it is dangerous to privilege speech based in reason above speech based in emotion. In using Matsuda's definition, however, I do not endorse a reason-emotion dichotomy. Indeed, I believe emotional speech is necessarily cognitive and that reason and emotion cannot be easily separated. When Jesse Jackson argues that the Black community should take responsibility for its contribution to crime in general and the drug trade in particular, he communicates his message with passion ("We are far more threatened by the dope than the rope [of the Ku Klux Klan]"; Bob Herbert, "Blacks Killing Blacks," *New York Times*, October 20, 1993, at A23, col. 5). The passion is a part of his message, and it is not the antithesis of reason.

Jackson's speech is also, of course, not an instance of persecutorial, hateful, and degrading speech. What marks out the persecutorial and hateful aspects of communication for sanction is not that they are emotional but that they implicate moral culpability, which ought to be present before sanctions are imposed.

172. Ronald Dworkin, *A Matter of Principle* (Cambridge, Mass.: Harvard University Press, 1985), 190 (emphasis added) (government must "treat all those in its charge as *equals,* that is, as entitled to its equal concern and respect." Ronald Dworkin, *Taking Rights Seriously* (Cambridge, Mass.: Harvard University Press, 1977), 272–73; Baker, *infra* note 180, at 278 (equal concern and respect as autonomous persons. This is a moral principle, not merely a political principle; not just a basis for political compromise or political unity, but a moral starting point.

Although I think that some such principle is one of the minimum conditions for legitimate government, I do not think the principle can generate the sweeping conclusions that many of its advocates educe. See generally Steven Shiffrin, "Liberalism, Radicalism, and Legal Scholarship," 30 *UCLA L. Rev.* 1103 (1983). Moreover, I think this argument might well be regarded by committed racists as circular. E.g., most liberals would claim that the compulsory education of eight-year-olds and our denying them access to many societal privileges and benefits them equal concern or respect but rather is a recognition of their circumstances. Some racists could similarly say that unequal treatment of people of color is appropriate to their circumstances and therefore does not deny them equal concern or respect as human beings. To answer this racist argument requires more than the invocation of a principle of equal concern and respect; it requires a substantive understanding of the principle. I do not propose to refute the racist here. Certainly, our legal system has rejected the racist understanding. I do not claim to offer arguments that would appeal to a racist.

173. The position of communists is more complicated. Communists argue that the system is so illegitimate and its evils so serious that it deserves to be overthrown. If they are correct, their contribution to the marketplace of ideas is valuable. There is, of course, a risk that an attempted overthrow might occur in circumstances where the evils are not sufficiently serious. Current law tries to address that possibility. See *Brandenburg v. Ohio* 395 U.S. 444 (1969).

If the Ku Klux Klan succeeds, in contrast, it is inevitably the case that the system is illegitimate.

174. For detailed presentation of a similar argument, see Harel, *supra* note 6. Robert Post argues, on the other hand, that the legitimacy of the system depends

on democratic dialogue, including speech that questions the assumptions of the system. Post, *supra* note 6, at 280–85. Although complete agreement among the citizens is not possible (*id.* at 281, 283), it is possible to subject the "political and social order to public opinion" and "to instill a sense of self-determination." *Id.* at 282. Post concedes that the achievement of "autonomous self-determination for both majority and minority is a complex and contingent question, dependent upon historical circumstances." *Id.* at 283. It seems plain to me that people of color in general and millions of others (perhaps most) do not have the sense of self-determination that Post argues is a necessary feature of democracy. Populist frustration about the failure of politicians to do the work of the people illustrates the point. It seems hard, therefore, to understand why racist speech causing harm should be constitutionally immunized in order to protect a self-determination that does not exist. More generally, Post denies that equality trumps dialogue. *Id.* at 292–93. Apart from invoking an argument about the difficulty of finding someone to interpret equality and positing that equality requires self-rule, Post's argument against the substantive theory of equality is that it would interfere with self-determination. This is puzzling, however. Clearly Post would not permit racial discrimination (or slavery) to be legitimized as a product of democratic dialogue, yet to limit the possible results of democratic dialogue is to limit both the reality of and the sense of self-determination. Of course, Post might respond that equality and other human rights can limit the output of public dialogue (thus limiting self-determination) but not the dialogue itself. In the end, however, it is easy to understand why self-determination is treated as an important value; it is difficult to understand why it would deserve the exalted place Post would provide. That we should strive for democracy is an insufficient answer because those who strive to limit public dialogue in the name of human rights also claim to be operating from democratic principles. Any definition of democracy is contested.

175. Many, of course, would object that courts should not evaluate the contribution of particular categories of speech to the marketplace of ideas (see, e.g., Massey, *supra* note 6, at 113), but they have certainly done so in the context of fighting words (*Chaplinsky v. New Hampshire,* 315 U.S. 568, 572 (1942)), obscenity *Paris Adult Theatre I v. Slaton,* 413 U.S. 49, 61 (1973)), and defamation (*Gertz v. Robert Welch, Inc.,* 418 U.S. 323, 340 (1974)). Determining that a category of speech is at odds with a foundational premise of the system is not only consistent with these precedents but also less open-ended.

Massey contends that "[p]ublic discourse cannot be defined normatively, for any such attempt is hinged to some ideological notion of what our collective identity *should* be." *Id.* at 113 (emphasis in original). My argument is that we must be hinged to an ideology of equality of persons, or else our government has no claim to our respect. That is, a democratic system presupposes some minimum conditions of our collective identity.

176. John Stuart Mill, "On Liberty," in *Essential Works of John Stuart Mill,* ed. Max Lerner (New York: Bantam Books, 1965), 269. Of course, it may do exactly the opposite. See Kretzmer, *supra* note 6, at 462–65.

177. For some there is a deep-seated ambivalence concerning racist speech. A desire for racist speech to go away coincides with a desire for the racist "to just come out and say it." For some, the harm of racist speech coincides with some

vindication in that racism has been exposed. Some would argue that they would rather bear racist insults in order to know who the racists are, but they, in my judgement, are an atypically hardy bunch.

178. For discussion of the harm, see sources cited *supra* note 168.

179. Cf. Delgado, "Words That Wound," *supra* note 6, at 146: "Because they constantly hear racist messages, minority children, not surprisingly, come to question their competence, intelligence, and worth. . . . If the 'majority defines them and their parents as no good, inadequate, dirty, incompetent, and stupid,' the child will find it difficult not to accept those judgments." See also *id.* at 147.

180. See, e.g., C. Edwin Baker, *Human Liberty and Freedom of Speech* (New York: Oxford University Press, 1989); David A. J. Richards, *Toleration and the Constitution* (New York: Oxford University Press, 1986); and Martin Redish, "The Value of Free Speech," 130 *U. Pa. L. Rev.* 591 (1982). For analysis of some of the confusion surrounding the notion of autonomy, see Richard H. Fallon, Jr., "Two Senses of Autonomy," 46 *Stan. L. Rev.* 875 (1994).

181. Expressions of racism may further self-expression while at the same time inhibiting human development. See Delgado, "Campus Antiracism," *supra* note 6, at 379: "[S]ocial science writers hold that making racist remarks impairs, rather than promotes, the growth of the person who makes them, by encouraging rigid, dichotomous thinking and impeding moral development."

182. This does not mean that preferences in conflict with other principles or amendments are suspect. My claim is that the principle of equal concern and respect is foundational in the sense that it is necessary for a legitimate Constitution. That could not be said of federalism or separation of powers, for example.

On the problems associated with taking people's preferences as given, see Cass R. Sunstein, "Democracy and Shifting Preferences," in *The Idea of Democracy,* ed. David Copp, Jean Hampton, and John E. Roemer (New York: Cambridge University Press, 1993), 196; Joshua Cohen, "Moral Pluralism and Political Consensus," in *id.* at 270.

183. A racist speaker need not necessarily argue this way, however. See *supra* note 172.

184. The claim of communists is different in this respect. Communists affirm the equality principle; they deny it has been empirically carried out. To the extent that communists argue against free speech, it seems to me that they are in the same position as the Ku Klux Klan, but the harm of that speech is not in the same league as racist speech. As to the marketplace value of communist speech, see *supra* note 173.

It might be argued that, because the principle of equal concern and respect is subject to varying interpretations, an argument of this sort has "slippery slope" problems. I would note first that this objection does not deny that the speech of the Klan is at odds with the principle of equal respect for persons. It rather worries that the same argument will be used in damaging ways in other contexts. As a practical matter, I think the objection is unfounded. Nor need I rely on the limited form that the argument plays in the analysis that follows.

The argument that creating an unprotected category of racist speech should be avoided because it would lead to other unprotected categories has to suppose that judges who would otherwise not have created new categories would do so because of the racist speech category. Apart from the speculative character of the argument, I am not prepared to assume that the creation of a new category of unprotected speech that followed from or bore a close resemblance to a racist speech category would necessarily be bad. It seems that the issue should turn on the facts—as it should with racist speech. For slippery slope arguments, see Linzer, *supra* note 6, at 205–19; Post, *supra* note 6, at 315–317.

185. Speakers who reject the premise of the system might argue that having been saddled with its disadvantages, they should not be denied its benefits. The problem with this argument is that from the perspective of the system, they have not been disadvantaged; they had no entitlement to mistreat others, and they have not themselves been otherwise mistreated.

186. Cf. John Rawls, *A Theory of Justice* 220 (Cambridge, Mass.: Belknap Press of Harvard University Press, 1971) ("The conclusion, then, is that while an intolerant [religious] sect does not itself have title to complain of intolerance, its freedom should be restricted only when the tolerant sincerely and with reason believe that their own security and that of the institutions are in danger").

187. See *supra* note 88.

188. For discussion of the harm, see sources cited *supra* note 168. To get at the point another way, if John Rawls's "veil of ignorance" (Rawls, *supra* note 186, at 136–42) yields the principle that the basic structure should be arranged to maximize the chances of the least advantaged members in society (the "difference principle." *id.* at 75–83), it seems clear that decision makers applying such a principle would seek laws against racist speech targeting historically disadvantaged groups—unless, as I will suggest, such laws would make matters worse.

It might be objected, however, that liberty rights take priority over the difference principle (*id.* at 243–51), so that the racist's right of free speech should prevail. But this objection is flawed. The justification of the priority of the liberty principle over the difference principle depends on the assumption that such a priority secures the primary good of self-respect (*id.* at 543–48). This assumption is particularly dubious with hate speech. More interesting is the argument that the audience, including members of the disadvantaged class, has an interest in hearing such speech.

189. Although conceptions of respect and autonomy are not without meaning, the same problem arises in many other contexts as well. See generally Shiffrin, "Liberalism," *supra* note 172, at 1147–70.

190. See generally Shiffrin, *supra* note 49, ch. 1; Schauer, "Categories and the First Amendment: A Play in Three Acts," 34 *Vand. L. Rev.* 265 (1981).

191. 418 U.S. 323 (1974).

192. *Id.* at 325.

193. The Court indicated both that it would not lightly abandon state interests compensating individuals for defamatory falsehoods (*id.* at 341) and it was "especially anxious to assure to the freedoms of speech and press that 'breathing space' essential to their fruitful exercise" (*id.* at 342).

194. Strict scrutiny is not applied. See *supra* text accompanying notes 73 to 86.

195. *American Booksellers Ass'n v. Hudnut*, 771 F. 2nd 323 (7th Cir. 1985), *aff'd*, 475 U.S. 1001 (1986) (when content discrimination is present, antipornography ordinance is automatically unconstitutional).

196. See generally Shiffrin, *supra* note 49, ch. 1.

197. Many of those who maintain the assumption that we can have it all are those who do not share in the risks of failure, and who have not directly experienced the harms associated with racist speech. But see *supra* note 11.

198. I do not think this would be true in all circumstances. See *infra* note 219.

199. Of course, ACLU liberals might think such an ordinance violates the meaning of America, but they would not engage in racist speech as a form of protest.

200. Neuborne, *supra* note 6, at 380; Strossen, *supra* note 19, at 559.

201. David O. Sears, "Symbolic Racism," in *Eliminating Racism: Profiles in Controversy*, ed. Phyllis A. Katz and Dalmas A. Taylor (New York: Plenum Press, 1988) ("Symbolic Racism"); Robert M. Entman, "Blacks in the News: Television, Modern Racism and Cultural Change," 69 *Journalism Quarterly* 341 (1992); Donald R. Kinder and David O. Sears, "Prejudice and Politics: Symbolic Racism Versus Racial Threats to the Good Life," 40 *Journal of Personality and Social Psychology* 414 (1981) ("Prejudice and Politics"); John B. McConahay and Joseph C. Hough, Jr., "Symbolic Racism," 32 *Journal of Social Issues* 23 (1976); David O. Sears, Carol P. Hensler, and Leslie K. Speer, "Whites' Opposition of 'Busing': Self-Interest or Symbolic Politics?" 73 *American Political Science Review* 369 (1979); David O. Sears and Donald R. Kinder, "Whites' Opposition to Busing: On Conceptualizing and Operationalizing Group Conflict," 48 *Journal of Personality and Social Psychology* 1141 (1985). See also sources cited *supra* note 167.

202. Kinder and Sears, "Prejudice and Politics," *supra* note 201, at 416.

203. *Id.* at 414.

204. See sources cited *supra* note 201.

205. Derrick Bell, *Faces at the Bottom of the Well* (New York: Basic Books, 1992); Robert Miles, *Racism* (New York: Routledge, 1989); David T. Wellman, *Portraits of White Racism* (New York: Cambridge University Press, 1993); Lawrence Bobo, "Group Conflict, Prejudice, and the Paradox of Contemporary Racial Attitudes," in *Eliminating Racism: Profiles in Controversy*, ed. (Phyllis A. Katz and Dalmas A. Taylor (New York: Plenum Press, 1988), 85 ("Group Conflict"); Lawrence Bobo, "Whites' Opposition to Busing: Symbolic Racism or Realistic Group Conflict?" 45 *Journal of Personality and Social Psychology* 1196 (1983); Richard H. McAdams, "Relative Preferences," 102 *Yale L.J.* 1, 91–103 (1992); Jim Sidanius, Erik Devereux, and Felicia Pratto, "A Comparison of Symbolic Racism Theory and Social Dominance Theory as Explanations for Racial Policy Attitudes," 132 *Journal of Social Psychology* 377 (1992).

206. Bobo, "Group Conflict," *supra* note 205, at 109 (emphasis added). Lawrence Bobo, e.g., one of the most articulate critics of the theory of symbolic racism, settles for the moderate conclusion that "*alongside* our traditional concern with individual prejudice, we should recognize the importance of group conflict."

207. Scott Cummings, "White Ethnics, Racial Prejudice, and Labor Market Segmentation," 85 *American Journal of Sociology* 938 (1980); H. Edward Rans-

ford, "Blue Collar Anger: Reactions to Student and Black Protest," 37 *American Sociological Review* 333 (1972).

208. Bell, *supra* note 205, at 9.

209. Sears, "Symbolic Racism," *supra* note 201, at 56–57.

210. Of course, penalties could be set at a very high level, and this might reduce the number seeking to be martyrs, but it would also intensify the martyrdom and concomitantly fan the racism.

211. To reiterate, I am not claiming that nontargeted racist speech fails to cause injury. But see Charles H. Jones, "Proscribing Hate: Distinctions Between Criminal Harm and Protected Expression," 18 *Wm. Mitchell L. Rev.* 935, 951 (1992) (arguing that the presence or absence of targeting determines whether offense is present or cognizable harm by drawing on a definition of harm from Joel Feinberg, *Harm to Others* [New York: Oxford University Press, 1984], 33–36). Much of the critical race scholarship convincingly argues (see sources cited *supra* note 168) that even nontargeted racist speech harms many individuals and the community. Moreover, sanctions would offer some generalized relief. But, if imposing sanctions promotes more racism than exists in the status quo (admittedly, a contestable claim), the case against sanctions is correspondingly strong.

212. Richard Delgado has observed that British and Canadian laws against racist speech met with initial resistance, which has now largely subsided. Delgado, "Campus Antiracism," *supra* note 6, at 371. This observation might be used to support the notion that racial polarization is not triggered by racist speech legislation (Delgado used it to argue that fears of censorship proved to be misplaced, *id.*). Whether or not racial polarization was fostered in Britain and Canada, the prospects in the United States seem more bleak. To be sure, racism exists in both Britain and Canada, but in the United States racism has been central to election campaigns, and it seems to occupy a more central place in the national consciousness.

Delgado argues that laws against racist speech could play a substantial role in controlling racism, suggesting such laws and rules would 'create a public conscience and a standard for expected behaviour that check *overt* signs of prejudice.' Nor is the change merely cosmetic. In time, rules are internalized, and the impulse to engage in racist behavior weakens." *Id.* at 374, quoting Gordon Allport, *The Nature of Prejudice*, 25th anniversary ed. (Cambridge, Mass.: Addison-Wesley, 1979), 470–71 (emphasis in original). In response, I concede that this is sometimes true; the Civil Rights Act of 1964 provides a good example of the phenomenon of an antiracism law eventually becoming internalized. On the other hand, antiracist rules can create backlash. Many have argued that busing and affirmative action programs have had such effects. Of course, backlash is only one factor to be used in making determinations about such programs. The issue I am raising is whether racist speech regulations are likely to produce such a backlash, and how much of a difference that should make in assessing their desirability.

As I suggest later, the rise of the anti–"political correctness" campaign exemplifies the resistance I believe more general racist speech regulation would face. Indeed, racist speech regulation in other countries has been accompanied by an *increase* in racial violence. Kevin Boyle, "Overview of a Dilemma: Censorship Versus Racism," in *Striking a Balance: Hate Speech, Freedom of Expression and*

Non-Discrimination, ed. Sandra Coliver, Paul Gordon, "Racist Violence: The Expression of Hate in Europe" in *id*. at 9–17. I do not push this point because there might have been an even greater increase in racial violence in the absence of such legislation. The same point applies to increased racial violence on college campuses.

Finally, as I also suggest later, the argument I make here is tentative and necessarily speculative.

213. Proposed antipornography legislation seems to be quite different. With exceptions, the commercial distributors of pornography are in the main less ideologically committed than members of the Klan or the neo-Nazis; thus, deterrence is likely to be more effective. Similarly, the misogynist messages of pornography are less explicit than the racist messages of the Klan or the neo-Nazis; thus, suppression of obscenity or pornography is likely to be regarded as an unconstitutional suppression of (1) speech and (2) a political ideology by many fewer Americans. On the other hand, if society attempted generally to suppress nontargeted hate speech against women, I would expect the general public to regard such an attempt as unconstitutional.

I should be clear that the risk about which I am concerned is increased racism and its consequences, not a risk to the First Amendment. Some might argue that the creation of a racist speech exception to the First Amendment would lead the public to believe that in First Amendment jurisprudence all that matters is whose ox is being gored, and that any such reaction would trigger public cynicism about the First Amendment. With all the cynicism in this country, however, the First Amendment seems to have been untarnished. I am not worried that public respect for the First Amendment would be diminished in ways that would be otherwise damaging.

214. *City of Richmond v. J. A. Croson Co.*, 488 U.S. 469, 493 (1989).

215. This is a common claim, and I believe it to be true, but it has yet to be "supported by any systematic evidence." Paul Burstein, "Affirmative Action and the Rhetoric of Reaction," *American Prospect* 138, 143 (Summer 1993).

216. This is true at least at the time of application (why else would they apply?), and I am not aware of any study showing that beneficiaries are generally dissatisfied with their decisions to apply and accept the benefits of such programs, although, of course, there are prominent examples of individuals who are now dissatisfied.

217. Indeed, the relentless right-wing media campaign against "political correctness" underscores the capacity of hate speech regulations to foment racial hostility.

218. On the other hand, the aspect of my proposal that limits sanctions to speech attacking members of historically oppressed groups (borrowed from Matsuda, *supra* note 6) is likely to be politically unpalatable in many contexts. To the extent that it is, it seems better to drop that aspect than to drop prohibitions altogether. Apart from the politics of the "second best" (an issue she has yet to address), I agree with Matsuda.

219. One exception to my general view would be speech in the workplace. Nontargeted speech in that context can create a hostile environment. In that context, however, free speech issues are taken far less seriously. See MacKinnon, *supra* note 6, at 49–50. Some of the reasons may be an intuition that the work-

place is not a place for free speech (an intuition I do not share, but which helps to explain why the issue has been regarded as more sensitive in universities); the sense that racist workplace speech is actually discrimination; and perhaps a general appreciation for the special difficulty of working under such conditions. One of the general themes of MacKinnon's *Only Words, supra* note 6, is to ask whether it makes any sense to recognize sexual and racial harassment by words in the workplace but not in other contexts as discriminatory conduct.

Another exception to my general view would occur in the context of what the *public* would regard as threats (regrettably, this class of speech is narrower than what *victims* would regard as threatening). Public sympathy for racist speakers who issue direct threats will be low. At least, the question of whether to define speech as targeted or nontargeted should be affected by the presence of threats. Certainly, if a small group is threatened by a nontargeted racial epithet, worries that the imposition of sanctions would be counterproductive diminish substantially.

Finally, the likelihood of a counterproductive reaction is substantially reduced in some "captive audience" situations. When, for example, nontargeted racist graffiti are placed in dorms and other common living spaces in contexts where the manifest intent is to injure or humiliate a captive audience, the perpetrator is far less likely to be regarded by the public as engaging in protected dialogue. Here again, the line between targeted and nontargeted speech tends to dissolve.

220. See *supra* note 4.

221. Cf. West. *supra* note 4, at 65: "In American politics, progressives must not only cling to redistributive ideals, but must also fight for those policies that — out of compromise and concession—imperfectly conform to those ideals. Liberals who give only lip service to those ideals, trash the policies in the name of *realpolitik*, or reject the policies as they perceive a shift in the racial bellwether give up precious ground too easily."

222. See generally Mitchell Cohen and Dennis Hale, eds., *The New Student Left: An Anthology* (Boston: Beacon Press, 1967).

223. See generally Delgado and Stefanic, "Images," *supra* note 6. I do not mean to suggest that more speech is never helpful. It cannot erase injury, however, and it will not eliminate the racist character of society.

224. Too many people assume that vagueness is always fatal in First Amendment analysis; much vagueness is tolerated in First Amendment doctrine, and it should be. Take defamation. Some statements are defamatory; some are not. Sorting out the differences is not always easy, but that does not make the tort of defamation unconstitutional. The amount of vagueness that is tolerable depends in part on the importance of the governmental interest, the extent to which the regulation furthers the interest, the possibility of less restrictive alternatives, and the impact of the vagueness on protected speech.

225. My conclusion is, therefore, contingent on empirical conditions. In many other societies, the case for broader racist speech regulations seems stronger, and the experience with such regulations, albeit mixed, seems to have been positive in many jurisdictions. Sandra Colliver, ed., *Striking a Balance: Hate Speech, Freedom of Expression and Non-Discrimination* (London: University of Essex, 1992).

226. For the broader contention that people of color (or other oppressed groups) should have veto power over issues that affect them directly, see Iris Mar-

ion Young, *Justice and the Politics of Difference* (Princeton, N.J.: Princeton University Press, 1990). 184.

227. In addition, victims of discrimination may be particularly acute in determining the circumstances in which, and the extent to which, discrimination arises. On the other hand, identifying what the "general will" of people of color is could be quite tricky. People of color are divided on the issue of hate speech regulation. How much of a majority does one need in order to defer? Does one need a sense of the amount of information held by those who have opinions? I do not purport to resolve questions like these. I only mean to observe that deference is appropriate, but that the determination to defer could be undermined by diversity of opinions.

228. Practitioners of outsider jurisprudence would probably do so as well, but especially as an instrument for securing justice for the marginalized; the emphasis of the perspectives is different.

229. People will be not converted merely because they are punished (Minow, *supra* note 6, at 1403), and "re-education" of the perpetrator is not a promising form of punishment. Grey, *supra* note 6, at 88 n.19

230. This is not to assume that all individuals will move for redress; much of the writing about the injuries caused by racist speech makes clear that flight may be a more frequent reaction than confrontation. But the availability of the remedy is what justice seems to require. Victims of physical assault might not pursue redress, but they deserve an available remedy.

231. The same statements are likely in most circumstances to cause broader injury to individuals not explicitly targeted and may be intended to do so, but that harm would not be the basis for regulation.

232. I do not see any particular grounds for optimism. See generally Bell, *supra* note 205.

Chapter IV
Dissent and Injustice

1. Some might worry that reactionary dissent will prevail, however. I would argue that worrying about reactionary corporate control is misplaced because we already have it. To worry about the ascendance of militiamen is to give too much credit to sensational media reports, to ignore the infiltration of law enforcement agencies, to exaggerate the contribution an emphasis on dissent might have, and to underestimate human beings.

2. Not all dissent combats injustice, nor is the combating of injustice the only value implicated in promoting dissent. Nonetheless, I restrict myself to the injustice aspect in this chapter. For an excellent presentation of the need for supporting dissent outside institutions from a postmodernist perspective, see William E. Connolly, *The Ethos of Pluralization* (Minneapolis: University of Minnesota Press, 1995); and William E. Connolly, *Identity/Difference: Democratic Negotiations of Political Paradox* (Ithaca, N.Y.: Cornell University Press, 1991) (*Identity/Difference*). The suggestion that society should nurture dissent is also well, but differently, presented in Ian Shapiro, *Democracy's Place* (Ithaca, N.Y., Cornell University Press, 1996); Robin West, "Foreword: Taking Freedom Seriously," 104 *Harv. L. Rev.* 40, 96 (1990); Vincent A. Blasi, "The Checking Value in First Amendment

Theory," 1977 *Am. Bar Found. Res.J.* 521 (emphasis on dissent to governmental action by press). For a brief but powerful discussion, see also C. Edwin Baker, *Human Liberty and Freedom of Speech* (New York: Oxford University Press, 1989), 118–21.

3. Jack Balkin argues that a main purpose of democracy and of our Constitution is to eradicate unjust hierarchies. One way of looking at much of this chapter is that it fits the First Amendment into that general interpretation. J. M. Balkin, "The Constitution of Status," 106 *Yale L.J.*, 2313 (1997). Note, however, that neither Balkin nor I would suggest that the exclusive purpose of the First Amendment is to combat unjust hierarchies. In addition, I do not believe it is possible to eliminate unjust hierarchies. For a related claim, which I also support, see David Lyons, "Normal Law, Nearly Just Societies, and Other Myths of Legal Theory," 1992 *Conference of the U.K. Association for Legal and Social Philosophy*, 13: "We have no plausible theory which is capable of supporting the claim that there is normally a moral presumption favoring obedience to the law. And we are unlikely to discover such a theory, because it is implausible to suppose that minimal requirements of moral decency have normally been satisfied by the sorts of law to which the vast majority of people have actually been subjected throughout most of legal history and to which the vast majority of people are being subjected today."

4. For incisive commentary on the psychology of the slide from difference to resentment, see Connolly, *Identity/Difference, supra* note 2, at 80–81.

5. See generally Michael Walzer, *Spheres of Justice: A Defense of Pluralism and Equality* (New York: Basic Books, 1983).

6. This theme permeates John Stuart Mill's *On Liberty*, ed. David Spitz (New York: Norton, 1975). See also Charles E. Lindblom, *Inquiry and Change: The Troubled Attempt to Understand and Shape Society* (New Haven, Conn.: Yale University Press, 1990), 69, 118–35.

7. As Samuel Scheffler, *Human Morality* (New York: Oxford University Press, 1992), 143, puts it:

[P]eople have a strong interest in achieving forms of personal integration that tend to have the effect of encouraging moral conservatism, and although this fact has its advantages, it also suggests that the reliability of the "commonsense" moral instincts shared by the members of a given society may depend to a significant extent on the justice or injustice of the society in question. In a seriously unjust society, well-intentioned people may have internalized moral attitudes that make the injustice of their institutions genuinely difficult for them to perceive, and all their instincts may testify to the society's moral soundness. By contrast, the people who find the injustices easier to perceive may be people who were already alienated from society in one way or another, and precisely because of their socially marginal status they may be dismissed by many well-intentioned and well-integrated people as mere cranks or gadflies. In an unjust society, however, the cranks and gadflies may be able to see some things more clearly than those who are better integrated.

8. Some worry that dissent will be too effective and bring about instability. Would that it be so! One person's instability is frequently another person's escape from domination. But, conceding that some forms of stability are harmful overall, promotion of dissent is unlikely to wreak havoc. The impulse to conform is strong,

and encouragement is not control. In a regime serious about encouraging dissent, most citizens would still free ride, waiting for others to speak up. More would speak up, but chaos is not around the corner. Even crediting the stability concern, the risk is worth taking because injustice permeates the status quo. Risking instability is better than accepting injustice.

9. For insightful, but quite different, perspectives on power, see Duncan Kennedy, *Sexy Dressing Etc.* (Cambridge, Mass.: Harvard University Press, 1993); Nancy Hartsock, "Foucault on Power: A Theory for Woman?" in *Feminism/Postmodernism*, ed. Linda J. Nicholson (New York: Routledge, 1990).

10. John Rawls, *A Theory of Justice* (Cambridge, Mass.: Belknap Press of Harvard University Press, 1971).

11. John Rawls, *Political Liberalism* (New York: Columbia University Press, 1993).

12. *Id.* at 303–4 (emphasis added).

13. Rawls, *Theory, supra* note 10, at 226. See also Rawls, *Political Liberalism, supra* note 11, at 324–31.

14. Rawls, *Theory, supra* note 10, at 226–27. See also Rawls, *Political Liberalism, supra* note 11, at 327 ("beyond the scope of a philosophical doctrine to consider in any detail the kinds of arrangements required to insure the fair value of the equal political liberties").

15. Rawls, *Political Liberalism, supra,* note 11, at 19. See also *id.* at 202–3.

16. Rawls, *Political Liberalism, supra,* note 11, at 19. See also *id.* at 202–3.

17. *Id.* at 206. See also *id.* at 205. Samuel Scheffler argues that those who are not victims of injustice in an unjust society have a moral duty to combat it and that one of the advantages of a just society is that it makes fewer moral demands, leaving people freer to pursue their own advantage. Scheffler, *supra*, note 7, at 139–40 (1992). Cf. Judith N. Shklar, *American Citizenship: The Quest for Inclusion* (Cambridge, Mass.: Harvard University Press, 1991), 6–7: "Good citizens . . . support the public good as it is defined by their constitution and its fundamental ethos. [T]he possibility of tension between personal morality and citizenship is always possible and even likely, and there are, of course, regimes so terrible that good people are bound to be bad citizens there. . . ." I would suggest without further ruminations on the nature of citizenship that good citizens resist the public good as defined by the Constitution to the extent such a definition is unjust.

18. *Id.* at 199–200.

19. See also Charles E. Larmore, *Patterns of Moral Complexity* (New York: Cambridge University Press, 1987), 66 ("Whatever the limits to its neutrality, equal respect is neutral with regard to the ideals of skepticism, experimentalism, and autonomy"). See also *id.* at 43–44 (general perspective on neutrality).

20. Stephen Gardbaum, "Liberalism, Autonomy, and Moral Conflict," 48 *Stan. L. Rev.* 385 (1996). Others have denied that neutrality between and among conceptions of the good is a necessary feature of liberalism. See, e.g., William A. Galston, *Liberal Purposes: Goods, Virtues, and Diversity in the Liberal State* 79–117 (Cambridge: Cambridge University Press, 1991); Vinit Haksar, *Equality, Liberty and Perfectionism* (Oxford: Oxford University Press, 1979); William A. Galston, "Defending Liberalism," 76 *American Political Science Review* 621 (1982); and Steven Shiffrin, "Liberalism, Radicalism, and Legal Scholarship," 30 *UCLA*

L. Rev. 1103 (1983). Brian M. Barry, *Justice as Impartiality* (New York: Oxford University Press, 1995), 131, 161, would not permit conceptions of the good, including autonomy, to be constitutionally privileged but would permit some conceptions of the good, including autonomy, to be advanced by a legislature.

21. See, e.g., Joseph Raz, *The Morality of Freedom* (New York: Oxford University Press, 1986).

22. Richard Rorty, *Contingency, Irony, and Solidarity* (New York: Cambridge University Press, 1989), 60–61, can be read for the proposition that dissent should be encouraged although the idea is underdeveloped, subject to the same objections I make against Mill, and proceeds from an unattractive epistemology (see my comments on postmodernism in chapter one).

23. Mill, *supra* note 6, at 6, 19, 58, 66.

24. *Id.* at 53–69.

25. *Id.* at 56.

26. *Id.* at 56–60.

27. *Id.* at 18.

28. *Id.* at 46.

29. John Stuart Mill, *Principles of Political Economy*, ed. Sir William Ashley (Fairfield, N.J.: A. M. Kelley, 1987).

30. John Stuart Mill, *Considerations on Representative Government* (South Bend, Ind.: Gateway Editions, 1962), 32.

31. See *id.* at 22–23.

32. See *supra* text accompanying note 25.

33. Mill, *supra* note 6, at 46.

34. Mill, *supra* note 30, at 179–83.

35. Mill, *supra* note 6, at 63.

36. Mill, *supra* note 30, at 34.

37. More rarely, journalists praise themselves for a function they often serve. See Joan Konner, "Publishers Note: Without Fear or Favor," *Columbia Journalism Review* 4, quoting Adolph Ochs: "The *New York Times* . . . so far as possible—consistent with honest journalism—attempts to aid and support those who are charged with the responsibility of government." According to Konner, Ochs "set the standards against which journalism continues to be measured." *Id.*

38. The level of discussion, however, is notoriously superficial. For a penetrating discussion, see Ronald K. L. Collins and David M. Skover, *The Death of Discourse* (Boulder, Colo.: Westview Press, 1996).

39. Not entirely separate from the perception of the Christian right as Other, or a fringe group, the media tends to be somewhat more favorable to pro-choice groups than to pro-life groups and usually exhibits little patience with negative stereotyping of gays. See Howard Kurz, "Beyond the Fringe, a New Skittishness," *Washington Post National Edition*, May 17–23, 1993, at 25, cols. 1–4.

40. For insightful discussion of the negative impact of advertising on democratic commitments, see C. Edwin Baker, *Advertising and a Democratic Press* (Princeton, N.J.: Princeton University Press, 1994); Collins and Skover, *supra* note 38.

41. See John Morton, "The Business of Journalism: Value of Newspapers Will Fall in War," *Washington Journalism Review*, March 1991, 56: "Advertising typi-

cally accounts for 80% of revenue and all the profit at most newspapers; these days circulation revenue does not even cover the cost of the paper a daily is printed on."

42. International Commission for the Study of Human Problems, *Many Voices, One World: Toward a More Just and More Efficient World Information and Communications Order* (London: K. Page, 1980), 110.

43. See generally Erving Goffman, *Gender Advertisements* (New York: Harper and Row, 1979). This problem is not confined to advertising. See Mary E. Becker, "The Politics of Women's Wrongs and the Bill of Rights," 59 *U. Chi. L. Rev.* 453 486–90 (1992).

44. Joanne Lipman, "Sexy or Sexist? Recent Ads Spark Debate," *Wall Street Journal,* September 30, 1991, at B1, col. 4, quoting Ron Anderson of ad agency Bozell.

45. Thus one junior ad executive states, "You've always got to be conscious of who your customer is. It may offend some groups—but they aren't your customers." *Id.* at B1.

46. See generally Catharine Mackinnon, *Feminism Unmodified: Discourses in Life and Law* (Cambridge, Mass.: Harvard University Press, 1987).

47. Sut Jhally, *The Codes of Advertising: Fetishism and the Political Economy of Meaning in the Consumer Society* (New York: St. Martin's Press, 1987), 138–39.

48. Ronald K. L. Collins, "Bikini Team: Sexism for the Many," *Los Angeles Times,* November 20, 1991, at B5, col. 1. For the suggestion that some advertisers are in the process of changing their ways, see Joanne Lipman, "Farewell, at Last, to Bimbo Campaigns," *Wall Street Journal,* January 31, 1992, at B2, col. 4.

49. Some life insurance company commercials fit this description. More typically, even though commercials for the most part depict the world in rosy terms, the recipient is often made to feel anxious because her life does not measure up to the nostalgic characterizations of life portrayed in the commercial. Of course, the message is that possession of the advertised product will relieve the anxiety.

50. William Leiss, Stephen Kline, and Sut Jhally, *Social Communication in Advertising: Persons, Products, and Images of Well-being,* 2d ed. (Toronto: Methuen, 1990), 69: "[A]dvertisements . . . [link] new goods and styles with traditional images of well-being: the slower pace, quiet and serenity, open space, and closeness to nature of rural life; happiness of loved ones in a close family setting that includes multiple generations; the attainment of goals set in accordance with personal, rather than institutional, demands; the concern for quality and good taste in judging fine foods, wine and clothing. An advertisement's composition often connects background imagery with products having not the slightest intrinsic relation to it—the automobile or cigarette package displayed against a stunning picture of unspoiled wilderness, the liquor bottle set in a farmhouse room full of hand-crafted furniture—in a straightforward attempt to effect a transfer of the positive feelings evoked by the imagery to the product."

51. Ronald K. L. Collins and Michael F. Jacobson, "Commercialism v. Culture," *Christian Science Monitor,* September 19, 1990, at 19, col. 4. On the negative effects of advertising, see generally Ronald K. L. Collins and David M. Skover, "Commerce & Communication," 71 *Tex. L. Rev.* 697 (1993). For responses by

Alex Kozinski and Stuart Banner, Rodney A. Smolla, Sut Jhally, and Leo Bogart, see *id*. at 747–832.

52. For discussion of the impact of advertisers on the nonadvertising content of the mass media in both entertainment and public affairs contexts, see generally Ronald K. L. Collins, *Dictating Content: How Advertising Pressure Can Corrupt a Free Press* (Washington, D.C.: Center for the Study of Commercialism, 1992); C. Edwin Baker, "Advertising and a Democratic Press," 140 *U. Pa. L. Rev.* 2097 (1992). See also Cass R. Sunstein, *Democracy and the Problem of Free Speech* (New York: Free Press, 1993, 62–66.

53. See Mark Crispin Miller, *Boxed In: The Culture of TV* (Evanston, Ill.: Northwestern University Press (1988), 13 (emphasis added): "In 1959[,] one adman wrote a letter to Elmer Rice, explaining why the agency would not support a series based on the playwright's early realist drama *Street Scene*: " 'We know of no advertiser or advertising agency of any importance in this country who would knowingly allow the products which he is trying to advertise to the public to become associated with the squalor . . . and general "down" character . . . of *Street Scene*. . . . On the contrary, *it is the general policy of advertisers to glamorize their products, the people who buy them, and the whole American social and economic scene.*' " Advertisers generally are provided suitable surroundings for their products: "[W]ith few exceptions, prime time gives us people preoccupied with personal ambition. . . . If not surrounded by middle-class arrays of consumer goods, they themselves are glamorous incarnations of desire. The happiness they long for is private, not public; they make few demands on society as a whole, and even when troubled they seem content with the existing institutional order. . . . The sumptuous and brightly lit settings of most series amount to advertisements for a consumption-centered version of the good life, and this doesn't even take into consideration the incessant commercials, which convey the idea that human aspiration for liberty, pleasure, accomplishment, and status can be fulfilled in the realm of consumption. The relentless background hum of prime time is this packaged good life." Todd Gitlin, *Inside Prime Time* (New York: Pantheon 1983), 268–69.

54. For example, when *thirty something* aired an episode focusing on a one-night stand between two gay characters, ABC lost $1,000,000 in advertising. When the two characters reappeared on the show in the course of the depiction of a New Year's Eve party, they briefly discussed their one-night stand and gave each other a midnight kiss on the cheek. For this episode, ABC lost $500,000. "When Gay Means Loss of Revenue," *Los Angeles Times,* December 22, 1990, at F1. More recently, gay and lesbian characters have begun to appear on television with some regularity, but this is because of advertiser approval (perhaps the newly discovered recognition that gays and lesbians buy products).

Because of concern about the possibility of advertiser withdrawals, "producers frequently discuss the plots of their shows with a network before filming begins." Kevin Goldman, "NBC to Hold Show's Producers Liable for Advertiser Response to Gay Plot," *Wall Street Journal,* September 30, 1991, at B4, col. 3. Jeff Sagansky, president of CBS Entertainment, maintains, as an industry publication put it, that advertisers are "increasingly reluctant to back hard-hitting shows because special interest groups are more active in threatening boycotts." *Broadcasting*, February 15, 1993, at 12.

55. Controversial themes can be explored on network television, but they must be dealt with in a balanced way so that segments of the mass audience will not be offended. The line between balance and blandness is often thin. For treatment of the ways in which special interest groups pressure the networks to keep controversial material off the air or to minimize its offensive aspects and the ways in which the networks seek to handle the pressure, see generally Kathryn C. Montgomery, *Target: Prime Time: Advocacy Groups and the Struggle over Entertainment Television* (New York: Oxford University Press, 1989).

56. Jan Hoffman, "TV Shouts 'Baby' (and Barely Whispers 'Abortion')," *New York Times,* May 31, 1992, at 27.

57. *Id.*

58. *Id.*

59. Martin A. Lee and Norman Solomon, *Unreliable Sources: A Guide to Detecting Bias in News Media* (New York: Carol Publishing Group, 1990), 3. Like the sitcoms, the problem pursued in the action program is ordinarily solved by the end of the show. On television, therefore, problems can usually be resolved within the program hour or by a race to the local store to buy a product. It is a shame that political candidates can do no more than promise the instant solutions television encourages us to expect. For the suggestion that violent programming is motivated by the cheap production costs and its popularity in the global market rather than ratings in the United States, see Jeff Cohen and Norman Solomon, *Through the Media Looking Glass: Decoding Bias and Blather in the News* (Monroe, Maine: Common Courage Press, 1995), 62–63.

60. Sonia Shah, "The Index: TV Violence and Paranoia," 1 *Mediaculture Review,* February 1992, at 7–8.

61. Ben Bagdikian, *The Media Monopoly,* 3d ed. (Boston: Beacon Press, 1990), 8. See also Leiss, *supra* note 50, at 186, citing Gitlin, *supra* note 53: "[Networks] just want the audience to watch so that their time can be sold to advertisers. Networks have no economic need for good quality programming that challenges and excites the audience. Simple attention-getting, as opposed to communicating interesting and thought-provoking material, is enough. The components of a set network formula are occasionally adjusted for particular programs, making commercial television a form of 'recombinant culture' in which the same elements—sex, adventure, violence—are constantly rejuggled."

62. John Keane, *The Media and Democracy* (Cambridge, Mass.: Blackwell, 1991), 67; Gitlin, *supra* note 53, at 92. To some extent, however, the cheery face of American television is unconnected to advertiser dependence (though noncommercial television would be unlikely to sport programming frequently interrupted with sweeping vistas and soaring music). Few American viewers would want to see a steady diet of programming "downers." Nonetheless, it is possible that the happy atmosphere of American television has encouraged a pervasive demand for cheer. Consider the forced public displays of cheerful comaraderie on *your* local newscast *wherever* it may be.

63. G. Bruce Knecht, "Magazine Advertisers Demand Prior Notice of 'Offensive' Articles," *Wall Street Journal*, April 30, 1997, A1, col. 6. Ultimately, Chrysler

dropped its demand for early warnings but stated that it still did not want to be associated with controversial articles and indicated that it would reduce the number of magazines in which it would place ads because it would not be receiving early warnings. Other important companies that demand early warnings expressed surprise at Chrysler's move and stated that they planned no similar moves. G. Bruce Knecht, "Chrysler Drops Its Requirement for an Early Look at Magazines," *Asian Wall Street Journal*, 1997 WL-WSJA 1469426 (October 16, 1997).

64. *Id.* at A6, col. 5.

65. *Id.* at A1, col. 6.

66. See Baker, *supra* note 52, at 2164–67; Keane, *supra* note 62, at 77–78. By looking to ratings as a basis for continuing programming, television executives do not take the intensity of the preferences of viewers into account. *Id.* at 79.

67. See Edward L. Palmer, *Television and America's Children: The Crisis of Neglect* (New York: Oxford University Press, 1988), 21–25 (discussing why advertiser-supported television fails children).

68. Rick Du Brow, "NBC Faces a Prime-Time Identity Crisis," *Los Angeles Times*, March 14, 1992, at F1. See also W. Leiss, *supra* note 50, at 113 (discussing preference for reliable consumers over elderly, low-income, and rural consumers); Montgomery, *supra* note 55, at 107 (cancellation of high-rated shows with "rural skews"); Bill Carter, "Fall Network Schedules Offer Plenty of Choices (At Least for the Young)," *New York Times*, May 27, 1992, at C15.

69. See generally Tom Shales, "Murder They Wrote Off," *Washington Post*, May 19, 1996 at G01.

70. Bagdikian, *supra* note 61, at 116.

71. Herbert J. Gans, *Deciding What's News: A Study of CBS Evening News, NBC Nightly News, Newsweek and Time* (New York: Vintage Books, 1980), 216.

72. Deirdre Carmody, "Ms. Magazine Prepares for a Life Without Ads," *New York Times*, March 5, 1990, at D9, col. 2.

73. At the local broadcast level, cheery talk and the need for a happy story mixed in with the weather and sports do not leave much time for serious stories of any kind, let alone the entertaining of radical questions and critique.

74. Gans, *supra* note 71, at 277.

75. See David McReynolds, "Socialism Yes," *The Progressive*, April 1993, at 24, 26 (struggle for socialism not about which party controls Washington, but about economic power).

76. See Robert M. Entman, *Democracy Without Citizens: Media and the Decay of American Politics* (New York: Oxford University Press, 1989), 21: "[S]cholars find that coverage of presidential campaigns generally emphasizes the horse race (who's gaining, who's fading, and why) much more than the policy issues or records of the candidates." See also Sunstein, *supra* note 52, at 60–61; Jeffrey C. Goldfarb, *The Cynical Society: The Culture of Politics and the Politics of Culture America* (Chicago: University of Chicago Press, 1991), 5–6; Shanto Iyengar and Donald R. Kinder, *News That Matters* 127–29 (Chicago: University of Chicago Press, 1987); Emmet H. Buell, Jr., " 'Locals and "Cosmopolitans': . . . Newspaper Coverage of the New Hampshire Primary," in Garry R. Orren and Nelson W. Polsby, *Media and Momentum: The New Hampshire Primary and Nomination Politics* (Chatham, N.J.: Chatham House, 1987), 60–103; Henry R.

Brady and Richard Johnston, "What's the Primary Message: Horse Race or Issue Journalism?" in Orren and Polsby, *supra*, at 127–86; John Tierney, "Campaign Journal: Now Journalists Renege on Election Promises," *New York Times*, January 31, 1992, at A12, col. 5.

77. Coverage of the 1992 presidential election may have presented more about the issues than many prior elections, but coverage of most state and congressional elections followed the horse race pattern. Even in the 1992 presidential election, a six-week study of the period immediately following the Republican National Convention found that only 17 percent of the three major network's election stories focused on policy issues: "Several important topics such as education, crime, the military budget, racism, and the banking crisis were not the subject of any campaign reports during the six weeks studied." Jim Naureckas, "Unfair to Bush? Unfair to Clinton? Campaign Coverage Was Unfair to Voters," 5 *Extra!* December 1992, at 5, 6.

78. One of the more spectacular failures during the Clinton administration was the failure of the press to take the time to understand the positions of Lani Guiner. See generally Laurel Leff, "From Legal Scholar to Quota Queen," 32 *Columbia Journalism Review* 36 (September 1993/ October 1993).

79. See generally Thomas Ferguson and Joel Rogers, *Right Turn: The Decline of Democrats and the Future of American Politics* (New York: Hill and Wang, 1986). See also Jeff Cohen and Norman Solomon, *supra* note 59, at 12–18.

80. Jeffrey B. Abramson et al., *The Electronic Commonwealth* (New York: Basic Books, 1988), 98.

81. As Walter Karp has stated, "It is investigative journalism that wins the professional honors, that makes what little history the press ever makes, and that provides the misleading exception that proves the rule: the American press, unbidden by powerful sources, seldom investigates anything." Quoted in Lee and Solomon, *supra* note 59, at 18.

82. John R. Zaller, *The Nature and Origins of Mass Opinion* (Cambridge: Cambridge University Press, 1992), 315.

83. Watergate is the exception that proves the rule. It was a story pursued at great expense and great risk by one newspaper. Watergate reporting is to press practice as *LA Law* was to legal practice. As Gans observes, "The investigative reporting required for an exposé is expensive and not always productive, for reporters must usually be assigned to the story for weeks, if not months, thus making them unavailable for other stories; and sometimes, months of investigation may not produce a suitable story. As a result, most news media resort to investigative reporting only when they cannot get access any other way or, equally often, when they need a circulation or rating booster." Gans, *supra* note 71, at 118–19.

84. "[T]elevision news, and American news in general, reflects and sustains the 'official' view. Journalists rely heavily on officials and on routine channels of information—the press conference, the informal briefing, and the handout." Iyengar & Kinder, *supra* note 76, at 132. One study found that 78 percent of the sources for domestic and foreign stories in the *New York Times* and the *Washington Post* were public officials. Leon V. Sigal, *Reporters and Officials* (Lexington, Mass.: D. C. Heath, 1973), 124, table 6–5.

85. Quoted in Lee and Solomon, *supra* note 59, at 17.

86. Mark Hertsgaard, *The Press on Bended Knee: The Press and the Reagan Presidency* (New York: Farrar, Straws, and Giroux, 1988), 55. See also *id.* at 59 (quoting *Boston Globe* reporter stating that the *New York Times* is "shameless with the fawning profiles of White House officials who will later be leaking stories [to the authors of said profiles].") See also Entman, *supra* note 76, at 20: "Government sources and journalists join in an intimacy that renders any notion of a genuinely 'free' press inaccurate."

87. Hertsgaard, *supra* note 86, at 68. Despite the conventional wisdom depicting Reagan as an uncommonly popular president, polls show that his average approval rating over the course of his years in office place him fifth among the last nine presidents. Lee and Solomon, *supra* note 59, at 148. Despite press reports of a mandate for Reagan, only 27 percent of the eligible voting public cast a ballot for him in 1980, and his advisers were aware that his proposed policies were well to the right of the American public. See Hertsgaard, *supra* note 86, at 102, 106.

88. More precisely, the Democrats sold themselves to segments of the business community. See generally Ferguson and Rogers, *supra* note 79.

89. By contrast, the spectrum of political discussion is markedly broader in European countries. See Hertsgaard, *supra* note 86, at 70.

90. The policy issues that are discussed in election campaigns are also largely dictated by the candidates. An important policy question will ordinarily not be an issue in an election campaign unless the candidates make it an issue. Thus, in the 1988 election (though they were unaware of the magnitude of the problem), reporters in America knew that the savings and loan industry would be a major item on the agenda of the next presidency, but neither candidate sought to make it an issue, and the press did not make it an election issue. See generally Howard Kurz, *Media Circus: The Trouble with America's Newspapers* (New York: Times Books, 1993), 47–68. On the other hand, as the focus on Gary Hart in 1988 and Bill Clinton in 1992 shows, the media will raise character issues to the point of obsession even if the other candidates do not. See Tierney, *supra* note 76.

91. A particularly important example concerned welfare reform. The Congress and president were at odds mainly on the question of how many people to throw off the rolls. The press coverage reflected that debate until shortly before the president signed the bill. See Neil deMause, "Following the Parties' Line on Welcome 'Reform,'" 9 *Extra* 6 (November/December 1996); Janine Jackson, "Economic Pack Journalism," *id.* at 11.

92. The early hostile reporting on President Clinton's administration can be attributed to a number of factors that went beyond his job performance: (1) a response to criticism that the press had been hard on Bush and easy on Clinton in the latter days of the campaign (which itself was attributable to Clinton's standing in the horse race); (2) a sense that Clinton was a minority president without a mandate; (3) a response to the existence of powerful criticism by Republican leaders; (4) and anger over the way Clinton treated the national press after gaining the presidency (making himself and others around him less accessible than during the campaign and routing many stories to the local press while circumventing the national press). One of the better discussions of the press's treatment of President Clinton in his early months in the White House is Christopher Georges, "Bad

News Bearers," 25 *Washington Monthly* 28 (July/August 1993). The Whitewater issue was given short shrift during the campaign but major press treatment during the Clinton administration. It was pushed during the administration because Republican leaders pressed the issue. During the campaign, "a key reason elite media dropped the story was that the only newsmaker pressing it was Jerry Brown, who . . . was considered an anti-establishment candidate, whom journalists were more prone to deride than quote." Jeff Cohen and Norman Solomon, "Whitewater Under the Bridge: How the Press Missed the Story," 7 *Extra* 8, 9 (May/June 1994).

93. See "Holding His Ground," 9 *Extra* 5 (July/August 1996).

94. *Id.* at 60–61. Bernard C. Cohen, *The Press and Foreign Policy* (Princeton, N.J.: Princeton University Press, 1963), 28–30. See also Entman, *supra* note 76, at 18: "The least expensive way to satisfy mass audiences is to rely on legitimate political elites for most information."

95. See Mitchell Stephens, *A History of News* (New York: Viking Press), 267 ("[T]he working definition of objectivity subscribed to by modern journalists demands that they rely on 'responsible' sources for their information and attribute any potentially controversial statements to those sources. But in selecting the persons whose views they will publicize, journalists invariably demonstrate a bias— usually toward those invested by society with some credentials or authority").

96. See Gans, *supra* note 71, at 42: "Like the news of other countries, American news values its own nation above all, even though it sometimes disparages blatant patriotism. This ethnocentrism comes through most explicitly in foreign news, which judges other countries by the extent to which they live up to or imitate American practices and values." See also Michael Parenti, *Inventing Reality: The Politics of the Mass Media* (New York: St. Martin's Press, 1986), 113.

97. Quoted in Hertsgaard, *supra* note 86, at 64.

98. This is not a bizarre hypothetical. See generally Gabriel Kolko, *Confronting the Third World* (New York: Pantheon, 1988).

99. See Gans, *supra* note 71, at 270–71: "These days journalists and government are commonly thought to be in an adversary relationship, although government is not an adversary most of the time. As the major source of news, it is in many ways a member of the journalistic team; and even during the Watergate years, journalists continued to cooperate with many segments of the government, including the White House.

The principal source of cooperation is built into the source considerations, through their skew toward official sources; and into the symbiotic relationship between beat reporters and their sources, which inhibits reporters from displeasing them." See also *id.* at 132–36.

100. See *id.* Keane, *supra* note 62, at 103. For discussion of exclusion of access and other techniques used to discourage or retaliate against unfavorable reporting, see George C. Edwards, *The Public Presidency* (New York: St. Martin's Press, 1983), 128–33; Michael Baruch Grossman and Martha Joynt Kumar, *Portraying the President: The White House and the News Media* (Baltimore, Md.: Johns Hopkins University Press, 1981), 280–81, 288–93.

101. See Gans, *supra* note 71, at 274. See also Hertsgaard, *supra* note 86, at 72.

102. The more fragmented the market, the more outlets that will strive for a portion of the audience, a "niche." Although the existence of multiple channels tends to produce more attempts to reach a part of the audience, the networks still aim for a mass audience, and the nonmovie channels have advertising that tends to limit the presentation of partisan views.

103. For persuasive commentary suggesting that the real culprit may have been advertising, see Baker, *supra* note 52, at 2103–32. See *id.* at 2131: "In sum, there are economic reasons to expect, historical evidence to suggest, and contemporary consciousness to indicate that both the decline of political partisanship and the rise of objectivity were at least partly caused by newspapers' need to gain the circulation on which advertising income depends."

104. Stephens, *supra* note 95, at 262. See also Abramson, *supra* note 80, at 14.

105. See *id.*

106. Douglas Kellner, *Television and the Crisis of Democracy* (Boulder, Colo.: Westview Press, 1990), 47–48.

107. *Id.* at 9.

108. Jim Naureckas, "Gulf War Coverage," 4 *Extra!* May, 1991, at 3, 5. Apart from the cheerleading coverage afforded to the war, the mainstream media did not join a legal challenge contesting Pentagon censorship during the war. Indeed, the major news media did not *report* the existence of the lawsuit until after the war was over. Lee and Solomon, *supra* note 59, at xvi.

109. Lee and Solomon, *supra* note 59, xxi.

110. *Id.*

111. *Id.* See also Abramson, *supra* note 80, at 29: "[M]inority and novel political views are the ones least in the position to attract television attention or to buy promotional time. The range of political programming on television thus tends to be fairly homogeneous—aimed at the tastes and preferences of the widest possible mass audience." Are the typical talk show hosts right-wing or sensationalists or both? Why?

112. There is some evidence that progressive spokespersons have been denied access to television and radio public affairs programs because of a refusal of a defense department guest to appear with peace proponents. See Lee and Solomon, *supra* note 59, at 105.

113. Gans *supra* note 71, at 52. See also *id.* at 67–68.

114. See Gans, *supra* note 71, at 212. An ABC News Washington bureau chief observed in the mid-1980s that: "Today as never before our reporters are part of the town's elite, which seems a reasonable factor in explaining why there is less of an adversarial tone in the coverage [of Washington]." Quoted in Hertsgaard, *supra* note 86, at 44.

115. Gans, *supra* note 71, at 190–93.

116. Gans, *supra* note 71, 190–94; Hertsgaard, *supra* note 86, at 80, quoting one of the original producers of Nightline: "The political sensibilities of people in network television are mainstream, traditional and conservative; neither far left nor far right. . . . We share the same basic assumptions of bankers, lawyers and the rest of the establishment. You ain't going to see a bunch of radicals coming in here."

117. *Id.* at 30–31.

118. As Goldfarb, *supra* note 76, at 111, observes, the battle of the conservatives "has escalated. It is no longer primarily concerned with Godless communism but with liberalism."

119. Lee and Solomon, *supra* note 59, at 61.

120. Gitlin, *supra* note 53, at 269–70.

121. See generally Baker, *supra* note 52, at 2144–53; Collins, *supra* note 52.

122. Morton Mintz, "A Reporter Looks Back in Anger," 55 *The Progressive* 29, 29 (December 1991).

123. Quoted in *id.* at 32.

124. *Sixty Minutes* has broadcast many stories critical of particular businesses. Here again culprits exist, but the structure is not on trial, nor are valuable advertisers.

125. Lee and Solomon, *supra* note 59, at 185.

126. Of course, "reform" of corporations is not the goal of radicals. But the corporate media's relative silence about abuses arising in a capitalist system is itself the sort of abuse that radicals would decry.

127. Lee and Solomon, *supra* note 59, at 29.

128. Bagdikian, *supra* note 61, at x. See also *id.* at 42: "In the years after World War II, no standard newspaper in the country would accept ads from Consumers Union because its magazine, *Consumer Reports*, tested and reported, sometimes negatively, name brands advertised in Washington." See also Comment, "Cigarette Advertising and Freedom of Expression," *U. Toronto Fac. L. Rev.* 304, 322 (1990) (citing differences between coverage of tobacco health issues among magazines that relied heavily on tobacco advertising and those that did not).

129. Lee and Solomon, *supra* note 59, at 64.

130. *Id.*

131. Often it is very obvious. For example, ABC was planning to do a report on the dangers of fiberglass, which exists in 90 percent of American homes. The concern was that fiberglass may cause lung cancer. The fiberglass industry pressured the network, and the network pulled the story. Susan Douglas, "Human Nature and the Newsroom," 60 *The Progressive* 17 (July 1996).

132. Lee and Solomon, *supra* note 59, at 96. Sometimes the intervention is more obvious. After CBS came under new management in 1982, CBS Evening News producer Richard Cohen reported that the new managers "had a view of what kind of news makes for good ratings: more features, make it light and bright, soften it up. Don't be negative about the President, people don't want to hear that." Quoted in Hertsgaard, *supra* note 86, at 163. See also Abramson, *supra* note 80, at 285–86. The drive for ratings was successful, and the other networks began to imitate CBS. See Hertsgaard, *supra* note 86, at 176.

133. Lee and Solomon, *supra* note 59, at 93.

134. See, e.g., Gans, *supra* note 71, at 20: "[A] decade's content analysis of the news would not easily show the extent to which the economy is dominated by oligopolies." See *id.* at 45: "[T]he news rarely notes the extent of public subsidy of private industry, and it continues to describe firms and institutions which are completely or partly subsidized by government funds as private—for example, Lockheed." Of course, business scandals are frequently reported, much to the

chagrin of chambers of commerce and conservative think tanks, which charge that the media is unfair to business. For a powerful response, see Peter Dreier, "The Corporate Complaint Against the Media," in *American Media and Mass Culture*, ed. Donald Lazere (Berkeley: University of California Press, 1987).

135. The print press has more freedom here. If people do not like the editorial line of a newspaper, they may continue to buy it because of political columnists they like, the bridge column, or the movie ads. If they are offended by abortion references in a program, they will turn to another channel.

136. See Hertsgaard, *supra* note 86, at 77, quoting ABC reporter Sam Donaldson: "The press, myself included, traditionally sides with authority and the establishment." See also Iyengar and Kinder, *supra* note 76, at 133: "Television news may be objective, but it is far from neutral. The production of news takes place within boundaries established by official sources and dominant values. . . . [T]elevision news [is] an inherently cautious and conservative medium, much more likely to defend traditional values and institutions than to attack them."

137. Edward Herman and Noam Chomsky, *Manufacturing Consent* (New York: Pantheon, 1988), 1.

138. *United States v. Eichman,* 496 U.S. 310 (1990); *Texas v. Johnson,* 491 U.S. 397 (1989).

139. The leading case is *New York Times Co. v. Sullivan,* 376 U.S. 254 (1964).

140. *Brandenburg v. Ohio,* 395 U.S. 444 (1969).

141. The history of the doctrine involving advocacy of illegal action shows that the degree of protection greatly depends on the sociopolitical context in which the issues arise. See Steven H. Shiffrin and Jesse H. Choper, *The First Amendment: Cases—Comments—Questions,* 2d (St. Paul, Minn.: West Publishing, 1996), 3–59.

142. E.g., many believe that *Brandenberg* contains a clear and present danger test with teeth, but subsequent to *Brandenberg, Communist Party of Indiana v. Whitcomb,* 414 U.S. 441, 450 (1974), stated that advocacy of action in the future was sufficient to meet legal requirements. Similarly under *Brandenburg,* it is unclear how explicit the advocacy must be, whether the case applies to trivial offenses, and whether it applies to the private solicitation of crime.

143. See, e.g., Benjamin DuVal, "The Occasions of Secrecy," 47 *U. Pitt. L. Rev.* 579 (1986).

144. See *Connick v. Myers,* 461 U.S. 138 (1983) (assistant district attorney fired for challenging office policy).

145. *U.S. Civil Service Comm'n v. Letter Carriers,* 413 U.S. 548 (1973).

146. *Associated Press v. Walker,* 388 U.S. 130 (1967) (public figure plaintiff, a former army general, must show that defamatory statement was made knowing falsehood or with reckless disregard of the truth in order to recover in a defamation suit).

147. *Time, Inc. v. Firestone,* 424 U.S. 448 (1976) (divorce involving one of America's most prominent industrial families where wife had held numerous press conferences was not a "public controversy" and wife was not a public figure); *Gertz v. Robert Welch, Inc.,* 418 U.S. 323 (1974) (prominent Illinois attorney not a public figure).

148. *Tavoulareas v. Piro,* 817 F. 2d 762 (D.C. Cir. 1987).

149. The *Firestone* Court applied the term as described in note 147 *supra* but did not define it.

150. *Adderly v. Florida,* 385 U.S. 39 (1966) (demonstration on jailhouse grounds protesting arrests of other demonstrators and of racial segregation, including segregation of the jail, amounted to trespass unprotected by the First Amendment).

151. *United States v. Kokinda,* 497 U.S. 720 (1990) (solicitation of political contributions on sidewalk leading from parking lot to post office not protected under the First Amendment).

152. *Clark v. Community for Creative Non-Violence,* 468 U.S. 288 (1984) (sleeping outside in the winter as a protest against policies toward the homeless not permitted in a park across the street from the White House).

153. *Perry Educ. Ass'n v. Perry Local Educators' Ass'n,* 460 U.S. 37 (1983) (rival teachers union denied access to school mailboxes even though groups like the YMCA and other civic organizations were permitted access).

154. *U.S. Postal Service v. Council of Greenburgh,* 453 U.S. 114 (1981) (placement of material in mailboxes forbidden without a stamp).

155. *City Council of Los Angeles v. Taxpayers for Vincent,* 466 U.S. 789 (1984).

156. *Burson v. Freeman,* 504 U.S. 191 (1992) (no campaign material or soliciting of votes within one hundred feet of polling place).

157. *International Soc. for Krishna Consciousness v. Lee,* 505 U. S. 672 (1992) (solicitation of funds not permitted except in designated areas of large metropolitan airport). Distribution of literature is protected, however. *Lee v. International Soc. for Krishna Consciousness,* 505 U. S. 830 (1992).

158. *Heffron v. International Soc. for Krishna Consciousness,* 452 U.S. 640 (1981) (neither distribution of literature nor solicitation of funds permitted on fairgrounds except from licensed booths).

159. *Lloyd Corp. v. Tanner,* 407 U.S. 551 (1972). But cf. *Pruneyard Shopping Center v. Robins,* 447 U.S. 74 (1980) (state can require shopping center to give access to demonstrators). Taking *Tanner* and *Pruneyard* together, demonstrators or distributors of literature have access to shopping centers if, but only if, government requires it or the shopping center permits it. No First Amendment right of access exists.

160. 412 U.S. 94 (1973).

161. 424 U.S. 1 (1976).

162. For insight into the dimensions of the problem, see Roland S. Homet, Jr., "Fact-Finding in First Amendment Litigation: The Case of Campaign Finance Reform," 21 *Okla. City L. Rev.* 97 (1996); Jamin Raskin and John Banifaz, "Equal Protection and the Wealth Primary," 11 *Yale L. & Pol'y Rev.* 273 (1993).

163. *Id.* at 48.

164. *Buckley v. Valeo,* 519 F. 2d 821, 841 (D.C. Cir. 1975).

165. See Burt Neuborne, "One Dollar, One Vote," 263 *The Nation* 21 (December 2, 1996).

166. For an excellent short treatment of a major part of what deserves to be done, see Blasi, *supra* note 2.

167. Much socialization, however, is a prescription for conformity, passivity, and ignorance. Lindblom, *supra* note 6, at 71.

168. See Lindblom, *supra* note 6, at 68.

169. B. David Brooks, *Lessons in Character* (San Diego: Young People's Press, 1998).

170. *Id.* at xi.

171. I originally thought it would be appropriate to have students organized to challenge injustice within their own schools, and a strong teacher might do this. Most teachers would fear that administrators would somehow retaliate against them, however. Teachers, as a group, in my experience are not known for their willingness openly to fight an administration (except through their unions).

172. See Jack Zevin, *Social Studies for the Twenty-First Century: Methods and Materials for Teaching in Middle and Secondary Schools* (New York: Longman, 1992), 383 ("Decrease teacher control by transferring decision making and conclusion drawing to students wherever possible, particularly on those issues that involve values, while reserving the right to challenge statements that need to be tested").

173. Chris Sperry and Dave Lehman, "Democratic School Governance," 11 *Democracy & Education* 41 (Spring 1997). Consider also Jerilyn Fay Kelle, "To Illuminate or Indoctrinate," in *Educating Tomorrow's Valuable Citizen,* ed. Joan N. Burstyn (Albany: State University of New York Press, 1996), 59, 63: "It is difficult to argue that lecture or teacher-talk is effective in transferring knowledge of the kind that profoundly informs, and that inspires democratic attitudes and actions. Yet current practice remains faithful to 'imposition' as its primary medium, which creates experiences that reinforce authoritarianism and elitism, embody the antithesis of democratic attitudes and behaviors, and encourage citizen deference to unchallenged 'superiors.' We may pontificate in social studies classrooms about the United States of America's being a democratic society. We may even moralize about democratic virtues and behaviors. But if we don't afford students the opportunity within their schools to live in and be active members of a democratic community, they will not become active, participatory citizens in the wider society."

174. For further examples of less-than-educational programming used by broadcasters for educational purposes, see generally Marc Silver and Anna Mulrine, "Fall's Edutainment Fix," *U.S. News & World Rep.,* October 7, 1996, at 67. The problem stems from the FCC's misplaced reliance on the "good faith judgment of broadcasters" to classify shows as educational. In re Policies and Rules concerning Children's Television Programming, 11 F.C.R. 10660, 10701 (1996).

175. See, e.g., Reed E. Hundt and Karen Kornbluh, "Renewing the Deal Between Broadcasters and the Public: Requiring Clear Rules for Children's Educational Television," 9 *Harv. J.L. & Tech.* 11, 11 (1996); Reed E. Hundt, "The Public's Airwaves: What Does the Public Interest Require of Television Broadcasters?" 45 *Duke L.J.* 1089 (1996). For a spirited critique of the public trustee model, see Ronald J. Krotoszynski, Jr., "The Inevitable Wasteland: Why the Public Trustee Model of Broadcast Television Regulation Must Fail," 95 *Mich. L. Rev.* 2101 (1997).

176. Reed E. Hundt, "A New Paradigm for Broadcast Regulations," 15 *J.L. &
Com.* 527, 531 (1996).

177. *Id.* at 12.

178. Charles Firestone and Phil Jacklin, "Deregulation and the Pursuit of Fairness," in *Telecommunications Policy and the Citizen,* ed. Timothy R. Haight
(NewYork: Praeger, 1979), 107.

179. Christopher Wright, Deputy General Counsel, FCC, American Association of Law Schools Annual Meeting, Panel on Sex, Violence, Children, and the
Media, January 1997, Washington, D.C.

180. The chilling effect on reporters as a result of this "gap" has been recognized by other authors. See, e.g., Laura B. Choper, "The Charge Is Libel: The
Best Defense Is an Aggressive Offense When a Public Official Sues the Media,"
29 *Santa Clara L. Rev.* 999, 1023 n.68 (1989) ("In fact, the potential for libel
litigation has caused numerous reporters, writers, and publishers to reduce
coverage on controversial subjects and litigious individuals. . . . Hence, when reporters and editors decline to publish articles for fear of retributive libel litigation, media centralization further limits public access to information and results
in increased propaganda rather than open discussion and debate on matters of
public concern"). See also Lee Levine, "Judge and Jury in the Law of Defamation:
Putting the Horse Behind the Cart," 35 *Am. U.L. Rev.* 3, 92, 143–44, n.125
(1985).

181. *Brandenburg v. Ohio,* 395 U.S. 444 (1969).

182. Employees do not feel free to organize in the private sector under existing
law. See generally Risa Lieberwitz, "Current Trends in U.S. Labor Law," International Symposium on the New Trends of Labor Law in Selected Countries, Korea
Labor Institute, Seoul, Korea (November 9, 1995) (recommending reforms). See
also Kate Bronfenbrenner and Tom Juravich, "The Impact of Employer Opposition on Union Certification Win Rates: A Private/Public Sector Comparison," Economic Policy Institute, Working Paper No. 113 (Washington D.C. Economic Policy Institute October 1994), at 23 (pointing to absence of effective constraints
on employer behavior inhibiting organizing in the private sphere and calling for
expansion of worker rights and employer penalties).

183. Worker self-realization is also an important value in this context.

184. See generally *Toward an Information Bill of Rights and Responsibilities*
(Washington, D.C.: Aspen Institute, ed. Charles M. Firestone and Jorge Reina
Schement 1995).

185. *Regan v. Taxation with Representation of Washington,* 461 U.S. 540
(1983).

186. C. Edwin Baker, *Advertising and a Democratic Press* (Princeton, N.J.:
Princeton University Press, 1994), 83–117.

187. Baker's tax proposal could not directly apply to the broadcast medium
because it does not receive revenue from its audience, but similar concerns are
present.

188. Henry Geller has suggested for many years that commercial broadcasters
be required to subsidize public broadcasters through payment of a licensing fee
or usage fee based on a percentage of the commercial broadcaster's gross revenues.

See Shari O'Brien, "The Responsibility of the Electronic Press to Juvenile Audiences," 15 *Sw. U.L. Rev.* 643, 694 n.289 (1985).

189. I am grateful to Ed Baker for this suggestion.

190. See generally Matthew N. Kaplan, "Who Will Guard the Guardians? Independent Counsel, State Secrets, and Judicial Review," 18 *Nova L. Rev.* 1787, 1841 (1994) (criticizing administration bureaucracies for overclassifying security information); Brian Z. Tamanaha, "A Critical Review of the Classified Information Procedures Act," 13 *Am. J. Crim. L.* 277, 312–13 and n.199 (1986) ("The classification system has a well-documented history of chronic abuse resulting in the unnecessary or overclassification of information").

Congress recognized the problem of overclassification as a way of circumventing the Freedom of Information Act and authorized courts to inquire whether documents requested under the Freedom of Information Act were properly classified. 5 *U.S.C.* §552(b)(1)(B)(1982). But not everyone sues, and internal checks can provide some additional assistance against overclassification.

191. For defenses of vouchers in this context, see Bruce Ackerman, "Crediting the Voters: A New Beginning for Campaign Finance," *13 The American Prospect* 71 (Spring 1993); Edward B. Foley, "Equal-Dollars-Per-Voter: A Constitutional Principle of Campaign Finance," 93 *Colum. L. Rev.* 1204 (1994).

192. In the 1996 election, $200 million in public funds was devoted to the presidential election, but the candidates and parties raised $600 million private dollars. "Democracy v. Free Speech," 61 *The Progressive* 8, 9 (January 1997). For public expenditures to serve their purpose, private expenditures have to be controlled.

193. In support of proportional representation, see Douglas J. Amy, *Real Choices/New Voices: The Case for Proportional Representation Elections in the United States* (New York: Columbia University Press, 1993); Enid Lakeman, "The Case for Proportional Representation," in *Choosing an Electoral System,* ed. Arend Lijphart and Bernard Groffman (New York: Praeger, 1984), 41–51. Note, "The Constitutional Imperative of Proportional Representation," 94 *Yale L.J.* 163 (1984). But see, e.g., Bruce E. Cain, *The Reapportionment Puzzle* (Berkeley: University of California Press, 50–51; Ferdinand A. Hermans, "Representation and Proportional Representation," in *Choosing an Electoral System, supra,* at 15–30; Peter H. Schuck, "The Thickest Thicket: Partisan Gerrymandering and Judicial Regulation of Politics," 87 *Colum. L. Rev.* 1325, 1362–64 (1987). Cf. Sanford Levinson, "Gerrymandering and the Brooding Omnipresence of Proportional Representation: Why Won't It Go Away?" 33 *UCLA L. Rev.* 257 (1985) (rehearsing rights-based arguments in favor of proportional representation and structural arguments against it).

194. See generally (Wilma Rule and Joseph F. Zimmerman, eds., *United States Electoral Systems: Their Impact on Women and Minorities* (New York: Greenwood Press, 1992); Darren Rosenblum, "Geographically Sexual? Advancing Lesbian and Gay Interests Through Proportional Representation," 31 *Harv. C.R.-C.L. L.Rev.* 119 (1996).

195. See Amy, *supra* note 193, at 140–52.

196. *Id.* at 76–98.

197. A cumulative voting system would also be progressive. See Lani Guinier, *The Tyranny of the Majority* (New York: Free Press, 1994), 149, 153:

> [M]odified at-large systems used in corporate governance, such as cumulative voting, should be considered. Under a modified at-large system, each voter is given the same number of votes as open seats, and the voter may plump or cumulate her votes to reflect the intensity of her preferences. Depending on the exclusion threshold, politically cohesive minority groups are assured representation if they vote strategically. Similarly, all voters have the potential to form voluntary constituencies based on their own assessment of their interests. As a consequence, semiproportional systems such as cumulative voting give more voters, not just racial minorities, the opportunity to vote for a winning candidate. . . .
>
> "In balancing the fears of balkanization against observations about existing alienation, I conclude that exclusiveness is a greater evil than controversy, that passivity does not equal contentment, and that differences need not be permanently enshrined in the electoral configuration. Modified at-large election systems encourage continuous redistricting by the voters themselves based on the way they cast their votes at each election. Whatever differences emerge, therefore, are those chosen by the voters rather than imposed externally on the voters based on assumptions about demographic characteristics or incumbent self-interest. These voter-generated differences may infuse the process with new ideas; diversity of viewpoint can be enlightening. Finally, the modified at-large system may simply reflect a necessary transition phase from power politics to principled politics. But, whether it succeeds in that respect, it at least has the benefit in infusing the process with more legitimacy from the perspective of previously disenfranchised groups.

See generally Lani Guinier, "No Two Seats: The Elusive Quest for Political Equality," 77 *Va. L. Rev.* 1413 (1991).

Chapter V
The Politics of Free Speech

1. *First Nat'l Bank of Boston v. Bellotti,* 435 U.S. 765 (1978) (business corporations have First Amendment right to spend money to influence the outcome of initiative campaigns).

2. E.g., Philip Morris purchased the exclusive right from the National Archives to be the official corporate sponsor of the bicentennial celebration of the Bill of Rights and participated in an extensive advertising campaign that associated its name with the First Amendment. See generally *Tobacco Issues (Part 2): Hearings Before the Senate Subcommittee on Transportation and Hazardous Materials of the Committee on Energy and Commerce,* House of Representatives, 101st Cong., 1st and 2d sess., 1–172 (1989–1990). As discussed in chapter two, many believe that the *Liquormart* case is a prelude to sweeping protections for tobacco companies.

3. *Hudgens v. NLRB,* 424 U.S. 507 (1976).

4. *Miami Herald Pub. Co. v. Tornillo,* 418 U.S. 241 (1974) (statute affording a right of reply to persons attacked in the media declared unconstitutional).

5. *R.A.V. v. City of St. Paul,* 112 Sup. Ct. 2538 (1992). For extensive discussion, see chapter three.

6. *American Booksellers Ass'n v. Hudnut,* 771 F.2d 323 (7th Cir. 1985), *aff'd,* 475 U.S. 1001 (1986) (Indianapolis pornography statute crafted by Catharine MacKinnon and Andrea Dworkin declared unconstitutional).

7. Mary E. Becker, "The Politics of Women's Wrongs and the Bill of 'Rights,' " *59 U. Chi. L. Rev.* 453 (1992); see also Mary Becker, "Conservative Free Speech and the Uneasy Case for Judicial Review," 64 *U. Colo. L. Rev.* 975 (1993).

8. Richard Delgado and Jean Stefanic, "Images of the Outsider in American Law and Culture: Can Free Expression Remedy Systemic Social Ills?" 77 *Cornell L. Rev.* 1258, 1259 (1992).

9. *Id.*

10. Morton J. Horwitz, "Rights," 23 *Harv. C.R.-C.L. L. Rev.* 393, 398 (1988).

11. David Kairys, *With Liberty and Justice for Some* (New York: New Press, 1993), 57. See generally *id.* at 39–97.

12. Mark Tushnet, "An Essay on Rights," 62 *Tex. L. Rev.* 1363, 1387 (1984). Jack Balkin has pointed to an "ideological drift" in the political valence of the First Amendment. He suggests that what "was sauce for the liberal goose increasingly has become sauce for the more conservative gander." J. M. Balkin, "Some Realism About Pluralism: Legal Realist Approaches to the First Amendment," 1990 *Duke L.J.* 375, 383.

13. See, e.g., Horwitz, *supra* note 10; Alan Freeman, "Racism, Rights and the Quest for Equality of Opportunity: A Critical Legal Essay," 23 *Harv. C.L.-C.R. L. Rev.* 295 (1988); Frances Olsen, "Statutory Rape: A Feminist Critique of Rights Analysis," 63 *Tex. L. Rev.* 387, 401 (1984); Peter Gabel, "The Phenomenology of Rights-Consciousness and the Pact of the Withdrawn Selves," 62 *Tex. L. Rev.* 1563 (1984); Tushnet, *supra* note 12; Karl E. Klare, "Labor Law as Ideology," 4 *Indus. Rel. L.J.* 450, 468–82 (1981); Duncan Kennedy, "Critical Labor Law Theory: A Comment," 4 *Indus. Rel. L.J.* 503 (1981); Duncan Kennedy, "The Structure of Blackstone's Commentaries," 28 *Buffalo L. Rev.* 205, 351–62 (1979).

The arguments of the critical theorists have triggered critical reactions from liberals, leftists, feminists, and critical race theorists, among others (not that these categories are all mutually exclusive). For a sampling of the diverse responses, see Sheri Lynn Johnson, "Confessions, Criminals, and Community," 26 *Harv. C.R.-C.L. L. Rev.* 327 (1991); Judith Scales-Trent, "Black Women and the Constitution: Finding Our Place, Asserting Our Rights," 24 *Harv. C.R.-C.L. L. Rev.* 9 (1989); Richard Delgado, "Critical Legal Studies and the Realities of Race," 23 *Harv. C.R.-C.L. L. Rev.* 405 (1988); Kimberle Crenshaw, "Race, Reform, and Retrenchment: Transformation and Legitimation in Antidiscrimination Law," 101 *Harv. L. Rev.* 1331 (1988); Harlon Dalton, "The Clouded Prism," 22 *Harv. C.R.-C.L. L. Rev.* 435, 441 (1987); Robert A. Williams, "Taking Rights Aggressively: The Perils and Promise of Critical Theory for People of Color," 5 *J. Law & Inequality* 103 (1987) ("Aggressively"); Patricia Williams, "Alchemical Notes: Restructuring Ideals from Deconstructed Rights," 22 *Harv. C.R.-C.L. L. Rev.* 401, 404–5 (1987) ("Alchemical"); Elizabeth M. Schneider, "The Dialectic of Rights and Politics: Perspectives from the Women's Movement," 62 *N.Y.U. L. Rev.* 589 (1986); Michael J. Perry, "Taking Neither Rights-Talk nor the 'Critique of Rights' Too Seriously," 62 *Tex. L. Rev.* 1405 (1984); Edward Sparer, "Fundamental Human Rights, Legal Entitlements, and the Social Struggle: A Friendly Critique of the Critical Legal Studies Movement," 36 *Stan. L. Rev.* 509, 514 (1984).

14. Frederick Schauer, "The Political Incidence of the Free Speech Principle," 64 *U. Colo. L. Rev.* 935 (1993).

15. He assumes in the main that those with power and wealth are relatively conservative and in the main that those with less power are relatively liberal.

16. Schauer, *supra* note 14, at 942.

17. Cf. Robin West, *Caring for Justice* (New York: New York University Press, 1997), 161–62: "[P]rotection of cultural dissent is of course a great virtue of our constitutional system. But what too often goes unacknowledged by the liberals and libertarians who trumpet it is that it comes at a heavy price: the constitution protects the culture dissented from no less than the dissent. Where the culture is extremely powerful, pervasive, and all-encompassing, and the forces of dissent relatively weak, what constitutionalism ensures first and foremost is that the potential powers of the state will not be allied with the forces of dissent. Nor, of course, can the powers of the state be employed against dissent—at least in theory, and at least much of the time. But whether (and when) the benefits of the promise of state neutrality—a promise as often breached as upheld in practice—outweigh the loss of the constitutionally forbidden alliance of the state with cultural dissent, is an *empirical,* although difficult, question. It is one which cannot be answered by definitional fiat, and it is simply a mistake for liberals and libertarians to assume otherwise." Although I will refer to the "free speech principle" throughout, the monistic connotation of the phrase is quite misleading. It distracts from the complexity of free speech as a practice and from the extent to which free speech refers to a multiplicity of sometimes conflicting values. See generally Steven H. Shiffrin, *The First Amendment, Democracy and Romance* (Cambridge, Mass.: Harvard University Press, 1990), 5–6, 104–5; Steven Shiffrin, "The First Amendment and Economic Regulation: Away from a General Theory of the First Amendment," 1212, 1252 (1983). Schauer has long understood this. See generally Schauer, "Categories in the First Amendment: A Play in Three Acts," 34 *Vand. L. Rev.* 265 (1981). His usage of the free speech principle is based on an understanding of what the public understands about the idea of free speech. I do not find his argument persuasive. See *infra* note 51. For criticism of Schauer's essay on this score and other aspects, see Steven D. Smith, "The Politics of Free Speech: A Comment on Schauer," 64 *U. Colo. L. Rev.* 959 (1993); and Steven L. Winter, "Fast Food and False Friends in the Shopping Mall of Ideas," 64 *U. Colo. L. Rev.* 965 (1993).

18. Schauer, *supra* note 14, at 942 n.37.

19. *Id.* at 951.

20. The most comprehensive discussion of the free speech principle from this perspective, and to my mind the most interesting, comes from someone who is a liberal in distinctive respects and a radical in others. C. Edwin Baker, *Human Liberty and Freedom of Speech* (New York: Oxford University Press, 1989) (embracing a free speech liberty principle for primarily nonconsequentialist reasons, but arguing that the liberty principle does not extend to business corporations or media corporations, though he would give substantial protection to the latter).

Other prominent work includes John Rawls, *A Theory of Justice* (Cambridge, Mass.: Belknap Press of Harvard University Press, 1971); Ronald Dworkin, *Taking Rights Seriously* (Cambridge, Mass.: Harvard University Press, 1977); Bruce A. Ackerman, *Social Justice in the Liberal State* (New Haven, Conn.: Yale University Press, 1980); and David A. J. Richards, *Toleration and the Constitution* (New York: Oxford University Press, 1986).

21. See, e.g., Isaiah Berlin, *Four Essays on Liberty* (London: Oxford University Press, 1969); John Stuart Mill, *On Liberty*, ed. David Spitz (New York: Norton, 1975); Richard Rorty, *Contingency, Irony, and Solidarity* (Cambridge: Cambridge University Press, 1989); and Richard Rorty, *Consequences of Pragmatism* (Minneapolis: University of Minnesota Press, 1982).

22. Of course, many on the left have deep attachments to the free speech principle (see Baker, *supra* note 20), and many liberals have not supported the free speech principle in times when it counted (see *infra* note 36).

23. Schauer, *supra* note 14, at 9 n.37.

24. It makes no difference for this analysis whether the free speech principle is embodied in the Constitution.

25. Schauer, *supra* note 14, at 954.

26. *Id.* at 957: "[T]here may be reason to believe that those who are politically or socially disadvantaged would urge [free speech] protection with caution, and that those who are politically or socially advantaged would welcome this greater protection with some enthusiasm."

27. Donald Lazere, ed., *American Media and Mass Culture* (Berkeley: University of California Press, 1987); John Keane, *The Media and Democracy* (Cambridge, Mass.: Blackwell, 1991), 38; John R. Zaller, *The Nature and Origins of Mass Opinion* (Cambridge: Cambridge University Press, 1992).

28. Many of the players (advertisers, owners, government officials, other sources) have power, and their agendas can compete. Sometimes that competition introduces themes of benefit to the left. Leaving the left aside, the question of whether media power on balance supports liberals or conservatives varies with the context (Franklin Roosevelt's presidency was no boon for conservatives, and I suspect that conclusion would have held even under modern media conditions). With respect to the left, the context has yet to vary sufficiently to make a difference.

29. See generally Michel Foucault, *The History of Sexuality: Volume I* 92–93 (New York: Vintage Books, 1980).

[P]ower must be understood in the first instance as the multiplicity of force relations immanent in the sphere in which they operate and which constitute their own organization; as the process which, through ceaseless struggles and confrontations, transforms, strengthens, or reverses them; as the support which these force relations find in one another, thus forming a chain or a system, or on the contrary, the disjunctions and contradictions which isolate them from one another; and lastly, as the strategies in which they take effect, whose general design or institutional crystallization is embodied in the state apparatus, in the formulation of the law, in the various social hegemonies. Power's condition of possibility, or in any case the viewpoint which permits one to understand its exercise, even in its more 'peripheral' effects, and which also makes it possible to use its mechanisms as a grid of intelligibility of the social order, must not be sought in the primary existence of a central point, in a unique source of sovereignty from which secondary and descendent forms would emanate; it is the moving substrate of force relations which, by virtue of their inequality, constantly engender states of power, but the latter are always local and unstable.

30. John B. Thompson, *Ideology and Modern Culture: Critical Social Theory in the Era of Mass Communication* (Stanford, Calif.: Stanford University Press, 1990), 24. See generally John Fiske, *Understanding Popular Culture* (Boston: Unwin Hyman, 1989). The theme recurs in many of the essays collected in Lawrence Grossberg, Cary Nelson, and Paula Treichler, eds., *Cultural Studies* (New York: Routledge, 1992).

31. Here liberals and the rest of the left frequently divide. Liberals frequently look to governmental leaders for solutions; the rest of the left has a variety of theories of change, but there is considerably more importance placed on grassroots democratic organizing. See, e.g., Richard Flacks, *Making History: The Radical Tradition in American Life* (New York: Columbia University Press, 1988); Tom Hayden, *Trial* (New York: Holt, Rinehart, and Winston, 1970), 150–68; Paul Potter, "Intellectuals and Power," in *The New Student Left,* ed. Mitchell Cohen and Dennis Hale (Boston: Beacon Press, 1967), 16, 20.

32. For activist advice on the manipulation of the mass media, see Charlotte Ryan, *Prime Time Activism: Media Strategies for Grassroots Organizing* (Boston: South End Press, 1991). Whatever one thinks of the importance of grassroots organizing as a source of change, I doubt the mass media is more powerful now than it was in the sixties. To be sure, newspapers are more likely to be part of a chain, and ownership of newspapers is less diverse. But the rise of video alternatives to the networks has fragmented the mass audience in the broadcasting medium (though network audiences are still substantial). In various stages of media technology, a variety of social movements have received substantial attention, e.g., feminism, ecology, gay rights, and animal rights. The rise of the Internet and the World Wide Web has made and will continue to make such organizing much easier.

33. The left is deeply divided about the results of social movements. Liberals tend to see social movements as spurring progressive change, though many of them are uncomfortable with some forms of collective resistance that most of the radical left find appropriate. On the importance of such resistance to the left, see Todd Gitlin, *The Sixties* (New York: Bantam Books, 1987), 84–85. On its impact, see Francis Fox Piven and Richard A. Cloward, "Normalizing Collective Protest," in *Frontiers in Social Movement Theory,* ed. Aldon D. Morris and Carol McClung Mueller (New Haven, Conn.: Yale University Press, 1992). Many radicals see the results of social movements as governmental co-optation taking the life out of social movements without substantially changing the character of the power structure; others produce more optimistic assessments. For thoughtful discussion of this issue, see Flacks, *supra* note 31, at 243–54. See generally Charles J. Stewart, Craig Allen Smith, and Robert E. Denton, Jr., *Persuasion and Social Movements,* 3d ed. (Prospect Heights, Ill.: Waveland Press, 1994).

34. James MacGregor Burns and Stewart Burns, *A People's Charter: The Pursuit of Rights in America* (New York: Knopf, 1991), 453–54. On social move-

ments generally, see Aldon D. Morris and Carol M. Mueller, eds., *Frontiers in Social Movement Theory* (New Haven, Conn.: Yale University Press, 1992).

35. See generally Baker, *supra* note 20, chs. 5 and 6.

36. On political repression in America, see generally Bud Schultz and Ruth Schultz, eds., *It Did Happen Here: Recollections of Political Repression in America* (Berkeley: University of California Press, 1989); and Robert Justin Goldstein, *Political Repression in Modern America* (Kent: Ohio State University Press, 1978). Many liberals have contributed to the assaults on leftist social movements. Liberals played a substantial role in the treatment of World War I protestors. See Richard Polenberg, *Fighting Faiths: The Abrams Case, the Supreme Court, and Free Speech* (New York: Viking Press, 1987) (liberals controlled the War Emergency Division of the Justice Department.) They also followed along with the censorship of McCarthy and, of course, Harry Truman. If one sticks with Schauer's terminology, it would have to be said that many of those who voted for Clinton and Dukakis—who think of themselves as liberals—have not exhibited devotion to the free speech principle when it counted. See Ellen W. Schrecker, *No Ivory Tower: McCarthyism and the Universities* (New York: Oxford University Press, 1986); and Manning Marable, "A New American Socialism," *The Progressive*, February 1993, at 20, 21. Of course, many liberals did exhibit such devotion, and many of those paid the price.

37. Schauer does not enter the debate. He proceeds entirely from a philosophical perspective, one that assumes the free speech principle will be respected.

38. Some might argue that this means that the left no longer needs judicial review and is unlikely to benefit from a Rehnquist Court. See Becker's work, *supra* note 7. Notice that my argument in this chapter is that the free speech principle benefits the left, not that judicial review of free speech cases benefits the left. Obviously, the Rehnquist Court could manipulate the free speech principle to damage the left. In many cases, it has. See generally Kairys, *supra* note 11.

39. More generally, critical race theorists have argued that rights have been an important tool for mobilizing the disempowered and their allies. As Robert A. Williams, Jr., argues, "The frequent attacks by CLS on both rights and entitlement discourse represent direct frontal assaults on the sole proven vehicle of the European-derived legal tradition capable of mobilizing peoples of color and their allies." Williams, "Aggressively," *supra* note 13, at 121. See also Dalton, *supra* note ; Delgado, *supra* note 13; Williams, "Alchemical," *supra* note 13. Other liberal or left critics of CLS have argued in the same vein, see Schneider, *supra* note 13; Sparer, *supra* note 13. In turn, the recognition that rights rhetoric is important in the building of activist movements has been conceded by some critical theorists who are otherwise critical of rights. See, e.g., Kennedy, "Critical Labor Law Theory," *supra* note 13, at 505–6; Freeman, *supra* note 13, at 332.

40. The left would be particularly, but not exclusively, concerned with threats to the progressive press.

41. Such an interpretation of the principle, albeit popular in the commentary, overlooks the extent to which government has power to manage its own resources. See Steven Shiffrin, "Government Speech," 27 *UCLA L. Rev.* 565, 587 n.122, 644–45 (1980). That is, as I suggested in chapter four, broadcasters are licensees of public airwaves. This does not mean, however, that government could comman-

deer all of the public airwaves. See generally Matthew L. Spitzer, "The Constitutionality of Licensing Broadcasters," 64 *N.Y.U. L. Rev.* 990 (1989) or that there
are no limitations on how government manages its resources. See Mark G. Yudof,
*When Government Speaks: Politics, Law, and Government Expression in
America* (Berkeley: University of California Press, 1983).

42. Some members of the left might favor incumbent protection programs, if
the incumbents were the right people. Other members of the left would regard a
commitment to democracy as more important.

43. I do not assume the left will take control of the government in my lifetime.
Moreover, I assume it is in the left's interest for liberals rather than conservatives
to be in power.

44. Liberals divide on important free press issues, defamation law in particular.
Liberals and the left divide over the question of privacy and the press.

45. Some libertarians' views are more complicated than a laissez-faire principle
suggests. C. Edwin Baker, e.g., subscribes to a strong principle of human liberty
on primarily non-consequentialist grounds but does not include for-profit corporations within the liberty principle. His approach allows for substantial intervention in the market. See Baker, *supra* note 20.

46. On the other hand, Schauer's thesis does not depend on the association of
conservatives with libertarians. It is enough for his purposes to associate conservatives with concentrations of power. Among conservatives it may be that libertarians are more likely to oppose policies that assist concentrations of power.

47. Owen M. Fiss, "Why the State," 100 *Harv. L. Rev.* 781, 783 (1987). See
generally Owen M. Fiss, *Liberalism Divided: Freedom of Speech and the Many
Uses of State Power* (Boulder, Colo.: Westview Press, 1996). See also Jerome A.
Barron, "Access to the Press-A New First Amendment Right," 80 *Harv. L. Rev.*
1641 (1967). For rich elaboration of a New Deal for speech, see Cass R. Sunstein,
Democracy and the Problem of Free Speech (New York: Free Press, 1993).

48. *Id.* at 786.

49. *Id.* at 793, citing *Columbia Broadcasting System v. Democratic National
Committee*, 412 U.S. 94 (1973).

50. It does not solve all problems by any means. As I argued in chapter three,
the analysis of hate speech issues is quite complicated using a dissent lens.

51. Schauer argues that one virtue of the laissez-faire principle is that it is easy
for the public to understand. Schauer, *supra* note 14, at 955. But there is no reason
to believe that the public would find it appreciably more difficult to understand a
free speech model based on a rich public debate or, as I would prefer—the dissenter. If we are to contemplate an unthinking public, the image of the dissenter
seems just as plausible as the marketplace of ideas metaphor, particularly when
one remembers that commercial advertising went without constitutional protection for more than a century and a half without public complaint—a result that
is hard to fit with a marketplace model. If we are to contemplate a thinking public,
we would have to recognize that the laissez-faire principle is not accepted by it.
The public opposed constitutional protection for flag burning. In discussing that
issue, President Bush referred to a dissent model, not a marketplace model: "As
President, I will uphold our precious right to dissent, but burning the flag goes
too far and I want to see that matter remedied." *New York Times*, June 28, 1989,

at B7. Presumably the public would support aspects of many of the standard exceptions to First Amendment protection. Thus, the public, whatever its divisions on free speech issues, already holds complicated views on free speech issues. If simplicity is a virtue here, that feature is entitled to little weight.

52. Racist speech is more complicated, though in the end, as I explain in chapter three, I protect most of it as well, i.e., all racist speech not directly targeted at particular individuals or small groups is fully protected.

53. *Austin v. Michigan State Chamber of Commerce,* 494 U.S. 652 (1990).

54. See the discussion in chapter two.

55. *Prune Yard Shopping Center v. Robins,* 447 U.S. 74 (1980). Dissenters, however, have no First Amendment right of access to shopping centers.

56. *Red Lion Broadcasting Co. v. FCC,* 395 U.S. 367 (1969), reaffirmed in *Metro Broadcasting v. FCC,* 497 U.S. 547 (1990); *Columbia Broadcasting System v. FCC,* 453 U.S. 367 (1981).

57. See *R.A.V. v. City of St. Paul,* 112 Sup. Ct. 2538 (1992) (suggesting that regulations aimed at racial harassment—whether by speech or conduct—might be constitutional).

Index